Youth in Transition

VOLUME III

DROPPING OUT –
Problem or Symptom?

JERALD G. BACHMAN
SWAYZER GREEN
ILONA D. WIRTANEN

SURVEY RESEARCH CENTER

INSTITUTE FOR SOCIAL RESEARCH
THE UNIVERSITY OF MICHIGAN
ANN ARBOR, MICHIGAN

ISR Code No. 3322

The research reported herein was performed pursuant to a contract with the Office of Education, U. S. Department of Health, Education, and Welfare. Contractors undertaking such projects under Government sponsorship are encouraged to express freely their professional judgment in the conduct of the project. Points of view or opinions stated do not, therefore, necessarily represent official Office of Education position or policy.

First Published 1971
Second Printing 1976

Library of Congress Catalog Card Number: 79-630045
ISBN 87944-112-7 clothbound

Published by the Institute for Social Research
The University of Michigan, Ann Arbor, Michigan 48106

Manufactured in the United States of America

PREFACE

This book is the third in a series of monographs documenting the Youth in Transition project, a longitudinal study of young men conducted by the Survey Research Center* under the primary sponsorship of the United States Office of Education.** The study is, in the broadest sense, an exploration of the effects of social environments, with special emphasis on the impact of school and work environments.

The present volume deals with the causes and effects of dropping out of high school. Since the start of the Youth in Transition project, a careful examination of "the dropout problem" has been one of our central objectives. It was clear from other studies that dropouts were different from stayins in many respects. But to what extent were these differences the *result* of dropping out? The research task, in our view, was to distinguish between causes and effects, between problems and symptoms. To do so required a research design which would follow students from the start of high school until the time when some had dropped out and the rest had graduated.

Distinguishing between causes and effects of dropping out is not simply a point of academic interest; it is a matter of great practical importance. The usual conclusion drawn from dropout statistics is that things get worse for someone who drops out of high school, and throughout the last decade our national policy in education has included a vigorous "anti-dropout campaign." The findings presented in this volume, based on more than six years of research, have direct bearing on the soundness and wisdom of that campaign.

In the first volume of this series, we argued that theoretical and practical aims can be mutually facilitating in social research. The work reported here was conducted with both aims in mind, and we have tried to reflect both practical and scientific emphases

*The Survey Research Center is one of four divisions of the Institute for Social Research of The University of Michigan; the other centers are: Research Center for Group Dynamics, Center for Research on the Utilization of Scientific Knowledge, and Center for Political Studies.

**Additional support for some phases of the research has been provided by the United States Department of Labor and the United States Department of Defense.

iii

in our style of reporting. We have included the detailed data and statistical relationships that are necessary for the scientific reader, but we have also tried to keep technicalities in the background and display our findings in ways that are meaningful to a broader audience. We hope we have done justice to both levels of reporting.

Guidelines for Using this Book

The table of contents provides a fairly detailed summary of the material in this volume, but a brief overview may be useful here. The first part of the book is introductory; Chapter 1 presents some major issues in the study of dropouts and Chapter 2 describes the research design. The next part of the book deals with those things which precede (and in large measure cause) dropping out; Chapter 3 deals with family background and ability, Chapter 4 treats school experiences and attitudes, Chapter 5 deals with a variety of personality and behavior dimensions, and Chapter 6 provides a summary and evaluation of all these factors that predict dropping out. The next part of the book concentrates on the effects of dropping out; Chapter 7 summarizes the changes in personality and behavior which do or do not occur after dropping out, and Chapter 8 compares the job outcomes of dropouts and stayins. Chapter 9 presents the dropouts' own views about why they left school and what it has meant to them. Chapter 10 summarizes the findings and considers some of their short-range and longer-range implications.

The reader less concerned with technical matters may want to skim over much of Chapter 2, and the last half of Chapter 6. Those wishing a fairly concise treatment of factors which predict dropping out can use the first part of Chapter 6 as a summary of the material in Chapters 3 through 5. And, of course, those wishing only an overview of findings may prefer to turn directly to the final chapter.

The present analysis of dropping out represents one part of the larger Youth in Transition project. This volume is designed to stand alone; however, it sometimes relies heavily on earlier work, and we have chosen not to repeat in detail those topics reported elsewhere. Accordingly, some readers may find it useful to refer to Volumes I and II in this series for further information on study design, sampling procedures, details of measurement content, interrelationships among family background factors, and the like.

Acknowledgements

The Youth in Transition project began in 1965 with Jerald Bachman and Robert Kahn as principal investigators. Since that time Bob Kahn has been involved in a wide range of research activities and administrative responsibilities. He has, nevertheless, maintained an interest and involvement throughout the lifespan of this project. His investment in the present volume began with his share in the initial planning and launching of the research, continued through the years of data collection and analysis, and included his very helpful review of the manuscript. These and many other contributions to the Youth in Transition project are deeply appreciated.

Other colleagues have made major contributions to the Youth in Transition project over a period of some years. Martha Mednick, Terrence Davidson, Lloyd Johnston, and Jerome Johnston have given much hard work and creative thought.

We appreciate the help of others who read portions of the manuscript and offered suggestions: Frank Andrews, David Bowers, Angus Campbell, Martin Frankel, and Martin Gold.

We are grateful to Diane Davidson for editorial work and final supervision of manuscript preparation, and to Patricia Veerkamp for typing and many other kinds of assistance.

We appreciate the work of William Haney, Douglas Truax and Lee Behnke in arranging the publication of this volume.

Many others at the Institute for Social Research helped to collect and analyze the data reported here. Thanks are due to the members of the Sampling, Field, and Coding Sections, and the Computer Services Facility.

A good many people have served on the Youth in Transition project staff during the past six years. Some have already been noted above, but it is a pleasure to acknowledge them all in the listing that follows.

Youth in Transition Project Staff (Past and Present)

Allison Arscott	John French, Jr.
Jerald Bachman	Swayzer Green
Joy Bingham	Penni Holt
Lynn Bozoki	Sally Iman
Janet Bumpass	Mary Jacobs
Robert Cope	Jerome Johnston
Diane Davidson	Lloyd Johnston
Terrence Davidson	Robert Kahn

Rita Lamendella
Judith Long
Martha Mednick
Haydee Navarro
Roberta Niaki
Guttorm Norstebo
Patrick O'Malley
Karen Paige
Janice Plotkin

Philip Rappaport
Joel Raynor
Willard Rodgers
Susan Shapiro
Claire Taylor
Barbara Thomas
Elizabeth vanDuinen
Patricia Veerkamp
Ilona Wirtanen

CONTENTS

TABLES

FIGURES

CONTENTS   xi

Chapter 1
DROPPING OUT–
A NATIONAL PROBLEM?

Dropping out of high school does not "just happen" to a young man. By the time he enters tenth grade many signs are there. If he comes from a poor and perhaps broken home, if he has a history of poor work and failure in school, if he engages in delinquent behavior outside of school, then he has a much greater than average chance of becoming a dropout. Dropping out is thus a *symptom* — a dramatic indicator of more basic problems and limitations that leave an individual ill-suited to the typical high school environment. Whether we assign the responsibility to the individual who drops out, or to the school environment he leaves, the fact remains that dropping out is symptomatic of something gone wrong.

But is dropping out anything more than a symptom? Is it also a problem in its own right? Granted that boys with problems are more likely to drop out, does dropping out add to their problems and make things still worse? Such questions go to the heart of a basic policy issue: Is it sensible to treat dropping out as a national problem, or are we merely "treating a symptom?"

The Youth in Transition project was designed to help answer this question. The project followed a nationwide sample of over two thousand young men from the start of tenth grade to a time nearly four years later. At the beginning of the study all of the young men were in school: by the end some had dropped out, most had graduated, and quite a few had gone on to college. In the chapters that follow we will see how those who would become dropouts were different from those who would stay in school and graduate; we will also see whether dropping out led to changes in personality, aspirations, and behaviors. Before turning to the findings, however, let us fill in a little of the background. We begin with a look at the national campaign to reduce dropping out in the 1960's.

The Anti-Dropout Campaign

When the Youth in Transition study was launched in 1965 there was already an aroused concern at the highest levels of government about the dropout problem. There was concern about the root causes, but it seemed clear that the first order of business was to get the dropouts back into school.

In 1961 Abraham Ribicoff, then Secretary of Health, Education, and Welfare, stated the issue in dramatic terms:

> Our high school dropout rate has reached fantastic proportions: 2.5 million of the 10.8 million students enrolled in grades 9—12 of the nation's public and non-public schools this fall will drop out before graduation.
>
> This is a problem of frightening implication representing a terrible waste of our youth and it is found—not just in the big cities—but in every state. The dropout rate ranges from 20-40 percent in the 50 states. I submit that the Federal Government has a responsibility here.
>
> We have sought and will continue to seek to strengthen the nation's schools in facilities, curriculum, counseling, and the quality and salaries of our teachers *so that we can hold our young people in school.* . . For in this democracy of ours, education is usually the key that unlocks the door to opportunity. (Ribicoff, 1961; italics added).

President Kennedy's messages on education contained a similar emphasis on improving schools *in order to* reduce the dropout rate:

> For the individual the doors to the schoolhouse, to the library, and to the college lead to the richest treasures of our open society: to the power of knowledge—to the training and skills necessary for productive employment—to the wisdom, the ideals, and the culture which enrich life—and to the creative self-disciplined understanding of society needed for good citizenship in today's changing and challenging world. (Kennedy, 1963).
>
> . . .we must stimulate interest in learning *in order to reduce the alarming number of students who now drop out of school* . . .we must give special attention to increasing the opportunities and incentives for all Americans to develop their talents to the utmost—to complete their education and continue their self-development throughout life. This means preventing school dropouts, improving and expanding special educational services, and providing better education in slum, distressed, and rural areas where the educational attainment of students is below par. . . (Kennedy, 1962; italics added).

President Johnson continued the campaign against dropping out with words such as these:

> Here's what despair looks like; it looks like a young man who has narrowed his whole world down to one city block. . . who is killing all his tomorrows one by one with pointless days. We must never slacken our efforts to put him and all youngsters like him back into America's future. *And the basic step is to get them back into school.* (Johnson, 1965; italics added).

These statements have not been cited simply to show the level of concern and publicity given to the dropout problem, but rather to illustrate a way in which the problem is frequently conceptualized. *The basic step is to get dropouts back into school.* Now of course the national leadership has recognized and emphasized the need for changes in the schools; but the implication clearly remains that even before such changes can be made, the dropout would be well-advised to return to school—his chances of "making it" in today's world would be much better if he went back to the classroom that he left. Figures on average earnings of dropouts versus stayins are brought in to buttress the argument: "You will earn this much more if you stay in school." (Often such figures make no distinctions between those who stay in school just until high school graduation and those who go on to higher education.)

Such a view of the dropout problem has led to a nationwide radio and television advertising campaign urging those in school to stay there, and those who have dropped out to return. We refer to this effort as the "anti-dropout campaign," with full awareness of the double meaning of the term. In one sense, the campaign has been a preventive effort directed against dropping out. But as a by-product of this effort, the campaign has also come to be directed against the dropout himself. No matter how good its intentions, the anti-dropout campaign has often criticized and ridiculed the dropouts. For example, teenagers are treated to the televised spectacle of a young man in a track suit trying to run a race in lead boots, and are told this represents the life of a dropout in today's society. More heavy-handed is a song written by Allan Sherman, presumably designed to make the dropout "image" altogether undesirable:

> Drop, dropouts out of school,
> Proud of the will to fail.
> You won't find us in the school hall—
> Look in the pool hall
> Or in the jail.
>
> Ignoramus, there you are,
> Sitting in your hopped-up car,
> And your brains ain't up to par
> And your ears stick out too far.
> (Sherman, 1964)

This sort of campaign leads to an interesting speculation. Suppose that the education offered during the last year or two of the typical high school really has very little effect upon the dropout-prone individual. What, then, do we do when we conduct a

national anti-dropout campaign that downgrades the status of dropouts, and perhaps encourages employers to make the diploma a
requirement when it need not be. It seems just possible that our
treatment of dropping out as a national problem has some of the
features of a self-fulfilling prophecy. Perhaps for some young
men the greatest disadvantage in being a dropout is measured not
in terms of the education they lost, but rather in terms of the
stigma they acquired.

In any event, approaching the dropout problem by persuading
individuals to stay in (or return to) the classroom must be based
on a simple and straightforward proposition—that things get worse
for individuals who drop out, and that this is the direct result of
having dropped out. In other words, dropping out is more than
just a symptom, it is a problem in its own right. That proposition
is a testable one, even with the limited measurement techniques
available in the social sciences; one of our basic purposes in this
book is to put it to the test.

Issues in the Study of Dropping Out

Is the Dropout Problem Really Growing?—it all depends on
how you look at things. A few years ago Schreiber put it this way:

> Paradoxically, the dropout problem surfaces at a time when
> the proportion of youngsters who quit school before graduating is
> lower than ever... At the same time, jobs have become increas-
> ingly specialized and technical, requiring greater amounts of formal
> education. The dropout has suddenly become a problem because,
> among other reasons, the range and number of jobs requiring little
> formal education has drastically diminished. And his predicament
> has become all the more visible, as more and more people accom-
> modate themselves to the nearly complete dominance of formal ed-
> ucation as the major path to fulfillment. (Schreiber, 1967, pp. 9-10).

In 1900 about ninety percent of male students failed to receive
high school diplomas. By 1920 this figure was about eighty percent.
It was not until the 1950's that the dropout rate was cut below half
(Zeller, 1966). The dropout rate declined to about thirty percent
by 1965 (Varner, 1967). Our own data suggest, as we shall see
below, that the dropout rate was still lower by the end of the 1960's.

So the proportion of dropouts has gone down, but so has the
proportion of jobs that are suitable and available for dropouts
(Beinstock, 1967; Swanstrom, 1967; Hathaway, et al., 1969; Persella, 1970). We could, of course, say the same thing about those
who do not continue their education beyond the point of high school
graduation. The percentage of graduates who do *not* go to college
is declining, but so is the percentage of jobs available to those

without college training. We will shortly take up this issue of post-high school education in greater detail; for the present it is sufficient to note that the job market is tougher for dropouts these days, but it is also tougher for those whose education ends with a high school diploma.

A Definition of "Dropout." Until now we have been following a fairly common practice found in the literature about dropouts (see Miller, et al., 1964)—we have been using the term without defining it, and without paying much attention to the various ways in which it could be defined. Very often "dropout" simply refers to all those who do not have a high school diploma (assuming they are part of a sample or cohort that is old enough to have completed high school). That is a fairly workable definition, except that it leaves some loose ends—the sort of problem created by an individual who leaves school but gets his diploma one or two or five years later by going to night school or by taking a standard examination. Thus this year's "dropout" could turn out to be next year's "stayin," depending upon the date of his belated diploma.

In the analyses reported herein, *we will define dropouts as those individuals who interrupt their full-time attendance in high school for more than a few weeks* (and for reasons other than illness). This means that an individual may drop out and later return to school for his diploma, but we will still consider that he was at one time a dropout, and for most analytic purposes we will group him with all other dropouts (some of whom may also have diplomas by the time this is written). Admittedly, the broad and inclusive nature of this definition does not permit differentiations among those who have dropped out at different stages of their education and for different reasons. It does not attempt to distinguish the so-called "pushout"—the individual who feels, sometimes quite accurately, that the people in the school want him to leave. Such distinctions are interesting matters for discussion, but they prove to be terribly difficult to translate into workable classifications. The present definition of dropouts is close enough to other uses of the term, it is consistent with our study design, and it is clear and meaningful—dropouts are individuals who interrupt their full-time high school education.[1]

---

[1]Our definition of "dropout" is largely consistent with a "standard" definition used by the NEA Project on School Dropouts and the U.S. Office of Education. According to the definition, a dropout is "a pupil who leaves school, for any reason except death, before graduation or completion of a program of studies and without transferring to another school" (Varner, 1967).

With Whom Shall We Compare the Dropouts? The definition of dropouts proved to be a fairly simple matter. A more difficult issue is this: What is an appropriate comparison group of non-dropouts? The answer depends on our purposes. If we are interested only in a gross description of differences between dropouts and everyone else, the answer is quite obvious: we compare dropouts with all stayins. Most studies of dropouts take this approach.

But suppose we are interested in the individual factors that predispose to dropping out—individual differences among those from similar school and home environments that lead one to drop out and another to stay in. In that case we might contrast the dropouts with a matched sample of individuals from the same schools and the same socioeconomic levels. (Such a sample was developed in this study, and was used extensively in preliminary analyses.)

To take still another position, suppose that our primary interest is learning how much of a difference it makes whether a young man finishes high school rather than dropping out. A useful comparison group, in that case, would be those who graduated from high school but went no further in their education. Combs and Cooley (1968) used this type of "control group" in their dropout analysis based on Project TALENT data.

The distinction between all high school graduates versus those graduates who do not continue their education beyond high school is of crucial importance in any analysis of the difference between dropouts and "stayins." If it is overlooked, a clear possibility exists that we will interpret a difference as lying between dropouts and stayins, when it is more meaningfully described as lying between those who enter college and those who do not.[2]

---

[2]If that distinction is not self-evident, an illustration may be of some help. Imagine a sample of 100 in which 20 have been identified as high school dropouts, 40 as graduates who did not continue their education, and 40 as graduates who continued with some form of post-high school education. Suppose those who went on to further education had a mean self-esteem score of 4 on a scale ranging from 1 to 5, while the other two groups each had mean scores of 3. This pattern would be described accurately as a difference between those who continued their education beyond high school and those who did not. However, a comparison which matched the dropouts with all stayins would also show a substantial difference in self-esteem: The dropouts would have a mean score of 3, but the group of all 80 stayins would have a mean score of 3.5 (since the 40 graduates who went on to further education had a mean score of 4, and the other 40 graduates had a mean score of 3).

What, then, is an appropriate comparison group for our analyses of dropouts? We have found it useful in most of our analyses to contrast three groups: at one end of the continuum are the dropouts, at the other end are those who have entered college or other post-high school education, and between them lie those who have not continued their formal education beyond high school graduation.

Educational Attainment as a Continuum

Does it make any sense to place dropping out and entering college on the same continuum? The question may be answered on both conceptual and empirical levels.

On the conceptual level, it seems useful to consider commitment to education as a broader dimension than one which distinguishes dropouts from stayins. Those who feel education is very important are not only less likely to drop out, they are also more likely to extend their education beyond high school. Certainly the idea of education as a key to success and occupational attainment does not disappear at the point of high school graduation. Our discussion earlier has reminded us that a college diploma is as important to many members of the present generation as a high school diploma was to the preceding generation. When jobs are scarce for dropouts, they are also likely to be scarce for those without post-high school training. Indeed, it requires no stretching of the imagination to see how the current campaign against dropping out of high school could be an equally persuasive argument to stay in (or return to) college: a good education is necessary if one wants to have a good job.

But there is more to education than its value as a credential and its ability to prepare one for job performance. For some, at least, education has intrinsic value—understanding how something works or learning something new can be satisfying in its own right. We expect such intrinsic motivation to be low for those who drop out of school. They may not be lacking in desire for intellectual stimulation, but they are not likely to desire the brand of stimulation provided by formal education. Those who do find stimulation in formal education are likely to desire more, and to satisfy that desire by entering college. This is not to say that all or even most who enter college do so for primarily intrinsic reasons. But it does seem reasonable to suppose that attitudes toward education will be most positive, on the average, among those who are aiming for college, and most negative among those who will become dropouts.

At the most general level the treatment of educational attainment as a continuum assumes that most factors which relate to dropping out of high school also relate, in an opposite direction, to extending one's education beyond high school. We have argued briefly that such an approach is conceptually plausible. And it is obviously parsimonious. The question remains: does such a continuum of educational attainment hold up at the empirical level—does it fit the data?

The evidence is quite clear and consistent. Along a variety of relevant dimensions, the dropouts and the college entrants are found at opposite ends of the scale, with the others (the non-college-bound high school graduates) located in the middle and often closer to the dropouts. The data will be presented in detail in the chapters to follow, but one finding is worth previewing because it bears directly on the conceptual argument presented above.

Measures of positive and negative school attitudes, first obtained when the respondents were beginning tenth grade, show sharp differences between those who later dropped out (Group 1), those who ended their education at high school graduation (Group 2), and those who went on to further education (Group 3). Moreover, the average scores for these three groups are spaced at nearly equal intervals, i.e., the differences between Group 1 and Group 2 are just about the same magnitude as the differences between Group 2 and Group 3.[3]

We conclude, then, that this simple continuum of educational attainment makes sense at both the conceptual and empirical levels. It will illuminate much of the analytic work to follow.

Purposes of this Volume

Our purposes have been suggested above. In this section we review and make them more explicit. In addition, we note some of the limits on this volume—the things we have not included.

Studying the Causes of Dropping Out. The longitudinal design of the Youth in Transition study is well-suited to an examination of many factors of personal background, ability, attitudes and behaviors that predispose to dropping out of high school. We will begin our analysis by looking at a number of family background and ability dimensions that relate to dropping out, building on the analysis of family background effects reported in Volume II of this series (Bachman, 1970). Next we will look at school

---

[3]We have not yet done an adequate job of defining and describing Groups 1, 2 and 3. We will turn to that task in Chapter 2.

experiences and attitudes toward school which are predictive of later dropping out. Finally, we will examine patterns of affective states, self-concepts, values, aspirations, and behaviors which differentiate dropouts from stayins.

Studying the Effects of Dropping Out. It is one thing to learn that boys who are low in self-esteem, to take one example, are more likely to drop out of school; it is quite another matter if we find that dropping out has the effect of lowering self-esteem still further. If we had been interested solely in factors which *predict* dropping out, we could have used a much simpler longitudinal design. It would have been sufficient to collect the initial set of measures from a sample of high school students, and then find out later whether they dropped out of school. Our most basic interest, however, has been to learn what *effects* of dropping out can be detected. Accordingly, we employed a longitudinal design which administered the same measures at several points in time in order to assess changes. We will examine measures obtained at two, three, and often four points in time in order to learn more about the effects of dropping out. We are interested in determining whether dropping out does lead to measurable changes in self-esteem, self-concepts of ability, affective states, delinquency, occupational aspirations, and the like. In addition, we will examine the occupational outcomes of dropouts to see whether they attain poorer jobs than those of similar background and ability who have graduated from high school.

Studying Educational Attainment as a Continuum. When we began the analyses reported in this volume, our purpose was to focus specifically on causes and effects of dropping out of high school. However, as some of our discussion above has suggested, we found it impossible to pursue that purpose without giving careful consideration to post-high school education as well; indeed, we came to feel that the most important distinctions often relate to college entrance rather than high school graduation. We have thus concluded that we can best achieve our purposes by studying dropping out as part of a larger continuum of educational attainment.

Some Limitations. Perhaps the largest and most important limitation in our study is the fact that all respondents are male. At the start of this project it seemed clear that the dynamics of dropping out, career planning, occupational attainment, and the like are substantially different for boys and girls, and we decided to concentrate our efforts on boys. Recent reports from Project TALENT (Combs and Cooley, 1968) and by Hathaway et al., (1969a, 1969b) confirm this conclusion. Girls and boys tend to drop out for different kinds of reasons, and the effects of dropping out are somewhat different for girls and boys. It is worth noting that in both of the dropout studies cited above the researchers elected to analyze and report data separately for boys and girls.

Another limitation is less basic but should be mentioned. Because our study began with a sample of tenth-graders, we will have nothing to say about the small proportion of dropouts who leave school before the start of tenth grade.

One other limitation requires discussion here. The Youth in Transition project has focused a good deal of attention on the measurement of school characteristics. One of our interests in doing so has been to learn what characteristics of schools are associated with high dropout rates. That topic is presently being pursued as part of a large analysis effort dealing with school characteristics and outcomes, and will be reported separately in a later volume.

Summary

There has been a great deal of concern about "the dropout problem" during the last decade. National leaders at the highest levels have taken the position that the most important thing is to get the dropouts back into school. A nationwide radio and television campaign has been used to dramatize the disadvantages felt by young people who lack a high school diploma and the education that it signifies. All of this rests on the simple and straightforward proposition that things get worse for individuals when they drop out of school. One of the basic purposes of the research reported here is to put that proposition to the test.

Our intention is to examine both the causes and the results of dropping out among young men. To put it another way, we want to distinguish between dropping out as a *symptom* of prior difficulties, and dropping out as a *problem* in its own right, leading to new or increased difficulties. In seeking the causes of dropping out we will examine family background, abilities, school attitudes and experiences, and a variety of other individual characteristics. Our study of the effects of dropping out will make use of measures obtained at several points in time, in order to discover changes in self-esteem, self-concepts of ability, affective states, delinquency, occupational aspirations, and the like.

It is not always clear whether dropouts should be compared with all high school graduates or with only those graduates who do not continue their education beyond high school. We have found it useful to treat educational attainment as a continuum: at the one end are the dropouts, at the other end are those who have entered college or other post-high school education, and between them lie those who have not continued their formal education beyond high school graduation. This approach makes conceptual sense; moreover, it fits the data quite well, as we shall see in the chapters which follow.

Chapter 2
RESEARCH DESIGN: DISTINGUISHING PROBLEMS FROM SYMPTOMS

From the outset of the Youth in Transition study, it was recognized that dropping out is symptomatic of underlying difficulties and/or limitations. And this creates a problem in research design, as the following passage from our first volume indicates:

> Short of an experiment to decide randomly that some boys should be removed from school and others should not, there is no way of getting a "pure" measure of the *effects* of dropping out—there will always be some contamination with the causes of dropping out. When one attempts to assess the *effects* of dropping out, it is impossible to contrast "dropouts" with otherwise comparable "stay-ins" because the very fact of dropping out (or getting pushed out) is evidence of some *prior* difference. To put it another way, it is a contradiction to say, "Suppose two boys are identical, then one drops out of school and the other does not. . . ."
>
> The best available solution for this serious problem in research design is that provided by longitudinal design. . . . Our basic strategy is to measure as many prior conditions as possible, and then to contrast changes that occur following drop-out with changes that accompany continuing in school. The longitudinal design does not completely eliminate the bias of self-selection, and it is important that this be recognized. But in our view it is the best available strategy for dealing with this complex problem. (Bachman, et al., 1967, pp. 38–39).

The examination of changes requires that the same measures be used in a number of data collections at different points in time. This repeated use of the same measures is a basic feature in our effort to distinguish problems from symptoms.

We turn now to a more detailed review of the design and a description of the major analysis groups to be used throughout the rest of the volume. The chapter concludes with an estimate of the dropout rate among young men in the Class of 1969.

13

Research Design[1]

The research design for the Youth in Transition study is described in detail in the first volume of this monograph series (Bachman, et al., 1967, chapter 3). Briefly, the design centers around a nationally representative panel of over two thousand adolescent boys who agreed to be surveyed repeatedly at intervals of a year or more. The first data collection took place in the fall of 1966, when the subjects had just entered tenth grade. Additional data collections took place in the spring of 1968 (the end of eleventh grade for most boys), the spring of 1969 (just before most were graduated), and the spring and early summer of 1970.[2] The panel members, at the time of the initial survey, were clustered in 87 schools throughout the United States.[3] Additional data concerning school environments have been obtained from principals, counselors, and samples of teachers in each of the participating schools. This information is being used extensively in analyses focused on school effects, to be reported in later volumes in this series.

Initial Sample. The study began with a sample of 2213 tenth-grade boys located in 87 public high schools. The schools and boys were selected through a multi-stage sampling design in such a way that the probability of a school's selection was proportionate to its size (i.e., the estimated number of tenth-grade boys), and roughly equal numbers of boys (about 25) were selected from each school. The net effect of this design is to provide an essentially bias-free representation of tenth-grade boys in public high schools throughout the United States (see Bachman, et al., 1967, pp. 21-24).

Response rates must be considered at two levels. A total of 88 schools were originally invited to participate in the study; an affirmative response was obtained from 71, and replacement schools in the same sample areas were secured for all but one of the remaining schools. In the resulting 87 participating schools, 2277 boys were invited to participate in the study. A total of 2213 (over 97 percent) agreed to participate and provided essentially complete data.[4]

---

[1]Much of the material in this section is taken directly from the "Research Design" section of the second volume in this series (Bachman, 1970).

[2]This sequence of data collections represents an improvement over that projected in our first volume.

[3]A small additional panel, located in a limited number of "discretionary" schools, has also been surveyed; however, data from this supplementary panel are not reported in the present monograph.

[4]Some weighting of individual responses was necessary to correct some limitations in the sample; a detailed discussion of this procedure is presented in Bachman et al. (1967, pp. 126-127).

Data Collection Procedures. An overview of data collection procedures at all four points in time is provided here. A more detailed account of the initial data collection, including copies of the instruments, may be found in Volume I (Bachman, et al., 1970).

Time 1: October-November, 1966. The first part of this data collection consisted of a personal interview with each respondent, lasting just over two hours on the average. The interviewing was carried out in the schools during school hours by the Survey Research Center's staff of trained interviewers. One or two interviewers were assigned to each school.

After all interviewing had been completed in a school, the participants met as a group during school hours and spent a morning or afternoon completing a battery of tests and questionnaires. These group sessions were conducted by the interviewers, following standardized instructions.

Time 2: March-May, 1968. This data collection included a personal interview followed by a paper-and-pencil questionnaire, requiring a total of about three hours to administer. Many of the questions administered at Time 1 were repeated in order to obtain measures of change.

Since it was important to have the interviewing conditions as similar as possible for dropouts and stayins, it was considered undesirable to conduct these interviews in school buildings. It was also undesirable to collect the data in respondents' homes, since the potential lack of privacy might have interfered with frank and open answers to some rather personal questions. Accordingly, the interviews were conducted at "neutral sites"—locations such as library conference rooms, community centers, church basements, and the like. Interviewers arranged such locations in the same general neighborhood as the schools used at Time 1, then contacted respondents (usually by phone) to arrange individual appointments. Respondents were paid two dollars to help reimburse them for any transportation costs in coming to the interview site.

Time 3: April-June, 1969. This data collection was not part of the original design. It required separate funding, and had to be limited to questionnaires administered to groups of ten or fewer respondents. Most of the content area covered in earlier questionnaires was repeated in this data collection, and some of the earlier interview material was converted to questionnaire form. Administration time was somewhat over two hours.

As in the case of the Time 2 data collection, neutral sites were used for the group administration of questionnaires by Survey Research Center interviewers. Respondents were paid five dollars to cover time and transportation costs.

Time 4: June–July, 1970. This final data collection, taken a year after most respondents graduated from high school, involved both interview and questionnaire segments. The personal interview lasted about two hours on the average, and covered many of the questions treated in earlier interviews as well as new questions about post-high school work and/or educational experiences. The questionnaire material also repeated many questions used in earlier data collections, and lasted about an hour and a half.

Interviewing was carried out individually by appointment, again using neutral sites. Because of the length of the session, and the fact that many respondents were now working and might thus consider their time worth more money, a payment of ten dollars to cover time and transportation was considered appropriate.

Respondents Who Moved. Whenever a respondent changed his place of residence between data collections, a considerable effort was made to locate him at his new address and have the interviewer in that area arrange a data collection. In many cases this was possible, but some young men were not contacted either because we were unable to learn the new address, or because the new address was not within 50 miles of an interviewer.

At Time 4 an attempt was made to include panel members who had participated in earlier data collections, but then joined the military service and were located on bases not accessible to our interviewers. A total of 66 such servicemen were sent a special mail version of the instruments, consisting of the standard questionnaire plus questionnaire versions of some interview items. Completed forms were returned by 49 respondents.

Response Rates in Later Data Collections. The response rates for all four data collections are summarized in Table 2-1. As the table indicates, the greatest loss in respondents occurred between Time 1 and Time 2. At each follow-up data collection, of course, there were those who could not be located at all; however, the relatively large drop in participation from Time 1 to Time 2 reflects the loss of those individuals who were willing to go along with a survey conducted in school, but were unwilling to come to a neutral site to be interviewed "after hours."

When a respondent refused or was unable to participate in one of the data collections, the interviewer made an effort to determine his student status. As a result, it was possible to classify as dropouts or stayins many of the boys who did not complete all four data collections.

The follow-up information on some non-respondents indicated that dropouts were much more likely than others to "drop out" of

TABLE 2-1

RESPONSE RATES ACROSS TIME

	Number of Respondents	Percent of Original Sample (N = 2277)	Percent of Time 1 Panel (N = 2213)
TIME 1 (Fall, 1966)	2213	97.2%	100%
TIME 2 (Spring, 1968)	1886	82.8%	85.2%
TIME 3 (Spring, 1969)	1799	79.0%	81.3%
TIME 4 (Summer, 1970)	1620	71.1%	73.2%

participation in the later data collections. This difference in non-response rate and its implication for the study are discussed below.

Analysis Groups

We argued in earlier sections that we should distinguish not just between dropouts and stayins, but also between those who do and do not continue their education beyond high school. Thus it will be useful to define three broad classes of individuals.

Group 1 consists of those who dropped out of high school or, more specifically, those who interrupted their full-time school progress for more than a few weeks. Some of those in Group 1 dropped out and then attained high school diplomas; in Appendix D we examine these individuals (Subgroup 1a) separately from those who dropped out and had not attained a diploma by mid-1970 (Subgroup 1b).

Group 2 consists of those who graduated from high school without ever having dropped out (as defined above), and who were *not* primarily engaged in post-high school education in the first half of 1970. These are the high school graduates who were primarily engaged in work roles or military service at Time 4. This group includes a few individuals who tried college as full-time students in the fall of 1969, but did not continue; it also includes some who were taking one or two classes in 1970, but did not consider themselves *primarily* students in post-high school education during that time.

Group 3 consists of those who were primarily engaged in post-high school education during the first half of 1970. (This category does not necessarily exclude all dropouts, since it is possible to drop out of high school but later go on to graduate and then enter higher education. In fact, 10 of our respondents followed just such a course, and could thus be categorized in both Group

1 and Group 3; however, since we required mutually exclusive categories for analytic purposes, we made the arbitrary decision to classify all of them in Group 3).

Now let us consider how our respondents may be sorted into the analysis groups defined above. We shall begin with those who are easiest to classify—the ones who continued their participation throughout the course of the longitudinal study, and thus gave us complete interview data on their status as of Time 4 (mid-1970). Column A of Table 2-2 presents the distribution of the Time 4 participants into Groups 1, 2 and 3. The analysis groupings shown in Column A are the ones we will use to examine *changes* that may result from dropping out or entering college, since only those individuals who remained participants at Time 4 have provided us with the "after" measures necessary to assess the effects of both college and dropout experiences.

Other analyses will focus on factors which cause (or predict to) dropping out, and for such purposes it will be useful to add to our analysis groupings those individuals who did not participate in the Time 4 data collection but whom we are able to classify as dropouts, stayins, college entrants, etc., on the basis of Time 3 responses and/or interviewer-provided data. Such classifications are not perfectly accurate, and they involve some degree of compromise. For example, there were about one hundred non-respondents whom the interviewers identified simply as having graduated from high school. In such cases the respondents were arbitrarily assigned to Group 2, even though some probably were college students in 1970 and thus belonged in Group 3. Column B of Table 2-2 presents the distribution of those who participated when the study began in the fall of 1966 but did not complete the Time 4 data collection.

Differences Between Respondents and Non-respondents at Time 4. We have stressed the importance of the Time 4 participants as those who will be used to examine *changes* resulting from dropping out of high school or entering college. The question then arises, can we generalize from these respondents to those who did not continue their participation throughout the study? A comparison of Columns A and B in Table 2-2 indicates that this is not possible at a general, undifferentiated level. Less than 10 percent of the Time 4 participants were dropouts, whereas 22 percent of the non-participants were identified as dropouts (and many of those who could not be classified are surely dropouts also).

Now suppose we ask our question in a more sophisticated manner: *within each analysis group,* are there important differences between those who participated at Time 4 and those who did not?

TABLE 2-2

CLASSIFICATION OF RESPONDENTS INTO ANALYSIS GROUPS
(Table entries are unweighted numbers of cases)

	A. Time 4 Participants	B. Left Study Before Time 4	C. Total
Group 1: Dropouts	157	129	286
(Subgroup 1a: diploma)	(32)		
(Subgroup 1b: no diploma)	(125)		
Group 2: Graduate/no post-high school education	620	176	796
Group 3: Post-high school education	843	71	914
Unclassified	-	217	217
Total	1620	593	2213

The answer to this question is contained in the data presented in later chapters, especially Chapter 7, but we can preview those data here. In general, the initial scores for intelligence, socioeconomic level, self-concepts, affective states, aspirations, etc., obtained at the start of tenth grade are about the same for those dropouts who participated at Time 4 as for those non-participants who were identified as having dropped out. This conclusion for analysis Group 1 also applies to Groups 2 and 3. In other words, the proportions falling into analysis Groups 1, 2 and 3 are quite different for Time 4 participants and non-participants, but within each analysis category there is little difference in background, ability, and personality dimensions between those who continued their participation through Time 4 and those who did not. This conclusion is most encouraging, for it means that even when we are limited to the 157 dropouts available at Time 4 our findings are likely to be applicable to dropouts in general. It also means that the several rather arbitrary classifications mentioned earlier did not lead to any apparent distortion of the analysis groups taken as a whole.

How Distinct and Different Are the Analysis Groupings? We've just noted that the analysis groupings can be used to uncover a good deal of consistency between those who did and did not participate at Time 4; and we will see in the following chapters that there are some large differences between the analysis groups in terms of background, abilities, attitudes, and behaviors. In short, the groupings are sufficiently accurate to be quite successful in our analyses.

At the same time we must acknowledge that no matter how accurately we assign individuals to the analysis groupings we have defined, the definitions themselves are quite broad and include a variety of individuals and experiences within them. Group 1, the dropouts, includes those who dropped out and later acquired diplomas (Subgroup 1a) as well as those who had not as of mid-1970 (Subgroup 1b). As we shall see, most dropouts express an intention to attain their diplomas, and no doubt some will do so. This makes it difficult to make any lasting distinction between the two dropout subgroups; more important, in our view, is the fact that both subgroups have in common the experience of having dropped out of the standard school program.

Group 3, those primarily engaged in post-high school education, also includes a diversity of respondents. Table 2-3 summarizes the several forms of post-high school education in which the Group 3 students were involved. While there are substantial differences between universities, liberal arts colleges, and junior or community colleges, the similarities between them seem even more important. It is somewhat harder to make the same case for technical or vocational schools; nevertheless, we concluded that those who described themselves as "primarily students" in technical and vocational schools had more in common with college students than with those in other categories. A basic distinction to keep in mind is the fact that Group 3 respondents are defined as those whose most important activity was being a student; thus, unlike Group 1 and Group 2 respondents, the respondents in Group 3 were not full-time members of the work force. (Given the fact that about 90 percent of those classified in Group 3 were attending a university or some form of college, we will often as a matter of convenience label this the "college" group.)

Group 2 is perhaps best defined in negative terms—those who did not drop out, but who did not go on to college. Of course, some individuals enter college several years after high school—often after a period of military service. Thus this categorization, like the others, is an arbitrary one dictated by convenience and by limitations in the time span of the study.

In sum, these are rough groupings, but useful ones. Moreover, the few distinctions we have been able to make here already go beyond those in most studies of dropouts (Miller, et al., 1964).

TABLE 2-3

TYPES OF POST HIGH-SCHOOL EDUCATION

Type of School	Number of Time 4 Respondents Attending
University	381
Liberal arts college	161
Junior or community college	154
Technical or vocational school	75
Other (engineering, teacher, business, agriculture college, etc.)	72

Estimated Total Percentage of Dropouts

We noted earlier the unfortunate, but understandable, fact of life that non-participation rates are much higher among dropouts than among stayins. Some, of course, were simply inaccessible— sometimes because they were in military service. But for others the explanation probably lies in the fact that the Youth in Transition study was closely linked to their school experience. In spite of our efforts to make all follow-up data collections "neutral" (conducted outside of school and using no school personnel), the fact remains that the study was initiated in schools and placed considerable emphasis on school-related issues and on long-range plans and aspirations. A dropout is likely to be sensitive about such matters, and this no doubt makes him hesitant to participate in further data collections. For these reasons and others, we estimate that we have complete data from less than half those who dropped out of high school.

Fortunately, in addition to the 157 dropouts who continued participation through Time 4, our interviewers were able to "track back" and identify another 129 of the original sample as dropouts. These two groups together account for 12.9 percent of the original sample of 2213 boys.

We are left, however, with 217 of the original sample (9.8 percent) who could not be identified as either dropouts or stayins. Surely some are dropouts—our problem is to estimate how many.

Let us begin by considering what we know about these 217 unclassified non-respondents. First, virtually all of them were non-participants as early as Time 3 (since all participants at Time 3 gave us sufficient information at that time to permit classifying them even if they did not participate at Time 4). Second, we know that the unclassified non-respondents at Time 3 had something in common with other non-respondents at Time 3 (those whom we *were* able to track back and classify)—all were unable or unwilling to participate in the Time 3 data collection. The dropout rate was about 49 percent among those Time 3 non-respondents we were able to classify; thus it seems reasonable to suppose that an equally high rate of dropping out occurred among those we could not classify. If so, then we would also expect a similarity between the two groups in terms of factors that predispose a boy to drop out, factors such as broken homes, low socioeconomic levels, limited academic ability, and the like. An investigation of such dimensions, mentioned in Chapter 3 and detailed in Appendix C, revealed that both sets of Time 3 non-participants (those we could track back and classify, and those we could not) were above average in those characteristics which predict dropping out. Indeed, what differences there were indicated that the dropout rate might have been slightly above 50 percent among the 217 whom we could not track back and classify.

The above analysis is admittedl y tenuous. There are some reasons to suppose that those non-respondents whom we were not able to track down might contain substantially more than fifty percent dropouts, since dropping out may be among the factors that make it difficult to track down an individual. We do think it is unlikely that substantially *fewer* than fifty percent of the unclassified individuals are dropouts. Thus our best guess is that our final estimate of the dropout rate does not overstate reality; it may be an understatement, but only by one or two percentage points.

Eighteen or Nineteen Percent of Tenth-Grade Boys Dropped Out. Based on the data summarized above, we would estimate a dropout rate of at least 18 percent, and perhaps as high as 19 or 20 percent, among our nationwide sample of public school tenth-graders (in the class of 1969). An independent source of information bearing on this estimate was available from principals' questionnaire data (collected in Spring, 1968); the data provided by principals indicate that 19 percent of all boys who start the tenth grade in the schools we sampled leave before graduating (not including those who transfer to other schools). Since this information applies to all boys in our cross-section of schools (not just to those in our sample), and since it was provided independent of our estimates above (and not examined until after the estimates were made), the convergence of estimates is most reassuring.

Any such summary figure nevertheless represents an oversimplification. It omits a few individuals who dropped out *before* the start of tenth grade. On the other hand, the figure includes as dropouts some who have already returned to school to attain their diplomas, and others who will do so in the future.

In spite of the oversimplifications, however, it seems clear that fewer young men were dropping out in the late 1960's than was the case even a few years earlier. One of the implications is that estimates of dropout rates, *including this one*, are transitory and require very frequent updating.

Some Non-Statistical Notes on Statistical Procedures

Although this monograph includes much statistical data, it is designed to be read by non-statisticians. We have tried to present findings in forms that will be meaningful to those with limited statistical training. This does not mean that we have avoided complex or sophisticated analytic procedures; rather, it means that we have tried to explain the results of such procedures in relatively non-technical terms.

Statistical Significance. It is important in survey research, as in other research methods, to distinguish between haphazard and systematic variation in any set of data. Tests of statistical significance represent *one* of the bases for making such distinctions (Winch and Campbell, 1969). However, it is difficult to arrive at significance levels based on a multistage clustered sample, and the problem becomes still more complex when we use multivariate analysis procedures. Accordingly, *it will not be our practice to declare certain relationships "statistically significant."* This does not mean that many of the relationships discussed in this monograph are not statistically trustworthy. On the contrary, given the size of our sample, virtually all of the relationships we interpret as *substantively* significant would easily meet conventional criteria of statistical significance. We deal with issues related to sampling errors, confidence intervals, and statistical significance in Appendix A.

Substantive Significance. Substantive significance is in large measure a matter of judgment. An author's judgment of substantive importance is reflected in the findings he chooses to present. Ideally, however, these findings are presented in forms that permit the reader to make his own judgments about their substantive significance. In this monograph we have adopted several practices designed to accomplish this purpose. Most important, we have tried to present findings in ways that will show the strength of the relationships involved; and when we contrast subgroups, we consider the extent to which they overlap as well as differ. The effect of this form of reporting may be to make some findings less dramatic, but hopefully more realistic. Another practice involves presenting more data than we can discuss, so that when a reader wishes to examine a set of findings closely he is able to do so. Much of this extra information has been placed in appendices, although some also appears in tables and figures within chapters. In either case, it is assumed that most readers will need and use somewhat less than the total amount of statistical data provided.

Summary

The design for the Youth in Transition study centers around a nationally representative panel of young men who were surveyed first in fall of 1966, when they were entering tenth grade, and again in the spring of 1968, the spring of 1969, and the early summer of 1970. Three major categories of respondents were identified: Group 1—dropouts; Group 2—graduates with no post-high school education; Group 3—those primarily engaged in further education during the year following their high school graduation. These are rough groupings, but useful ones—and they represent a degree of analytic refinement seldom used in studies of dropouts versus graduates.

Non-response rates are higher among dropouts than among graduates, and this presents some analysis problems. Taking this into account, we estimate a dropout rate of at least 18 percent, and perhaps as high as 19 or 20 percent, among our nationwide sample of young men (those who entered tenth grade in 1966). The dropout rate is clearly going down—fewer young men were dropping out in the late 1960's than was the case even a few years earlier. This serves as a reminder that any estimate of dropout rate, no matter how accurate, applies only to a specific and rather limited period in time.

Chapter 3
IMPACT OF FAMILY
BACKGROUND AND ABILITY

Popular wisdom holds that family background and environment have a great deal to do with whether or not a youth will drop out of high school. A number of dropout studies (Varner, 1967; Orshansky, 1968; Hathaway, 1969) support this view. In this chapter we consider eight family background dimensions and note the ways in which they are related to dropping out. We also examine several dimensions of intellectual ability, and consider whether some of the effects of family background can appropriately be viewed as operating "through" intelligence or reading ability as intervening variables.

A fairly extensive study of family background characteristics and their impact formed the basis of the second volume in the Youth in Transition series (Bachman, 1970). The present chapter represents an extension of that analytic effort to deal with a new criterion dimension—dropping out of school. It will be helpful to lean rather heavily on our previous work for two reasons: First, Volume II provides much detailed information on the background dimensions and analysis techniques which require only brief summaries here. Second, many of the findings reported in Volume II provide a context within which to interpret our new data on dropping out.

Family Background

Our earlier analysis dealt with eight dimensions of family background, each measured when the respondents were starting tenth grade: socioeconomic level, family size (number of siblings), broken home, family relations, religious preference, parents' political preference, community size, and race. Most of these dimensions have already shown some association with such relevant factors as school attitudes, occupational aspirations, and college plans, and most are also related to dropping out of school. Our initial analyses for this volume were carried out with the full set of eight family background variables in order to maintain consist-

25

ency with Volume II. Those analyses are summarized in Appendix B. In the present chapter we will concentrate our attention on those background dimensions which show sufficiently large and reliable effects to warrant discussion. In addition, we will "take apart" one of the summary background measures, family relations, in order to examine its major component, parental punitiveness.

Socioeconomic Level. Socioeconomic level (SEL) is perhaps the most fundamentally important of the family background measures examined in the Youth in Transition study. It is related to most other background measures; indeed, what appear to be "effects" of other background dimensions can sometimes be attributed equally well (and with greater parsimony) to SEL.

The summary measure of SEL used in this study consists of six equally-weighted ingredients: father's occupational status, father's educational level, mother's educational level, number of rooms per person in the home, and a checklist of other possessions in the home.[1] These highly intercorrelated ingredients all relate to the quality of home environment available to children. (They are also, of course, likely indicators of genetic endowment; therefore, we cannot conclude that the relationship between SEL and dropout rates represents only the effects of environment.)

Socioeconomic level shows consistently strong relationships with measures of intelligence, vocabulary skill, and reading comprehension. Given strong correlations with measured ability, it is not surprising to find that SEL is also related to young men's perceptions of their own school ability; but it is important to note that even after intelligence and other background factors are controlled statistically, a moderate association remains between SEL and self-concept of school ability.

Socioeconomic level is associated with a number of other dimensions reflecting attitudes and behaviors relating to school. School grades are positively correlated with SEL; so are college plans and occupational aspirations. Negative attitudes toward school, test anxiety, and rebellious behavior in school are all greater among low SEL students.

We concluded in Volume II that socioeconomic level is important in shaping ability; but even after controlling for ability, SEL also has a positive influence on performance, aspirations, school attitudes, and important self-concepts. In short, the boy from a high socioeconomic home is doubly advantaged (Bachman, 1970).

---

[1]See Bachman (1970), especially Appendix B, for a detailed description of the summary measure of socioeconomic level.

Figure 3-1 presents the relationship between socioeconomic level and our measure of dropout/college entrance (i.e., analysis Groups 1, 2, and 3 as described in Chapter 1). The expected pattern appears sharp and clear—about 23 percent of those in the bottom SEL categories were classified as dropouts, whereas this was true of only 4 percent in the top category.

The above percentages of dropouts are actually underestimates, since we were unable to classify nearly 10 percent of our original sample. We argued in Chapter 2 that these "unclassifieds" probably dropped out in proportions equal to or greater than the dropout rate for the most appropriate comparison group—those other members of the original sample who also did not participate in later data collections but who could be tracked back and identified as either dropouts or stayins. If we assume that the dropout rate among the "unclassifieds" is the same as that for the "track-backs," and if we follow that approach separately within each category of SEL, we can arrive at an estimated dropout rate that represents an improvement over that provided by the solid bars at the bottom of Figure 3-1. Such an estimate has been made, and the procedures are detailed in Appendix C; the resulting estimated dropout rate is shown by the dashed line in Figure 3-1.

Our *estimated* dropout rate for those in the bottom SEL category is 30 percent or more, ample evidence that family background plays a vital role in whether a young man drops out of high school.

The relationship between socioeconomic level and college entrance is also quite strong, as indicated in Figure 3-1. Just over 10 percent of the young men in the bottom SEL category were primarily students (post-high school) in spring of 1970, compared with about three quarters of those in the top SEL category. This finding is scarcely surprising, especially since it conforms closely to data on college *plans* reported in Volume II. We note it here because it is so consistent with the view that "commitment to education" may be viewed as a continuum: at one end is the dropout, toward the other end is the college student, and somewhere in the middle is the youth who ends his education with high school graduation.

Family Size. Family size, or the number of siblings a boy has, shows a fairly substantial relationship with socioeconomic level. About half of our respondents reported two or fewer siblings, and within this range there is no appreciable association between family size and SEL. However, larger families tend also to be low in SEL. A similar pattern appears when family size is

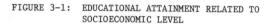

FIGURE 3-1:   EDUCATIONAL ATTAINMENT RELATED TO
              SOCIOECONOMIC LEVEL

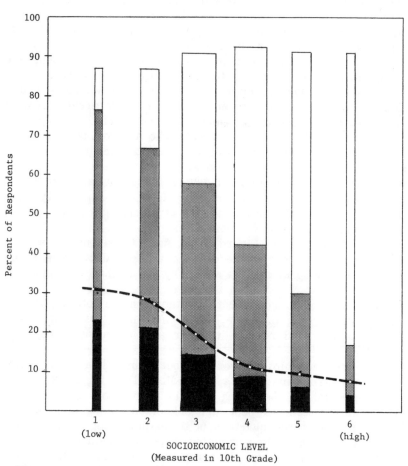

Group 1: High school dropouts
Group 2: Stayins who were not "primarily students" after high school
Group 3: Stayins who were "primarily students" after high school

- - - Dropout rate estimated from total sample (incl. "undiscovered dropouts")

Eta (treating educational attainment as a trichotomous criterion) = .37

NOTES: Width of each bar is proportionate to size of predictor subgroup.
        See Chapter 2 for complete definitions of Groups 1,2, and 3.

        This figure follows a standard format that will reappear through-
        out Chapters 3,4, and 5. A discussion of the several features of
        this format, including the procedures for estimating dropout rate
        for the total sample, is presented in Appendix C.

related to tests of intelligence and ability; as the number of siblings increases beyond two, average test scores gradually decline. When the effects of SEL are removed statistically, the relationship between family size and test scores is reduced but by no means eliminated.

The young men in our sample who came from small families were higher in self-concepts of school ability, academic achievement (grades), college plans, and occupational aspirations. Negative school attitudes were more prominent among those from larger families. Part of these relationships can be attributed to differences in socioeconomic level, but a portion of the effect remains in each case after controlling for SEL.

Family size is related to dropping out, as shown in Figure 3-2. Boys from large families were about three times more likely to drop out than those from small families. Another way of expressing the relationship is to note that dropouts average 3.6 siblings, the non-college stayins average 3.2, while the mean for college entrants in 2.4.

But is this really anything more than an indirect reflection of the lower socioeconomic levels of large families? Applying the same statistical techniques as were used in Volume II, we find that the effects of family size are diminished when SEL is controlled, but they do not disappear.[2]

Broken Home. Thus far our findings about dropouts are just what we would have expected based on the family background effects reported in Volume II. We reported that boys in poorer families, and those in large families, are disadvantaged in a variety of ways—and now we find that they also drop out of school more often than average. When we look at the effects of a broken home (absence of one or both parents) the similarity with findings in Volume II no longer obtains. We begin by reviewing our earlier conclusions:

> We have stressed the distinction between homes broken by death and those broken by separation (usually by formal divorce). With few exceptions, homes broken by death are similar to intact families in terms of socioeconomic level or number of siblings, whereas homes broken by separation are more often large families and those at low socioeconomic levels. Families disrupted by separation also tend to show poorer than average parent-son relationships, while those broken by death do not.

---

[2]The statistical procedure is Multiple Classification Analysis; the data are presented in Appendix B, the procedure is discussed briefly later in this chapter and outlined extensively in Volume II (Bachman, 1970, pp. 62-71).

FIGURE 3-2:   EDUCATIONAL ATTAINMENT RELATED TO
              FAMILY SIZE

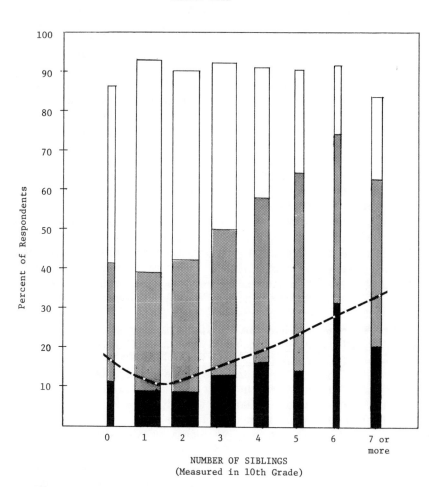

NUMBER OF SIBLINGS
(Measured in 10th Grade)

■ Group 1: High school dropouts
▩ Group 2: Stayins who were not "primarily students" after high school
□ Group 3: Stayins who were "primarily students" after high school

– – –Dropout rate estimated from total sample (incl. "undiscovered dropouts")

Eta (treating educational attainment as a trichotomous criterion) = .25

NOTES: Width of each bar is proportionate to size of predictor subgroup.
         See Chapter 2 for complete definitions of Groups 1,2, and 3.
         See Appendix C for further information and for data underlying
         figures.

Boys from homes broken by separation are a bit below average in accomplishments, aspirations, and other factors associated with SEL. It appears, however, that nearly all of these differences in homes broken by separation can be attributed to their lower SEL. Once SEL is controlled, there is little if any unique effect attributable to separated families.

Boys who have lost a parent due to death show virtually no differences from those living with both natural parents. Differences no doubt exist, but they are not large or general enough to be visible in terms of our criterion dimensions.

These findings are not the result of an exhaustive study of the effects of broken homes. On the other hand, if the loss of a parent—usually the father—due to death or separation is often a crippling experience to a young man, we should expect to see some greater indication of it in the dimensions we have been examining. As it stands, we find that once we control for differences in SEL, there is surprisingly little evidence that boys from broken homes are worse off than their classmates from intact homes. (Bachman, 1970, pp. 193-194)

We did find the above evidence surprising, because we expected in advance that broken homes would show some unique effects on self-esteem, or occupational aspirations, or college plans, or delinquency. But the differences did not appear in our data collected in tenth grade. (Or if they did appear, they were too small and inconsistent for us to consider them meaningful.)

The findings on dropout rates require that we revise our earlier conclusion—broken homes do make a measurable difference. The data are summarized in Figure 3-3. Of those coming from intact homes at the times they entered tenth grade, 11.5 percent were later identified as dropouts; the comparable percentages are 16.5 for those from homes broken by death, and 19.6 for those from homes broken by separation. The estimated dropout rates, shown by the dashed lines in Figure 3-3, heighten the distinction between intact homes and broken ones. A reasonable conclusion is that dropping out of high school is about twice as likely among boys from broken homes.

We noted in our summary of Volume II that homes broken by divorce or separation are lower in socioeconomic level, and that factor alone might account for some of the differences noted above. Controlling SEL eliminates the small difference in dropout rate between homes broken by death and those broken by divorce or separation. However, both forms of broken homes remain well above average in dropout rate after we control SEL.

Our finding that dropping out is perhaps twice as likely among boys from broken homes is important enough to require careful interpretation. First of all, we must recall that the percentages

FIGURE 3-3:   EDUCATIONAL ATTAINMENT RELATED TO
              BROKEN HOME

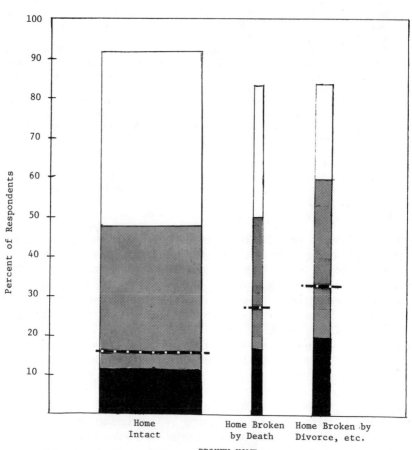

BROKEN HOME
(Measured in 10th Grade)

■ Group 1:   High school dropouts
▨ Group 2:   Stayins who were <u>not</u> "primarily students" after high school
☐ Group 3:   Stayins who <u>were</u> "primarily students" after high school
━━Dropout rate estimated from <u>total</u> sample (incl. "undiscovered dropouts")

Eta (treating educational attainment as a trichotomous criterion) = .14

Notes: Width of each bar is proportionate to size of predictor subgroup.
        See Chapter 2 for complete definitions of Groups 1,2, and 3.
        See Appendix C for further information and for data underlying
        figures.

reported here are based on relatively small subgroups, and thus cannot be interpreted with great precision. In addition, we must keep clearly in mind the limits of the relationship. Dropping out occurs *relatively* more often in broken homes. Does this mean that a boy from a broken home will *probably* become a dropout? No indeed—as Figure 3-3 indicates, the great majority of boys from broken homes do not drop out. And it would be equally mistaken to conclude that most dropouts are the products of broken homes: about two-thirds come from homes that are intact.

Family Relations. A single, general-purpose measure of family relations (or parent-son relations) was developed using 10 items having to do with parental punitiveness and 11 items dealing with closeness to parents and the feeling that parents are reasonable. The items in this scale are fairly subjective; thus there is much room for subtle distortion and misinterpretation of response scales, all of which can occur without a respondent even recognizing it. This measure is not strongly associated with other family background dimensions, but there is some tendency for parent-son relations to be better in smaller, intact families high in socioeconomic level.

The family relations measure shows strong relationships with a number of measures of interest to us here. The better a boy reports getting along with his parents, the higher is his self-esteem, his self-concept of school ability, his attitudes toward school, and his feelings of personal efficacy. The poorer the family relations he reports, the more likely the boy is to admit to delinquency, rebellious behavior in school, test anxiety, and negative school attitudes. Considerable caution was exercised in reporting these findings in Volume II, for *all* of the measures mentioned above are highly subject to bias or distortion.

The problems of bias are diminished, however, when a measure of family relations obtained at the start of tenth grade is related to subsequent objective behaviors such as dropping out and college entrance. Our analysis revealed that a substantial correlation does indeed exist between family relations and dropout/college entrances: the better a boy reported getting along with his parents at the start of tenth grade, the less likely he was to drop out of high school and the more likely he was to enter college.

Parental Punitiveness. An exploration of the separate components of the family relations measure revealed that the relationship with dropout/college entrance is attributable almost entirely to the 10 items dealing with parental punitiveness. Indeed, an index of the parental punitiveness items alone shows a slightly

TABLE 3-1

ITEMS COMPRISING THE PARENTAL PUNITIVENESS INDEX

1. How often do your parents completely ignore you after you've done some-
    thing wrong?

2. How often do your parents act as if they don't care about you any more?

3. How often do your parents disagree with each other when it comes to raising
    you?

4. How often do your parents actually slap you?

5. How often do your parents take away your privileges (TV, movies, dates)?

6. How often do your parents blame you or criticize you when you don't
    deserve it?

7. How often do your parents threaten to slap you?

8. How often do your parents yell, shout, or scream at you?

9. How often do your parents disagree about punishing you?

10. How often do your parents nag at you?

stronger association with dropout/college entrance than does the
total family relations scale. The ingredients for the parental
punitiveness index are presented in Table 3-1. The relationship
between punitiveness and dropout/college entrance is displayed in
Figure 3-4. The pattern for dropping out is curvilinear; there was
little difference in dropout rate among the lowest three or four
categories of punitiveness, but beyond that dropping out occurred
more frequently as (reported) punitiveness increased. College
entrance is also related to punitiveness; boys who reported their
parents as relatively low in punitiveness were about twice as likely
to enter college as those who rated their parents very high on this
dimension.

There are at least two different interpretations of this relationship. Perhaps the most obvious one is that patterns of parental punitiveness are among the causes of educational attainment.
But it is also possible that "good kids" do not get punished very
much while "bad" dropout types do. Certainly more of the behavior patterns which precede dropping out (e.g., delinquency and
rebellious behavior in school) could trigger parental punitiveness.
It may well be that both interpretations are valid to some degree,
and that parental punitiveness is part of a complex network of
actions and reactions that precede dropping out.

(It is of interest to note that the very lowest level of rated
punitiveness shows a 10 percent lower proportion of college en-

FIGURE 3-4: EDUCATIONAL ATTAINMENT RELATED TO
PARENTAL PUNITIVENESS

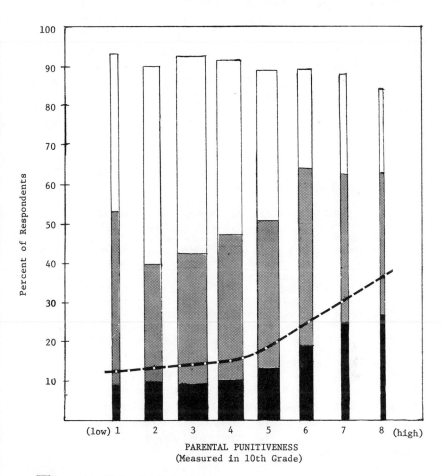

PARENTAL PUNITIVENESS
(Measured in 10th Grade)

■ Group 1: High school dropouts
▨ Group 2: Stayins who were not "primarily students" after high school
□ Group 3: Stayins who were "primarily students" after high school

— —·Dropout rate estimated from total sample (incl. "undiscovered dropouts")

Eta (treating educational attainment as a trichotomous criterion) = .23

Notes: Width of each bar is proportionate to size of predictor subgroup.
See Chapter 2 for complete definitions of Groups 1,2, and 3.
See Appendix C for further information and for data underlying
figures.

trance than the next lowest levels. We suspect that this may reflect a certain type of response pattern rather than the relationship between *actual* punitiveness and college entrance. No doubt some respondents felt a need to represent their parents in the most attractive terms possible, and thus represented them as being very low in punitiveness by checking "Never" to most of the questions shown in Table 3-1. We suspect that this somewhat "unsophisticated" form of responding occurred a bit less frequently among the brighter collegebound respondents, and that this alone could account for the apparent drop in college entrance at the low end of the punitiveness scale.)

Religious Preference. The relationship between religious preference and dropout/college entrance is entirely consistent with our findings in Volume II:

> The difference in SEL and intelligence can account for most. . . effects of religion; in other words, a concise account of background effects would focus on SEL and intelligence and say rather little about effects of family religious preference. The one exception to this generalization involves the 59 Jewish respondents in our study. This subgroup, representing less than 3 percent of our total sample, has departed from the average in ways that cannot be attributed entirely to their above-average intelligence or socioeconomic level.
>
> Jewish respondents are higher than any other religious subgroup in self-esteem, a finding that is consistent with the earlier work of Rosenberg (1965). They are also well above average in political knowledge, occupational aspirations, and college plans. (Bachman, 1970, p. 196)

Our present analyses show a very similar pattern. Rates of dropping out and college entrance among Catholics were identical to those for the rest of the sample. Episcopalians were below average in dropout rate and somewhat above average in college entrance, while the reverse was true for Baptists. However, *all of these relationships virtually disappear* when we introduce statistical controls for SEL and other background dimensions.

The Jewish respondents again proved to be the exception. Throughout the study they displayed consistently high aspirations. By spring of 1970 a first major goal had been attained: over 90 percent had entered college. (This may be contrasted with 51 percent college entrance among the next highest religious category, the Episcopalians.) Not one of the Jewish respondents had dropped out of high school. Roughly half of the above effects can be attributed to intelligence, SEL, and other background factors; the effects remaining after such statistical controls are still quite large and important. The data certainly fit our earlier conclusions:

Our findings for Jewish respondents are based on only a few cases; taken alone, they must be treated with a good deal of caution. But the results presented here are consistent with other findings, and together they indicate that the family background of Jewish children is particularly supportive of high self-esteem and high levels of achievement orientation. (Bachman, 1970, p. 196)

One question which our earlier analysis left unanswered arose out of the fact that most Jewish respondents were clustered in only a few locations; 45 out of the total of 59 were located in just four high schools. Could it be that the high test scores and college entrance rates of the Jewish subsample simply reflect an accidental grouping into four outstanding schools? The question was answered by comparing Jewish with Gentile respondents in each of the four schools. The results are unequivocal. In every school the rate of college entrance was dramatically higher for the Jewish respondents than for Gentiles (87 to 100 percent versus 29 to 64 percent). In three of the four schools socioeconomic level was also higher for the Jewish respondents, but that difference was not sufficient to explain the larger difference in rate of college entrance.

In sum, only one category of religious experience seems to have any consistent and measurable effect on educational attainment (above and beyond the correlation between religion and SEL). The effect is rather large, but it applies to such a small subgroup that it does not add much to our overall prediction; accordingly, we would not designate religion (or the Jewish-Gentile distinction) as an important family background predictor in these analyses. But for the small subgroup that it involves, our prediction can be unusually accurate: to be Jewish is to graduate from high school and go on to college.

Race. We have treated race as a family background factor because of the large racial differences that exist along dimensions such as education, occupation, income, housing, and the like. Our earlier analyses indicated quite clearly that a careful examination of racial differences could not be accomplished simply by comparing blacks and whites:

Probably our most basic finding is the fact that the 256 black respondents in this study cannot be studied as a single subgroup. No less than three groups of blacks must be considered, based on different school (and community) environments: blacks in integrated schools, blacks in northern segregated schools, and blacks in southern segregated schools. . . .we first found in preliminary analyses that black students in integrated schools are very different from those in segregated schools in terms of test scores and socioeconomic level;

8

YOUTH IN TRANSITION

we then found that those in southern segregated schools are quite different from those in northern segregated schools. Given these differences in socioeconomic level and test scores, we decided that these three black subgroups would be examined separately throughout the monograph. (Bachman, 1970, p. 198)

Differences among racial subgroups in rates of dropping out and college entrance are displayed in Figure 3-5. The figure clearly indicates that here, as in Volume II, the largest and most interesting differences are not simply between blacks and whites, but rather between black subgroups.

Blacks who attended integrated schools (i.e., schools with no fewer than 40 percent whites) had dropout and college entrance rates almost identical to those of whites. The largest difference between the two categories involves missing data: we tracked back all but 9 percent of the whites, whereas we were left with missing data for 20 percent of the blacks who had attended integrated schools. The proportion of integrated blacks identified as dropouts is slightly (and nonsignificantly) lower than that for whites; however, this difference might be eliminated or reversed if we had dropout information on the missing data cases. Similarly, the rate of college entrance is three or four percentage points lower for integrated blacks, but if we remove the missing data cases from our calculations the difference is reversed—of those whom we were able to track down and identify at Time 4, post-high school education was 2 percent more frequent among blacks from integrated schools than among whites. None of these differences is at all statistically trustworthy; we have noted them simply to show how small they really are, and thereby indicate how little difference in educational attainment we have found between blacks from integrated schools and whites (from both integrated and segregated schools).

When we look at the groups of blacks from segregated schools, the findings are quite different. Of those from segregated schools who were identified at Time 4, roughly one-quarter were in post-high school education; the comparable figure was nearly one-half for blacks from integrated schools and for whites. Dropout rates were also substantially higher among blacks from segregated schools, especially those from three segregated schools in the North.[3]

Adjusting for test scores, SEL, and other background dimen-

----

[3]Volume II mistakenly reported the Northern segregated blacks as located in four schools; they were in fact located in only three schools.

FIGURE 3-5: EDUCATIONAL ATTAINMENT RELATED
TO RACE

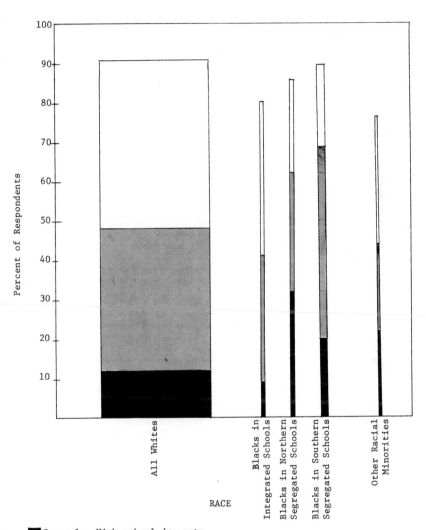

Group 1: High school dropouts
Group 2: Stayins who were not "primarily students" after high school
Group 3: Stayins who were "primarily students" after high school

Eta (treating educational attainment as a trichotomous criterion) = .15

NOTES: Width of each bar is proportionate to size of predictor subgroup.
See Chapter 2 for complete definitions of Groups 1,2, and 3.
See Appendix C for further information and for data underlying
figures.

sions has relatively little effect on the data for integrated blacks, since they are not sharply different from whites along these dimensions. What differences there are lie in the direction of suggesting slight over-achievement on the part of the integrated blacks. In the case of Southern segregated blacks, adjusting for background dimensions suggests that their rates of dropout and college entrance are not underachievement; if anything, their levels of academic attainment are a bit higher than their background data would have led us to predict.

More than one-third of the respondents we could identify from black Northern segregated high schools had dropped out. Some of that effect can be attributed to background differences, but roughly half of the effect remains after adjustments for family background. We are unwilling to draw conclusions based on only three schools; nevertheless, there is enough consistency between them to be worth noting. In each of the three schools, more than one-third of those we were able to track down had dropped out before graduating. And in each of the schools, the large majority of students were in general or vocational programs—only a few were in college preparatory programs. In some other respects the schools are not entirely similar. Two are large schools (over 2000 students) located in large mid-western cities; one in a residential neighborhood, the other in an industrial/commercial area. The third school is smaller, and located in a small town in the northeast.

Here, as in our second volume, the racial differences turn out to involve black students in segregated schools. We cannot begin to pinpoint the patterns of causation in this area, but our findings once again suggest the importance of school integration/segregation in patterns of racial differences.

Other Background Characteristics. Our examination of family background effects on dropping out and college entrance included two other dimensions, family political preference and the size of the community in which the respondent was raised. Neither of these background dimensions showed strong or consistent relationships with the criteria.

Intelligence and Verbal Skills

Dropouts frequently mention their inability to perform well in school as one of the reasons for dropping out. And, of course, entering and remaining in college depends upon intelligence and verbal skills to a considerable degree. In this section we will see how dropping out and college entrance are related to tests of intelligence, reading and vocabulary skills. Intelligence and verbal skills are highly overlapping, particularly as we have measured them; nevertheless, we shall find that they differ somewhat in their ability to predict dropout/college entrance.

Quick Test of Intelligence. The Ammons Quick Test (QT) is a brief measure of general intelligence (Ammons and Ammons, 1962). It was individually administered at the end of the Time 1 interview. Volume II in this series (Bachman, 1970) presents a further description of the test and its correlates in our data. For the present it will be sufficient to note that the test requires word recognition and reasoning ability, but it does *not* require that the respondent read or make written responses.

The relationships between the Quick Test and rates of dropping out and college entrance are clearly evident in Figure 3-6. Over two-thirds of those in the top category of intelligence entered college, whereas only 14 percent of those in the bottom category did so. The correlation between intelligence and dropping out is also strong; we *estimate* (taking account of nonrespondents) that over one-third of those at the bottom level of intelligence dropped out, whereas only 6 or 7 percent in the top category failed to graduate from high school.

The relationships noted above are strong, but a great deal of overlap between categories remains. Quite a number of those at the highest levels of intelligence did not go on to college, and some did not even finish high school.

We turn now to measures of reading and vocabulary skills. These dimensions seem more closely and specifically associated with school performance than does general intelligence, thus we might expect them to show stronger associations with our dropout/college entrance dimension.

General Aptitude Test Battery—Part J: Vocabulary. This test (abbreviated GATB-J) is part of the well standardized multifactor test battery developed by the United States Employment Service for vocational counseling (Super, 1957). The vocabulary test consists of 60 sets of four words each. Each set of words includes two which have either the same meaning or opposite meanings; the respondent is required to pick the correct pair from each set of four. The total time permitted was five minutes; since many respondents did not finish in this period, speed must be considered one of the components of successful performance in this test.

It should be noted that this test followed directly after another test which was also highly speeded. Thus those respondents who might be characterized as "test-wise" (i.e., skilled in the art of

FIGURE 3-6:   EDUCATIONAL ATTAINMENT RELATED TO
              QUICK TEST SCORES

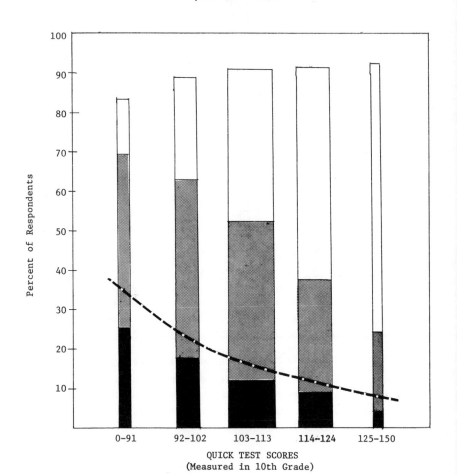

QUICK TEST SCORES
(Measured in 10th Grade)

▉ Group 1: High school dropouts
▨ Group 2: Stayins who were not "primarily students" after high school
☐ Group 3: Stayins who were "primarily students" after high school

⬛━━ Dropout rate estimated from total sample (incl. "undiscovered dropouts")

Eta (treating educational attainment as a trichotomous criterion) = .31

NOTES: Width of each bar is proportionate to size of predictor subgroup.
         See Chapter 2 for complete definitions of Groups 1,2, and 3.
         See Appendix C for further information and for data underlying
         figures.

test-taking) were likely to be warmed up and ready to take the GATB-J at full speed, recognizing that a high score depends more on working fast than on being entirely free from errors.

Figure 3-7 presents the relationship between the GATB-J vocabulary test and rates of dropping out and college entrance. The pattern is similar to that for the Quick Test of Intelligence shown in Figure 3-6, but the effects for the vocabulary test are a bit stronger. Of those who scored in the top category of the GATB-J, over three-quarters entered college, and practically no one dropped out.

Gates Test of Reading Comprehension. This test, taken from the Gates Reading Survey (1958), consists of 21 short passages arranged in order of increasing difficulty. The respondent's task is to insert into each passage two or three words selected from a list of five possibilities. A total of 20 minutes was allowed, which proved to be more than adequate for nearly all respondents. Thus this test, unlike the GATB-J did not depend significantly upon speed. Another way in which this test differs from both the GATB-J and the Quick Test is that it has a fairly low "ceiling" (i.e., a good many respondents were able to attain perfect or near-perfect scores), and it has a good deal of discrimination at the low end of the scale. In other words, it is a fairly sensitive measure of amount of reading deficiency, but it does not discriminate very well between good readers and outstanding readers.

The relationship between the Gates reading test and rates of dropping out and college entrance are shown in Figure 3-8. The figure shows the ability of this test to discriminate at the lower end of the scale, and indicates the special relevance of reading skill as a predictor of dropping out. Our *estimated* drop-out rate for those at the lowest levels of reading skill is greater than 40 percent.

Intelligence Versus Verbal Skills. In our view there is little to be gained from trying to maintain any sharp distinction between intelligence and verbal skills. Even if one were satisfied with such distinctions at the conceptual level, our measure of intelligence (like most others) is heavily dependent upon verbal skills. Nevertheless, there are some important differences between the three tests we have been examining, and we want to consider those differences here.

Our earlier analyses, presented in Volume II in this series, found fairly high correlations among the three tests (product-moment $r = .66$ to $.71$). All three measures were about equal in strength of relationship to family background dimensions, also to test anxiety ($r = -.25$ to $-.26$), college plans ($r = .29$ to $.31$), and

FIGURE 3-7:   EDUCATIONAL ATTAINMENT RELATED TO
              VOCABULARY SKILLS

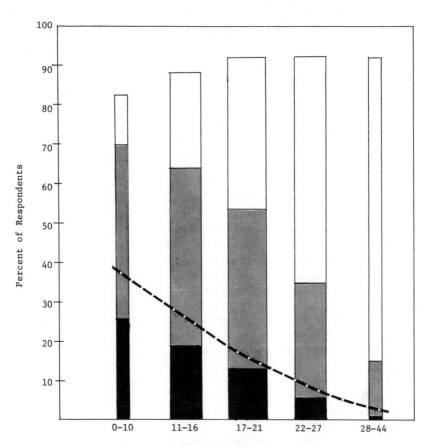

GATB-J TEST OF VOCABULARY SKILLS
(Measured in 10th Grade)

■ Group 1: High school dropouts
▨ Group 2: Stayins who were not "primarily students" after high school
☐ Group 3: Stayins who were "primarily students" after high school

▬ ▬ ▬ Dropout rate estimated from total sample (incl. "undiscovered dropouts")

Eta (treating educational attainment as a trichotomous criterion) = .40

NOTES: Width of each bar is proportionate to size of predictor subgroup.
        See Chapter 2 for complete definitions of Groups 1,2, and 3.
        See Appendix C for further information and for data underlying
        figures.

FIGURE 3-8: EDUCATIONAL ATTAINMENT RELATED TO
READING SKILLS

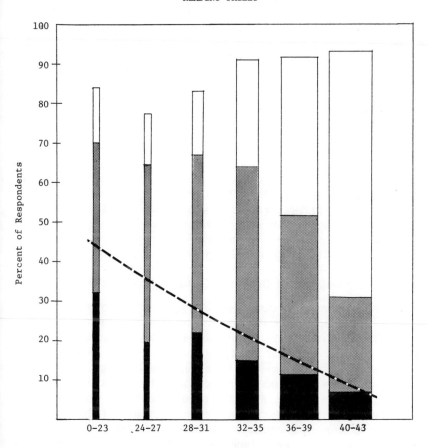

GATES TEST OF READING SKILLS
(Measured in 10th Grade)

▮ Group 1: High school dropouts
▨ Group 2: Stayins who were <u>not</u> "primarily students" after high school
☐ Group 3: Stayins who <u>were</u> "primarily students" after high school

▬ ▬ Dropout rate estimated from <u>total</u> sample (incl. "undiscovered dropouts")

Eta (treating educational attainment as a trichotomous criterion) = .37

NOTES: Width of each bar is proportionate to size of predictor subgroup.
See Chapter 2 for complete definitions of Groups 1,2, and 3.
See Appendix C for further information and for data underlying
figures.

occupational aspirations (r = .38 to .41). On the other hand, the GATB-J measure of vocabulary skill was superior as a predictor of (self-reported) grades in school (r = .44 versus .36 for the other tests) and self-concept of school ability (r = .50 versus .43 for the Quick Test and .38 for the Gates). In short, we found a good deal of overlap and similarity in the tests, but also some indication that the GATB-J is a bit more closely associated with academic accomplishments.

Those earlier results forecast the present findings in Figures 3-6, 3-7 and 3-8. The GATB-J vocabulary test shows the strongest association with our composite measures of dropout/college entrance (Eta = .40); the Gates reading test is next strongest (Eta = .37); and the Quick Test of Intelligence is least strong (Eta = .31).[4] In short, we can do a better job of predicting dropping out and college entrance when we use tests that are closely linked to academic performance. Given this conclusion, we will usually prefer the measures of vocabulary and reading skill rather than the more general test of intelligence when we relate intellectual abilities to the dropout/college entrance dimension.

Multivariate Prediction of Dropping Out and College Entrance

The relationships displayed in Figures 3-1 through 3-8 are essentially two-dimensional—the dropout/college entrance dimension, treated as a rough continuum, has been compared with a number of background and ability dimensions, taken one at a time. We have noted the changes in such relationships that occur when other dimensions are "statistically controlled," but we have deferred discussion of the analysis procedures used to accomplish this. We have also deferred any consideration of the *combined* predictive power of a number of background and/or ability dimensions considered simultaneously. Such analyses require the use of rather sophisticated multivariate techniques. One such technique which we have found particularly well-suited to our purposes is Multiple Classification Analysis (MCA). A very brief overview of MCA will be adequate for our purposes here.

Multiple Classification Analysis. Volume II of this series presented a fairly extensive description of MCA (Bachman, 1970, pp. 62-75), and a complete description of the MCA model and the

---

[4]The composite measure of dropout/college entrance involves giving a score of "1" to dropouts, a score of "3" to college entrants, and a score of "2" to everyone else. Some justification for the use of this summary measure is given in the following section and in Appendix C.

corresponding computer program is provided by Andrews, et al., (1967). The following summary overview is adapted from our discussion in Volume II.

MCA permits us to predict a criterion dimension such as dropping out of school using a number of predictor dimensions simultaneously. It computes a multiple correlation coefficient, R, which when squared provides an estimate of the total variance in the criterion explainable by all predictors operating together. It also provides an estimate (termed Beta) of the separate effect of each predictor as if it were uncorrelated with all other predictors—i.e., with other predictors "statistically controlled."

It may be helpful to think of MCA as a form of multiple regression analysis that has a good deal of extra freedom. Most important, it treats predictors as nominal scales. For some of our background dimensions, such as broken home or religious preference, this is essential. For others, it means that a curvilinear relationship (such as that for Parental Punitiveness shown in Figure 3-4) is not forced into a straight-line "compromise" estimate. In addition, MCA can handle a wide range of interrelationships among predictors, another important feature in dealing with highly intercorrelated dimensions such as family background factors and intellectual ability. Finally, MCA can handle missing data on any particular predictor simply by treating absence of data as another predictive category. This means that we do not lose all information on an individual simply because he has missing data on one of the predictor dimensions.

One other feature of MCA needs to be noted here. Like other forms of multiple regression, MCA assumes that the effects of predictor variables are combined *additively*; that is, it assumes that there is no interaction among predictors. This assumption is of critical importance, for it means that either the investigator must assume that no appreciable interaction exists (based on other findings, theory, or intuition), or he must search the data for such interactions prior to final application of the MCA technique. Our earlier analyses of family background explored this area carefully, and found only one important interaction—the triple interaction of race, region, and school integration that has already been incorporated into our multi-category "race" variable (Bachman, 1970, p. 69). Analyses of the present data on dropout and college entrance revealed no further substantial interactions among background and ability dimensions; thus we consider that the assumption of additivity is appropriate for the present analyses.

MCA can be used to predict either dichotomous criteria (e.g., dropouts versus stayins) or continuous criteria (e.g., income).

We argued earlier that it is appropriate to view our three category measure of educational attainment (dropout/high school only/college entrance) as a continuum. We have found that this trichotomy can be used rather neatly as a criterion dimension in Multiple Classification Analysis with no evidence of difficulty. Chapter 6 includes considerable data which support this assertion.

Joint Prediction from Family Background Measures. The most important family background dimension, in terms of ability to predict dropping out and college entrance, is socioeconomic level. Next most important are family size (number of siblings) and parental punitiveness. We found that coming from a broken home also makes a fairly large difference in likelihood of dropout and college entrance; however, this effect applies to only a minority of boys, and thus its impact on the total group is less than that of the other background factors mentioned above.

These four family background dimensions, SEL, family size, parental punitiveness, and broken home, were combined in a Multiple Classification Analysis predicting to our continuum of educational attainment (dropout/high school/college).[5] The resulting multiple R (adjusted) is .43; the unadjusted R^2 or proportion of variation explained is .193.

Intellectual Ability as an Intervening Variable. In Volume II we argued that intelligence came in the middle of the following causal sequence: family background influences intelligence which in turn influences various criterion dimensions. Such a variable in the middle of a causal sequence can be termed an *intervening variable*.

We found earlier in this chapter that measures of vocabulary and reading skill are preferable to a more general test of intelligence when predicting to educational attainment. Accordingly, we have chosen to consider such academic skills as intervening variables in the present analysis. The upper portion of Figure 3-9 presents a diagram summarizing this view of academic skills as intervening variables between family background and educational attainment.

Taken alone, the GATB-J test of vocabulary can account for .159 of the variance in our continuum of educational attainment (this estimate is simply the value of Eta squared). Likewise, the Gates reading test can account for .134 of the variance. The two tests overlap, but not completely; their combined ability to predict

---

[5]The remaining background characteristics seemed either less important or less reliable, and thus were not selected for inclusion in this phase of the analysis.

FIGURE 3-9

MODEL SUMMARIZING THE EFFECTS OF FAMILY BACKGROUND
CHARACTERISTICS AND ACADEMIC ABILITY

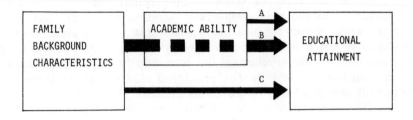

Arrow A: Effects of academic ability that are independent of the
effects of family background characteristics

Arrow B: Joint or "overlapping" effects of family background
characteristics and academic ability, which we <u>interpret</u>
as the effects of family background factors operating
<u>through</u> <u>academic</u> <u>ability</u> <u>as</u> <u>an</u> <u>intervening</u> <u>variable</u>

Arrow C: Effects of family background characteristics that are
independent of the effects of academic ability

Arrows A+B: Total effects of academic ability

Arrows B+C: Total effects of family background characteristics

Arrows A+B+C: Total effects of family background characteristics plus
academic ability

Given the data from Multiple Classification Analyses presented in the text,
we can fill in the model as follows:

$$A+B+C = 23.8\% \text{ of variance in educational}$$
$$\text{attainment (unadjusted)}$$
$$A+B = 17.8\%$$
$$B+C = 19.3\%$$

Therefore:

$$A = 4.5\%$$
$$B = 13.3\%$$
$$C = 6.0\%$$

variance in educational attainment is .178, with a multiple R (adjusted) of .42 (based on Multiple Classification Analysis).

Now we see that our ability to predict educational attainment is roughly equal whether we use family background dimensions (.193 of the variance) or tests of intellectual ability (.178 of the variance). But the most important question remains: how much better can we predict educational attainment if we consider family background and academic skills simultaneously? A Multiple Classification Analysis combining the four family background dimensions and the two test scores predicted .238 of the variance (unadjusted) and produced an adjusted multiple R of .49.

The increase in prediction when we add test scores to family background amounts to 4.5 percent in explained variance. That is certainly a noteworthy improvement, but the fact that it was not larger indicates that most of the variance explainable by test scores was already taken into account when we based our prediction on socioeconomic level and other family background dimensions. Stated another way, it seems that the impact of family background on educational attainment occurs largely *through* academic skills as intervening variables, rather than in ways that are largely independent of academic skills.

The lower portion of Figure 3-9 presents a more systematic treatment of academic skills as intervening variables. Based on that treatment, we conclude that most of the impact of family background does occur through academic skills as intervening variables; 13.3 percent of the variance can be interpreted in this manner. An additional 6.0 percent of the variance in educational attainment appears to be due to "unique" effects of family background—effects that are non-overlapping or independent of academic skills—effects that cannot be traced back to family background characteristics as we have measured them.

We do not consider our model or our measures to be so precise as this division of the explained variance may suggest. We have used exact numbers simply as a matter of convenience, and as a way of illustrating the sort of logic we followed. Nevertheless, we do consider our methods sufficiently valid to support this general conclusion: family background and intellectual ability are largely overlapping in their impact upon educational attainment. Our interpretation is that family background is a very major determinant of intellectual ability, which in turn is a vital ingredient in educational attainment.

Summary

A number of background and ability dimensions were related

to educational attainment. Among the family background characteristics, socioeconomic level (SEL) was most important; the higher
the family SEL, the more likely a boy was to enter college and
the less likely he was to drop out of high school. Other background
dimensions were also related to educational attainment; and while
controlling SEL reduced the strength of these relationships, it did
not eliminate them. Educational attainment was lower among boys
from large families. College entrance was less frequent among
boys from broken homes, especially those broken by divorce or
separation; and dropping out occurred roughly twice as often among
boys from broken homes. Educational attainment was also lower
among boys who reported high levels of parental punitiveness; this
relationship may reflect a complex pattern of parental actions and
reactions in relating to boys who have a history of getting along
rather poorly in school. The only difference in educational attainment which related to religious preference (after controlling
SEL) involved the 59 Jewish respondents in our sample; all graduated from high school and over 90 percent continued into further
education.

Racial differences in educational attainment centered around
black students in segregated schools, especially in three northern
schools. Blacks in integrated schools had dropout and college entrance rates almost identical to whites (from both integrated and
segregated schools). Our findings related to race are severely
limited by the small sizes of black subsamples, but the results
match our earlier findings in suggesting the importance of school
integration/segregation in patterns of racial differences.

Tests of intelligence and vocabulary and reading skills were,
of course, positively related with educational attainment—the
brighter and more skilled an individual, the less likely he was to
drop out and the more likely he was to enter college. While there
was a good deal of overlap between the intelligence test and the
measures of verbal skills, we were able to do a better job of predicting dropping out and college entrance when we used the tests
most closely linked to academic performance.

Using Multiple Classification Analysis in a sequence of applications, we found that the four most important family background
dimensions plus the tests of vocabulary and reading skill could
predict about 24 percent of the variance in educational attainment.
The family background characteristics and the verbal skill dimensions were found to be largely overlapping in their impact. We
interpret this as indicating that the impact of family background
on educational attainment occurs largely through academic skills
as intervening variables.

Chapter 4
SCHOOL EXPERIENCES AND ATTITUDES TOWARD SCHOOL

The boy who performs poorly in school and dislikes his experiences there is likely to drop out; the one who does well and enjoys school—or at least finds it acceptable—is likely to go on to higher education. These assertions are scarcely surprising; they are consistent with common sense, and they are supported by research (Bledsoe, 1959; Lichter, 1962; Varner, 1967; Combs and Cooley, 1968; Dentler and Warshauer, 1968). Our purpose in this chapter is to document the strength of the kind of relationships mentioned above, taking advantage of our longitudinal design to predict high school dropout and college entrance from attitude and behavior data obtained in tenth grade.

We have separated the substance of this chapter into four broad areas: school performance prior to tenth grade, course program and performance during tenth grade, general attitudes toward school, and rebellious behavior in school. The chapter concludes with a section on multivariate prediction.

School Performance Before Tenth Grade

The basic academic skills develop early. By the middle of elementary school the fundamentals of language—speaking, reading and writing—usually are mastered. And most students learn that in order to succeed in the classroom it is essential to adopt certain patterns of behavior and to conform to established rules and authority. Measures of success in school are formalized in report cards. Less formal communications about success or failure may occur daily in teacher-pupil interactions or through comparisons with peers.

Perhaps the most dramatic—and traumatic—indication of early failure in school occurs when a youngster is held back a grade. Even a failing grade on an exam or one poor report card can be upsetting, but such things can be overcome. However, when a boy does not get promoted to the next grade along with the rest of his class, *everyone knows he has flunked*. He will never catch

53

up with his class again. He will be a bit bigger than his new classmates and may mature somewhat earlier, but these usual sources of pride will be marred by the shared knowledge that "he should be a grade ahead."

Failing a Grade in School. Before they reached third grade, 9 percent of the respondents in our sample had been held back a grade. By the end of sixth grade another 10 percent had had this experience. By the start of tenth grade (the second start for about one percent), a total of 24 percent had been held back at least one grade. [1]

The relationship between failing a grade and later educational attainment is quite strong. More than half of the dropouts had failed a grade by the time they reached tenth grade; the same sort of failure had occurred for 27 percent of those who ended their education with high school graduation, and only 8 percent of those who went on to college. This does not mean, of course, that if a boy fails a grade he is more likely than not to become a dropout. As Figure 4-1 indicates, we *estimate* that about 40 percent of those in our sample who failed a grade in school later dropped out; but we also found that about 14 percent of those who failed a grade later went on to post-high school education. We estimate a 10 percent dropout rate among those who never failed a grade.

A boy who has been held back a grade is four times as likely to become a dropout compared with someone who has not. It would be tempting to argue from this that no one should ever fail a grade in school, lest he become a dropout. That conclusion may in the end prove to have some validity, but the present data are not sufficient to make the case. All we can say at this point is that being held back a grade is part of the past school experience of over half of the boys who later become dropouts; whether it is an important cause in its own right, or merely a very revealing symptom, remains to be demonstrated.

Classroom Grades. Another part of the school experience of boys who become dropouts is that they have a history of lower grades than those who graduate, and especially those who go on to college.

Classroom grades were investigated in our second volume, and found to be strongly related to ability and family background

---

[1]Three percent of the sample had been held back twice. A total of 4 percent had been skipped ahead a grade; preliminary examination of this latter subgroup revealed relatively few departures from the rest of the sample, thus it is not treated separately in this monograph.

FIGURE 4-1:   EDUCATIONAL ATTAINMENT RELATED TO
              GRADE FAILURE

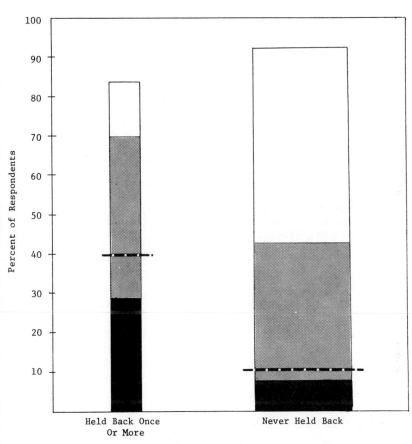

GRADE FAILURE

Group 1: High school dropouts
Group 2: Stayins who were not "primarily students" after high school
Group 3: Stayins who were "primarily students" after high school

━━• Dropout rate estimated from total sample (incl. "undiscovered dropouts")

Eta (treating educational attainment as a trichotomous criterion) = .37

NOTES: Width of each bar is proportionate to size of predictor subgroup.
        See Chapter 2 for complete definitions of Groups 1,2, and 3.
        See Appendix C for further information and for data underlying
        figures.

(multiple R = .43).   A summary description of the measure and the findings will be useful here.

> Our measure of academic performance is based on the following question, asked early in the interview: "What is the average grade you got in your classes last year?   Putting them all together, how would your grades average out?"   The respondent selected a grade from a list provided by the interviewer.   Since our subjects were just beginning tenth grade, their answers of course refer to the average grades they attained as students in the *ninth* grade.   There is evidence that the reports of grades obtained from the respondents are quite valid and reliable.   Part of that evidence involves relationships with background measures   and intelligence, reported below.
> . . .It was also possible to compare self-reported grades with some school records after the third data collection; the product-moment correlation is .71 (based on 920 cases).   One further bit of evidence suggests that the self-reports of grades are not distorted by the need for social approval; the correlation between the Crowne-Marlowe scale and grades is -.01. . .
> Academic achievement. . .is strongly related to measures of intelligence and academic ability, and also to family background factors.   About one-third of our prediction of grades may be described as unique effects of intelligence, another third as unique effects of family background, and the remaining third as background effects operating through intelligence as an intervening variable. (Bachman, 1970, pp. 168-172)

The relationships between ninth grade scholastic performance and later dropout and college entrance rates are shown in Figure 4-2.   The patterns are the strongest to be found in this monograph.   We estimate that over half of those with "D" averages in ninth grade dropped out, whereas only 2 percent of the "A" students did so.   Less than 8 percent of the "D" students went on to college while over 80 percent of the "A" students did.   In short, by the time a boy reaches the end of ninth grade, his academic performance can help a great deal in predicting dropping out or going on to college.

Self-Concept of School Ability.   A boy's academic performance can also tell *him* a good deal about his ability to do well in school.   We found in earlier analyses that academic performance correlates .48 with a measure of self-concept of school ability—an index of three interview items which ask the respondent to compare himself with other boys his age in terms of scholastic ability, intelligence, and reading skill (Bachman, 1970).   A summary of background factors relating to self-concept of school ability sounds very similar to the pattern summarized earlier for classroom grades:

> The most direct determinant of a boy's self-concept of school ability is his actual intelligence (Eta = .46).   But behind intelligence

FIGURE 4-2:   EDUCATIONAL ATTAINMENT RELATED TO
AVERAGE GRADES IN NINTH GRADE

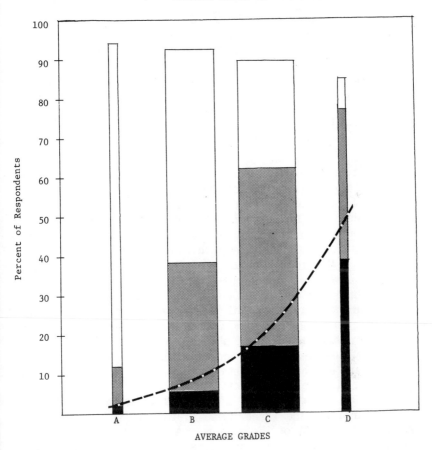

■ Group 1:   High school dropouts
▨ Group 2:   Stayins who were <u>not</u> "primarily students" after high school
□ Group 3:   Stayins who <u>were</u> "primarily students" after high school

▬ ▬ ·Dropout rate estimated from <u>total</u> sample (incl. "undiscovered dropouts")

Eta (treating educational attainment as a trichotomous criterion) = .42

NOTES: Width of each bar is proportionate to size of predictor subgroup.
See Chapter 2 for complete definitions of Groups 1, 2, and 3.
See Appendix C for further information and for data underlying
figures.

lie family background factors that are also important predictors. Self-concept of school ability is highest when family socioeconomic level is high, number of siblings is few, and family relations are reported as good. Much of the effect of these background factors is interpreted as operating via their impact on intelligence, but some of the effect is independent of measured intelligence. (Bachman, 1970, p. 103)

Figure 4-3 relates self-concept of school ability to dropout and college entrance rates. Again the relationships are strong and in the expected direction; the higher one's self-concept of school ability the less likely he is to become a dropout, and the more likely he is to enter college.

Figure 4-3 contains some additional information of interest. An examination of the width of the bars in that figure indicates that only a small proportion of the respondents gave themselves ratings on the "below average" side of the ability scale. (The response scale was deliberately designed to make it impossible for a respondent to rate himself simply as average—he had to choose a position on either side of that midpoint.) A total of about 18 percent of the respondents rated themselves "slightly below average" or lower; well over one-third of them went on to become dropouts, while only one in six entered post-high school education. For any student to rate himself "far below average" on such important dimensions as school ability and intelligence must represent an overwhelming admission of defeat. That rating does not appear in Figure 4-3 because only one individual in our sample of more than two thousand tenth-graders rated himself that low; shortly afterward he dropped out of school.

The "far above average" rating was used consistently (i.e., on two or more of the three items in the index) by only a little more than 3 percent of the sample. Apparently their self-concepts were fairly accurate, since less than 4 percent dropped out and 84 percent went on to college.

School Performance, Self-Concept, and Educational Attainment. The three dimensions we have considered in the above sections jointly account for about 26 percent of the variance in our continuum of educational attainment (multiple R = .51). These relationships are not surprising; but it is noteworthy that they represent a somewhat more accurate prediction than we can attain using a battery of family background information and test scores. When it comes to school performance, it appears that nothing succeeds like success—and nothing predicts to future success better than past success. The negative side of the equation holds equally well—the boy who has been held back a grade, who brings

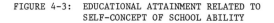

FIGURE 4-3:   EDUCATIONAL ATTAINMENT RELATED TO
SELF-CONCEPT OF SCHOOL ABILITY

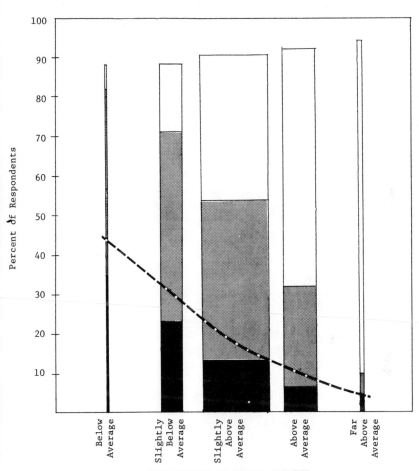

Group 1:   High school dropouts
Group 2:   Stayins who were <u>not</u> "primarily students" after high school
Group 3:   Stayins who <u>were</u> "primarily students" after high school

Dropout rate estimated from <u>total</u> sample (incl. "undiscovered dropouts")

Eta (treating educational attainment as a trichotomous criterion) = .35

NOTES: Width of each bar is proportionate to size of predictor subgroup.
See Chapter 2 for complete definitions of Groups 1,2, and 3.
See Appendix C for further information and for data underlying
figures.

home poor report cards, and who holds a low opinion of his scholastic ability is the one most likely to drop out of school.

(Would things be different if that boy described above had not been held back a grade and if his report card were not poor? Perhaps his self-concept would be different, given the absence of such clear feedback. And perhaps in some cases he would not drop out of school, since his efforts might not seem so fruitless. We recognize that the findings reported above can give rise to such speculations—after all, everyone wants to reduce "the dropout problem," so if bad report cards and being held back a grade lead to dropping out then perhaps we should abolish such practices. But that argument makes an assumption which goes far beyond the present findings—the assumption that the bad grades, etc., are not merely symptoms of school failure but are important causes of failure in their own right. The assumption may be true, at least to some degree in some cases. But to consider that this is the whole explanation is to indulge in a great and misleading oversimplification—one that ignores large and basic differences between dropouts and stayins in home environment and measured ability.)

Tenth-Grade Program and Performance

Program of Study. By the time they were starting tenth grade, over 40 percent of the young men in our sample said they were in the college preparatory program in their school. Over 60 percent of that group did indeed go on to college, while only an estimated 9 percent dropped out of high school.

The other programs of study, general, vocational, commercial, agricultural, etc., showed little variation in dropout rate; in each program an estimated 20 to 25 percent dropped out. College entrance was fairly low (15 to 17 percent) for those who were in vocational, commercial, or agricultural programs. About 30 percent of those in the general program entered college.

The finding that tenth-grade students in the college preparatory program are likely to go on to college, and unlikely to become dropouts, comes as no surprise. (And, of course, if we had based our prediction on eleventh grade or twelfth grade course of study, our prediction would have been substantially more precise.) But the fact that these matters are decided to a considerable degree by the time a boy enters tenth grade is worth noting. The tenth-grade college prep student has a better than 60 percent chance of being in college three years later; the chance for students in other programs is less than half that good.

Homework and Classroom Performance. One of the factors that might be expected to distinguish the potential dropouts and college entrants is time spent on homework. Surely this would seem to be a good measure of motivation, of commitment to education. We would expect the student bound for college to spend much more time on his homework than the student who is soon to drop out of school. Some differences do occur, although they are not nearly as dramatic as others presented in this chapter. Over 40 percent of the tenth-grade boys who later dropped out claimed that they spent ten or more hours a week on homework; 60 percent of the college-bound reported doing more than ten hours of homework.

Figure 4-4 presents the relationship between total time spent on homework (both in school and at home) and later rates of dropping out and college entrance. Of those who reported doing less than five hours homework, we estimate that about 33 percent became dropouts; the estimated dropout rate is about 11 percent for those doing twenty or more hours of homework. College entrance also shows some relationship to homework. Only 22 percent of the low homework group went on to college, whereas about half of those doing ten or more hours per week were college-bound. Most of the differences in rates of dropping out and college entrance occur among the lower ranges of homework time; once we go beyond ten hours the differences are relatively small.

(It may be worth noting that the total time reported for doing homework declined appreciably over the course of the longitudinal study. At the start of tenth grade a majority reported spending more than ten hours a week on homework; this dropped somewhat by the end of eleventh grade, and was substantially lower at the end of twelfth grade. It may be the case that high school students work harder at the start of tenth grade than they do later on, particularly when they are close to graduation. Possibly they find their assignments more difficult and time-consuming at the start of tenth grade. Another factor may be a difference in measurement; an interview question was used the first two times, while a paper-and-pencil questionnaire item had to be used at the end of twelfth grade. Perhaps the respondents were more frank about their actual homework efforts when they did not have to admit it in a face-to-face interview situation! Thus the possibility certainly exists that the homework times displayed in Figure 4-4 are a bit exaggerated on the average. Nevertheless, we consider the basic relationships between homework and educational attainment to be valid.)

A series of interview questions, using five-category response

FIGURE 4-4:   EDUCATIONAL ATTAINMENT RELATED TO
              HOURS SPENT ON HOMEWORK

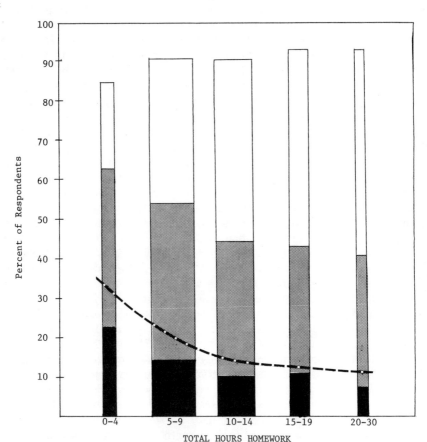

TOTAL HOURS HOMEWORK
(Measured in 10th Grade)

■ Group 1: High school dropouts
▓ Group 2: Stayins who were <u>not</u> "primarily students" after high school
□ Group 3: Stayins who <u>were</u> "primarily students" after high school

•—·Dropout rate estimated from <u>total</u> sample (incl. "undiscovered dropouts")

Eta (treating educational attainment as a trichotomous criterion) = .21

NOTES: Width of each bar is proportionate to size of predictor subgroup.
         See Chapter 2 for complete definitions of Groups 1,2, and 3.
         See Appendix C for further information and for data underlying
         figures.

scales, asked each respondent to rate his own classroom performance. As might be expected, the answers to these questions show
some relationship to dropping out and college entrance; however,
the patterns are not very strong. One of the questions asked,
"How hard do you think you work in school, compared to the other
students in your class?" Fully 68 percent of the respondents
chose the alternative "About average;" the others divided equally
between those who thought they worked harder than average, and
those who felt they worked less hard than average. Responses to
this question are related to dropout and college entrance rates in
Figure 4-5.

As Figure 4-5 indicates, dropping out was lowest, and college entrance highest, among those who said they worked "Harder."
However, those who claimed to work "Much harder" when compared with other students in their class were actually below average in later college entrance. It may be a good thing to work
somewhat harder than one's classmates, but it would appear that
those who see themselves as trying very hard are not so likely
to succeed. Or perhaps some who see themselves as not succeed-
ing try much harder but still are not highly successful.

Two other questions produced similar patterns, although
somewhat weaker than those displayed in Figure 4-5. One question
asked, "How close do you come to doing the best work you are able
to do in school?" The most frequent response was the midpoint
on the scale, "Somewhat close." However, the 27 percent who
rated their work as coming "Quite close" to their best were most
likely to enter college and least likely to drop out. Those who
rated themselves "Very close," the highest possible rating, were
not above average in college entrance. Those who said they were
"Not very close" or "Not at all close" to doing their best were
of course least likely to enter college, and more likely than average to become dropouts.

The remaining question asked, "How satisfied are you with
the way you're actually doing in school?" The responses to this
question revealed greater dissatisfaction than was indicated by the
other questions. The answer "Not very satisfied" was chosen by
37 percent, and another 6 percent chose "Not at all satisfied."
We estimate that one out of five among those "Not very satisfied"
with their schoolwork later dropped out; the rate for those "Not
at all satisfied" is estimated at one out of three. Among those
who were "Very satisfied" with their performance in school, less
than one in ten dropped out. College entrance was highest among
those expressing satisfaction with their schoolwork, lowest among
those expressing dissatisfaction.

FIGURE 4-5:   EDUCATIONAL ATTAINMENT RELATED TO
               SELF-RATING OF SCHOOL EFFORT
               COMPARED WITH OTHERS

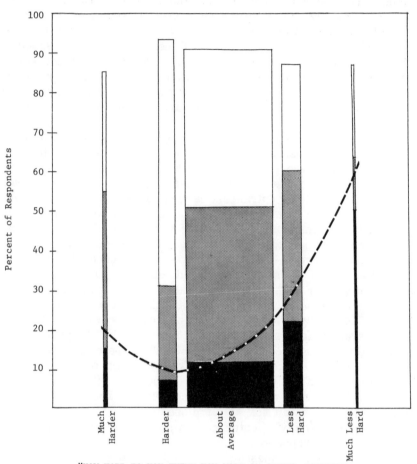

"HOW HARD DO YOU THINK YOU WORK IN SCHOOL COMPARED
TO THE OTHER STUDENTS IN YOUR CLASS?"
(Measured in 10th Grade)

■ Group 1: High school dropouts
▒ Group 2: Stayins who were not "primarily students" after high school
□ Group 3: Stayins who were "primarily students" after high school

•━━Dropout rate estimated from total sample (incl. "undiscovered dropouts")

Eta (treating educational attainment as a trichotomous criterion) = .23

NOTES: Width of each bar is proportionate to size of predictor subgroup.
        See Chapter 2 for complete definitions of Groups 1, 2, and 3.
        See Appendix C for further information and for data underlying
        figures.

In sum, the likelihood of college entrance is greatest among those who spend a good deal of time on their homework, who are quite satisfied with their schoolwork, and who see themselves as working somewhat harder than average. On the other hand, college entrance is no higher than average among those who say they are coming *very* close to doing their best in school, and working *much* harder than the other students in their class. This may indicate that some of those who feel they are working very hard are finding their high school work rather difficult; possibly the student whose high school work is a bit less of a struggle is the one most likely to continue into higher education.

Attitudes Toward School

A number of questionnaire items dealt with respondents' perceptions of, and attitudes toward, their high school environment. Potential dropouts, college-bound students, and others did not differ very much in their perceptions of school organization, teacher behavior, and the like. As would be expected, these groups did differ somewhat in their personal attitudes toward their courses and toward school in general. This section highlights some of those differences.

Interest in Courses. One item in the questionnaire asked the respondent to indicate, "How interesting are most of our courses *to you*?" Answers were generally favorable, albeit somewhat restrained. Only 7 percent were enthusiastic enough to check the answer "Very exciting and stimulating." The answers "Quite interesting" and "Fairly interesting" were each checked by about 40 percent. Ten percent rated their courses as "Slightly dull" and another 3 percent rated them "Very dull."

Interest in tenth-grade courses shows some relationship to later dropping out and college entrance, as Figure 4-6 indicates. Of those who rated their courses "Very dull," we estimate that over 40 percent later dropped out, while only about 16 percent entered college. Those who rated their courses "Quite interesting" were least likely to become dropouts, and most likely to enter college. Here, as in some of the relationships in the earlier section, the pattern is somewhat curvilinear. Those who claimed that their tenth-grade courses were "Very exciting and stimulating" turned out to have lower educational attainments than those who made the more modest claims that their courses were "Quite interesting" or "Fairly interesting."

Positive and Negative School Attitudes. In Volume II we introduced two indexes of attitudes or motivation toward school, the first based on 15 questionnaire items, the second based on 8 items.

FIGURE 4-6:   EDUCATIONAL ATTAINMENT RELATED TO
INTEREST IN SCHOOL COURSES

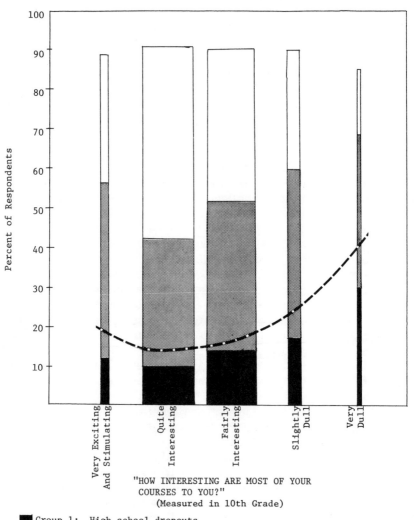

"HOW INTERESTING ARE MOST OF YOUR
COURSES TO YOU?"
(Measured in 10th Grade)

▇ Group 1: High school dropouts
▨ Group 2: Stayins who were <u>not</u> "primarily students" after high school
☐ Group 3: Stayins who <u>were</u> "primarily students" after high school

▪━▪ Dropout rate estimated from <u>total</u> sample (incl. "undiscovered dropouts")

Notes: Width of each bar is proportionate to size of predictor subgroup.
See Chapter 2 for complete definitions of Groups 1,2, and 3.
See Appendix C for further information and for data underlying
figures.

The first index, which we have termed *positive school attitudes,* contains items that stress the intrinsic value of education; for example, "I think school is important, not only for the practical value, but because learning itself is very worthwhile." . . .Every one of the items is endorsed by at least three-quarters of the respondents, who say they feel this way either "pretty much" or "very much." It should be noted that the items possess a great deal of social acceptability—they sound like the right thing to say, and it may be that some of our respondents are inclined to tell us what they think we want to hear. Taken at face value, the data certainly suggest that most tenth-grade boys have favorable attitudes toward school.

The second index, termed *negative school attitudes*, consists of eight items ranging from general dissatisfaction ("School is very boring for me, and I'm not learning what I feel is important") to a devaluation of school in comparison to other sources of experience ("A real education comes from your own experience and not from the things you learn in school"). The items indicating general dissatisfaction received little endorsement, on the whole, while the items stressing the relative superiority of experience outside school were endorsed more often. . .

The two scales are, of course, inversely related; the product-moment correlation between them is -.51. Thus in much of what follows we will be able to talk about both scales together, recognizing that a relationship for one will appear in the opposite direction for the other. (Bachman, 1970, pp. 106-108)

Our present findings, like those in Volume II, show opposite relationships for the two scales, with negative school attitudes having somewhat stronger effects. Figure 4-7 displays the association between negative school attitudes in tenth grade and later educational attainment. Two-thirds of the respondents admitted to having negative school attitudes only "A little" or "Not at all;" these individuals showed above average educational attainment. The lowest rate of college entrance and the highest dropout rate occurred among those who agreed with negative statements about school "Pretty much" or "Very much."

Value Placed on Academic Achievement. The questionnaire included a series of items designed to tap values that are generally approved in our society. Respondents were asked to rate each of a number of statements according to whether it represents (1) a very good thing for people to do, (2) a good thing. . ., (3) a fairly good thing. . ., (4) a fairly bad thing. . ., (5) a bad thing. . ., (6) a very bad thing for people to do. One of the scales, based on items developed by Scott (1965), consisted of the following four items related to academic achievement:

Studying constantly in order to become a well-educated person.
Working hard to achieve academic honors.

FIGURE 4-7:   EDUCATIONAL ATTAINMENT RELATED TO
NEGATIVE SCHOOL ATTITUDES

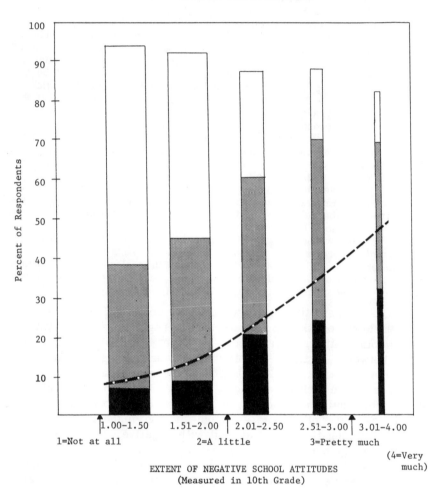

EXTENT OF NEGATIVE SCHOOL ATTITUDES
(Measured in 10th Grade)

■ Group 1:   High school dropouts
▨ Group 2:   Stayins who were not "primarily students" after high school
☐ Group 3:   Stayins who were "primarily students" after high school

‑ ‑ ‑ Dropout rate estimated from total sample (incl. "undiscovered dropouts")

Eta (treating educational attainment as a trichotomous criterion) = .33

NOTES: Width of each bar is proportionate to size of predictor subgroup.
See Chapter 2 for complete definitions of Groups 1,2, and 3.
See Appendix C for further information and for data underlying
figures.

Striving to get the top grade-point average in the group.

Studying hard to get good grades in school.

At the start of tenth grade a substantial majority (70 percent or more) rated each statement as a good or very good thing for people to do. As we note in a later chapter, those ratings declined throughout the course of high school: however, they still remained quite positive on the whole. Virtually all respondents continued to agree that it is at least a fairly good thing to pursue academic achievement.

Academic achievement value in tenth grade is moderately related to later educational attainment, as one might expect. Those who placed the highest value on academic achievement were most likely to go on to college, and least likely to drop out. Perhaps the more interesting question is this: What *changes* in academic achievement value occur as some boys drop out of high school and others graduate and go on into college? The answer to that question is somewhat surprising, as we shall see in Chapter 7.

Rebellious Behavior in School

A questionnaire segment consisting of 13 items asked respondents to report how frequently they engage in disruptive behavior in school, break rules, or do poor school work. The items covered such topics as fighting or arguing with other students, goofing off in class so others can't work, coming late to school or class, skipping class, coming unprepared, copying assignments, and cheating on tests. Each item asked the respondent to indicate how often he did each thing, using a response scale ranging from "almost always" to "never."

> "Seldom" or "never" is the most frequent response to questions about disruptions such as arguing with students or teachers, or doing things to make teachers angry. When it comes to things like being unprepared, or turning in sloppy or incomplete assignments, the frequencies tend to be slightly higher, but the modal response remains "seldom."
>
> A majority admit to at least occasional cheating on tests. Two percent say they almost always do so, 4 percent say it happens often, 15 percent say they cheat sometimes, and 38 percent say they seldom cheat. Forty percent say that they never cheat on tests. (Bachman, 1970, p. 166)

Figure 4-8 presents the relationship between rebellious behavior in tenth grade and later educational attainment; the pattern is essentially linear, and fairly strong. Of those least rebellious in tenth grade (the ones who answered "never" to most questions), less then 7 percent became dropouts. At the other end of the

FIGURE 4-8:   EDUCATIONAL ATTAINMENT RELATED TO
REBELLIOUS BEHAVIOR IN SCHOOL

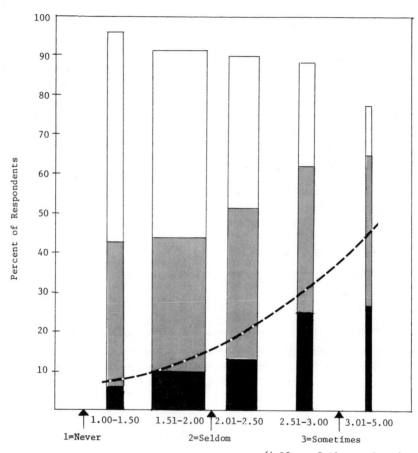

FREQUENCY OF REBELLIOUS BEHAVIOR IN SCHOOL
(Measured in 10th Grade)

■ Group 1: High school
▨ Group 2: Stayins who were <u>not</u> "primarily students" after high school
□ Group 3: Stayins who <u>were</u> "primarily students" after high school

■ ■ ■ Dropout rate estimated from <u>total</u> sample (incl. "undiscovered dropouts")

Eta (treating educational attainment as a trichotomous criterion) = .26

NOTES: Width of each bar is proportionate to size of predictor subgroup.
See Chapter 2 for complete definitions of Groups 1,2, and 3.
See Appendix C for further information and for data underlying
figures.

scale, of those who "often" engaged in rebellious behavior in school, we estimate that nearly half (about 45 percent) dropped out. College entrance was also related to scores on this scale; the greater the level of rebellious behavior, the lower the likelihood of going on to college.

Multivariate Prediction from School Experiences and Attitudes

Thus far in this chapter we have presented essentially two-dimensional relationships; we have looked at various aspects of school experience and attitudes, and then related them, one at a time, to a continuum of educational attainment (i.e., the dropout/college entrance dimension). How we shall see how well we can predict educational attainment when we look at a number of predictors jointly.

A series of Multiple Classification Analyses was carried out, beginning with nearly all of the dimensions reported in this chapter, and gradually eliminating predictors in order to find the smallest number which could account for most of the variance explainable by the total set.

At the end of the first stage of these analyses, we found that we could account for about 30 percent of the variance[2] in our continuum of educational attainment (multiple R = .55) using the following six predictors:

Grade failure in school (being held back a grade)
Average classroom grade (self-reported) in ninth grade
Self-concept of school ability
Positive school attitudes
Negative school attitudes
Rebellious behavior in school

The reader may recall that earlier in this chapter we noted that the first three predictors in the above list, which have to do with school performance primarily, were able to account jointly for about 26 percent of the variance in educational attainment. Thus the remaining three dimensions dealing with students' attitudes and reactions to the school experience were able to add another 4 percent to the explained variance.[3]

---

[2]This variance estimate, and those to follow, all include an adjustment for degrees of freedom.

[3]For those who may be interested in the last three variables taken alone, a separate MCA indicated that they can account for a total of about 13 percent of the variance in educational attainment; that is, of course, substantially less than the 26 percent explainable by the three performance-related variables.

The next step in our multivariate analyses involved a prediction using the two tests of intellectual ability, the GATB-J test of vocabulary and the Gates reading test, in combination with the six measures of school experiences and attitudes listed above. This combined set of eight predictors was able to account for about 32 percent of the variance in educational attainment. In other words, the two test scores contributed an additional 2 percent explained variance (beyond the 30 percent based on the six school experience and attitude dimensions).

These analyses illustrate, of course, the considerable degree to which the predictor variables overlap. It is not surprising to find that test scores do little to improve our prediction of educational attainment if we have already taken account of classroom grades, since test scores are highly correlated with grades.

The next major step in our multivariate analysis was to add family background predictors to see if they increased further our ability to predict educational attainment. Before going on to this step, however, we felt it would be useful if we could reduce the total of eight predictors to a somewhat smaller number. An examination of the beta weights from the Multiple Classification Analysis suggested that we could do almost as well with the following reduced set of predictors:

> Grade failure in school
> Average classroom grade in ninth grade
> Negative school attitudes
> GATB-J test of vocabulary
> Gates reading test

This combination of predictors was able to explain a total of about 31 percent of the variance in educational attainment, only 1 percent lower than our prediction using all eight variables.

The five predictors above were combined with the following family background dimensions in another multivariate analysis:

> Socioeconomic level
> Family size (number of siblings)
> Parental punitiveness
> Broken home

The total set of nine predictors explained about 34 percent of the variance in educational attainment (multiple R = .59), indicating that the family background predictors were able to explain an additional 3 percent of the variance above and beyond that explainable from school performance, attitudes, and test scores.

FIGURE 4-9

MODEL SUMMARIZING THE EFFECTS OF FAMILY BACKGROUND
CHARACTERISTICS, ACADEMIC ABILITY, AND
SCHOOL ATTITUDES AND PERFORMANCE

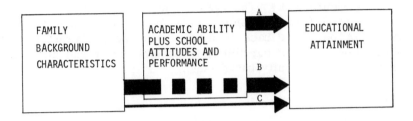

Arrow A: Effects of academic ability plus school attitudes and performance
            that are independent of the effects of family background
            characteristics

Arrow B: Joint or "overlapping" effects of family background
            characteristics and academic ability plus school attitudes
            and performance, which we <u>interpret</u> as the effects of family
            background factors operating <u>through</u> <u>academic</u> <u>ability</u> <u>plus</u>
            <u>school</u> <u>attitudes</u> <u>and</u> <u>performance</u> <u>as</u> <u>an</u> <u>intervening</u> <u>variable</u>

Arrow C: Effects of family background characteristics that are
            independent of the effects of academic ability plus school
            attitudes and performance

Arrows A+B: Total effects of academic ability plus school attitudes and
            performance

Arrows B+C: Total effects of family background characteristics

Arrows A+B+C: Total effects of family background characteristics plus
            academic ability plus school attitudes and performance

Given the data from Multiple Classification Analyses presented in the text,
we can fill in the model as follows:

$$A+B+C = 34.3\% \text{ of variance in educational}$$
$$\text{attainment (unadjusted)}$$
$$A+B = 31.4\%$$
$$B+C = 19.3\%$$

Therefore:

$$A = 15.0\%$$
$$B = 16.4\%$$
$$C = 2.9\%$$

In Chapter 3 we proposed a causal model indicating that family background has much of its effect *through* intellectual ability as an intervening variable (see Figure 3-9). We can expand that model to include school performance and attitudes along with the test scores as intervening variables. The expansion is displayed in Figure 4-9.[4] The results indicate that there is a good deal of impact from academic skills, performance and attitudes that cannot be traced back to family background characteristics; indeed, almost half of our ability to predict educational attainment is independent of family background.

Summary

Past educational success or failure proved to be a most important predictor of future educational attainment. Being held back a grade in school is one indicator of educational failure; we estimate a dropout rate of about 40 percent among those who have failed a grade in school, but only about 10 percent among those who were never held back. Classroom grades also were strongly related to educational attainment, especially college entrance; over 80 percent of the "A" students (in ninth grade) later went on to college, while less than 8 percent of the "D" students did so. Other variables were related to educational attainment: self-concept of school ability, self-rating of hard work in school, stated interest in course work, and other attitudes toward school.

A measure of rebellious behavior in school was strongly related to educational attainment; for those who "often" engaged in rebellious behavior in school, we estimate that nearly one-half later became dropouts.

An extension of the multivariate analyses begun in Chapter 3 indicated that about 34 percent of the variance in educational attainment was explainable when past school experience (grade failure, classroom grades, and school attitudes) was added to background and ability predictors. Our interpretation of the several multivariate analyses is that a good deal of impact from academic skills, performance and attitudes cannot be traced back to family background factors; almost half of our ability to predict educational attainment is independent of family background.

---

[4]It is tempting to consider more elaborate models in which academic skills are separated from performance and attitudes; however, we view these dimensions as so closely interrelated that such a separation would be artificial and misleading.

Chapter 5
DIFFERENCES IN PERSONALITY
AND BEHAVIOR

The title of this chapter is misleading in one sense, since we have already been dealing with aspects of personality and behavior; in Chapter 3 we examined dimensions of intelligence and academic skills, and in Chapter 4 we reviewed important school experiences and attitudes. Nevertheless, a number of additional "person characteristics" have been measured in the Youth in Transition study, and this chapter summarizes those most strongly related to educational attainment.

Our coverage includes such personality dimensions as needs for self-development and self-utilization, feelings of internal control (or personal efficacy), self-esteem, somatic complaints, negative affective states, feelings of independence, and impulses to aggression. Also reported are measures of values, ambitious job attitudes, and occupational aspirations. Finally, this chapter examines some dimensions of delinquent behavior which serve as powerful predictors of dropping out of school.

The Need for Self-Development

People go to school for purposes of self-development—at least that is why they are *supposed* to go to school. Accordingly, we might expect that those individuals who express a high need for self-development will be highest in educational attainment.

Fifteen questionnaire items were developed by Long (1967) to measure the need for self-development. Respondents were asked for self-ratings using such statements as: "When I am learning something new, I like to set a goal for myself and try to reach it; I look for opportunities to better myself; I would be unhappy in a job where I didn't grow and develop; If I had to lower my goals because I just couldn't make it, that would really hurt." A complete listing of the items in this scale is presented in Volume I of this monograph series (Bachman, et al., 1967).

Figure 5-1 presents the relationship between the need for self-development, as measured in tenth grade, and later educational

attainment. At the lowest level of self-development need, an estimated 27 percent dropped out; at the highest level of the need,
an estimated 12 percent dropped out. Sixty-two percent of those
who were highest in need for self-development entered college,
while only 21 percent did so among those lowest in self-development need. In short, our expectations are borne out by the data-
those tenth-graders who expressed the greatest need for self-
development reached the highest average levels of educational attainment.

Closely related to the need for self-development is the need
for self-utilization—the use of one's existing skills and abilities.
Long (1967) developed an eight-item measure of this dimension,
using questions such as the following: "I wish I had more chance
to use some of my skills; I'd like to bring my usual performance
in line with the best I've ever done; when the work I'm doing
doesn't give me the chance to do the things I'm good at, I am
dissatisfied." In Volume II of this series we related the measures of need for self-development and need for self-utilization to
each other, and to family background dimensions:

> The product-moment correlation between the two scales is .72.
> The two scales also display nearly identical relationships with back-
> ground dimensions. Thus it is doubtful that the scales have succeed-
> ed in measuring two separate components of self-actualization needs.
> At least for our present purposes, it will be convenient to consider
> these dimensions jointly. (Bachman, 1970, p. 114)

Data from the present analysis are fully consistent with our
earlier conclusion; the two need scales do a nearly identical job
of predicting educational attainment (the 15-item self-development
scale predicts slightly better than does the 8-item self-utilization
scale). Perhaps further attempts at measuring these two need
dimensions will be more successful in separating them. For the
present, however, it appears that both scales are effective to some
degree—educational attainment is greatest among those who express a need to develop, and use, their skills and abilities.

Internal Versus External Control of One's Fate

Is dropping out likely to occur most often among those who
feel that matters are "in the hands of fate"? Are college entrants
most likely to be those who think that they control their own destinies?

Rotter (1963, 1966) has used the term "internal control" to
designate the feeling that an individual controls his own fortunes,
while "external control" refers to the notion that one is swept

FIGURE 5-1: EDUCATIONAL ATTAINMENT RELATED TO
NEED FOR SELF-DEVELOPMENT

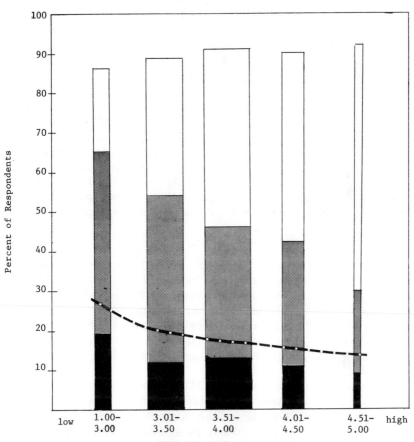

NEED FOR SELF-DEVELOPMENT
(Measured in 10th Grade)

Group 1: High school dropouts
Group 2: Stayins who were not "primarily students" after high school
Group 3: Stayins who were "primarily students" after high school

—— Dropout rate estimated from total sample (incl. "undiscovered dropouts")

Eta (treating educational attainment as a trichotomous criterion) = .18

NOTES: Width of each bar is proportionate to size of predictor subgroup.
See Chapter 2 for complete definitions of Groups 1, 2, and 3.
See Appendix C for further information and for data underlying
figures.

along by outside events. Twelve items from Rotter's (1966) I-E (internal-external) Scale were included in the questionnaire. The relationship between this personality dimension (measured in tenth grade) and educational attainment is shown in Figure 5-2. Among those highest in internal control, the estimated dropout rate was about 12 percent; the rate was about twice as high among those at the external control end of the scale. Those who felt they controlled their own affairs were also more likely to enter college, as the figure shows.

Coleman found that an important correlate of school achievement is "the extent to which an individual feels that he has some control over his own destiny" (Coleman, 1966, p. 23). Our present findings confirm and extend that conclusion; a feeling of personal control is one of the factors that *predicts* to later educational attainment. Long before the events actually occurred, those destined to drop out indicated below average feelings of personal efficacy, while those bound for college were above the average.

Self-Esteem and Affective States

Dropouts are thought to be low in self-esteem and high in negative affective states such as depression, resentment, and anomie (Cervantes, 1965; Zeller, 1966; Hathaway, et al., 1969). The findings reported in this section confirm those relationships to some degree, and indicate that negative affective states and low self-esteem *precede* dropping out. In addition, college entrance is predicted by relatively high self-esteem and less negative affective states.[1]

Self-esteem. Coopersmith (1967, p. 5) defines self-esteem as ". . .a *personal* judgment of worthiness that is expressed in the attitudes the individual holds toward himself." Rosenberg (1965, p. 31) uses similar terms: "When we speak of high self-esteem, then, we shall simply mean that the individual respects himself, considers himself worthy. . . Low self-esteem, on the other hand, implies self-rejection, self-dissatisfaction, self-contempt."

The measure of self-esteem used here consists of ten questionnaire items, six adapted directly from the scale developed by Rosenberg (1965) and four developed by Cobb, et al. (1966). Our earlier analyses of self-esteem found it to have (a) a small positive correlation with intelligence and somewhat higher correlations

---

[1]The measures discussed in this section have all been described more fully in earlier volumes in this series (Bachman, et al., 1967; Bachman, 1970).

FIGURE 5-2:   EDUCATIONAL ATTAINMENT RELATED TO
              INTERNAL CONTROL

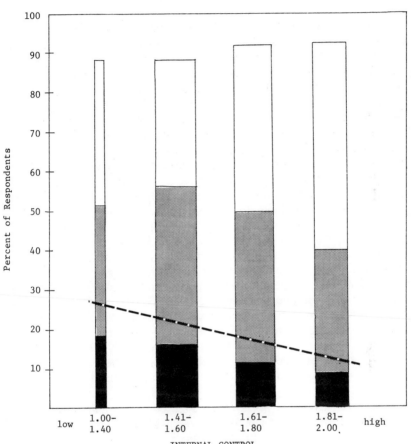

Group 1: High school stayins
Group 2: Stayins who were <u>not</u> "primarily students" after high school
Group 3: Stayins who <u>were</u> "primarily students" after high school

Dropout rate estimated from <u>total</u> sample (incl. "undiscovered dropouts")

Eta (treating educational attainment as a trichotomous criterion) = .17

NOTES: Width of each bar is proportionate to size of predictor subgroup.
         See Chapter 2 for complete definitions of Groups 1,2, and 3.
         See Appendix C for further information and for data underlying
         figures.

with self-concept of school ability and self-reports of grades, (b) a small positive correlation with socioeconomic level, and (c) a fairly strong correlation with our measure of family relations (Bachman, 1970).

The relationship between self-esteem and educational attainment is shown in Figure 5-3. Self-esteem differences are most strongly related to college entrance; 56 percent of those at the highest self-esteem level went on to enter college, while only half as many did so among those lowest in self-esteem.

We estimate that about one-fourth of those lowest in self-esteem dropped out of high school, whereas dropping out occurred only half as often among those highest in self-esteem. It is important to note, however, that this relationship distinguishes dropouts from those who enter college, but it does not really differentiate between dropouts and those who end their education with high school graduation—there was very little difference in average self-esteem between these two categories, but both were noticeably lower than those who went on to college.

Negative Affective States and Somatic Symptoms. Our earlier analyses of affective states dimensions revealed fairly high intercorrelations among six scales: Irritability, General anxiety, Anxiety and tension, Depression, Anomie, and Resentment. Accordingly, a single composite measure was constructed from these scales. "The term negative affective states seems an appropriate summary of these dimensions. A respondent scoring high on this composite measure would say that he sometimes, often or almost always feels: depressed, bored, useless, left out, worried about many things, jealous, resentful, tense, and irritable" (Bachman, 1970, p. 131).

Negative affective states are related to educational attainment, although the effects are not very strong. Those who reported the most negative affect were above average in dropout rate (an estimated 27 percent) and below average in college entrance (31 percent). Among those low in negative affect, the dropout rate was low (an estimated 12 percent) and college entrance was somewhat above average (45 to 48 percent).

Closely related to the negative affective states index is a self-report measure of somatic symptoms (the product-moment correlation between the two measures is .54). The somatic symptoms measure is an 18-item checklist of physical complaints adapted from the questionnaire used by Gurin, et al. (1960) in the study *Americans View their Mental Health.* In general, our respondents reported few symptoms, as might be expected for young men in tenth grade. Nevertheless, some differences in amount of symp-

FIGURE 5-3: EDUCATIONAL ATTAINMENT RELATED TO
SELF-ESTEEM

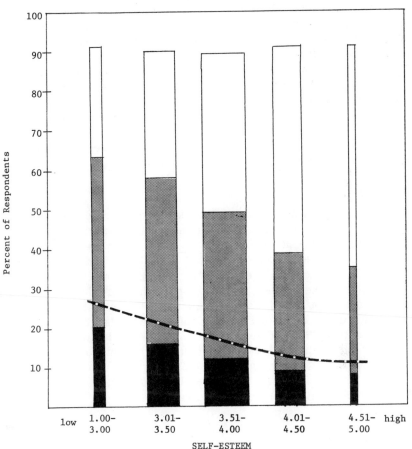

Group 1: High school stayins
Group 2: Stayins who were <u>not</u> "primarily students" after high school
Group 3: Stayins who <u>were</u> "primarily students" after high school

—— Dropout rate estimated from <u>total</u> sample (incl. "undiscovered dropouts")

Eta (treating educational attainment as a trichotomous criterion) = .19

NOTES: Width of each bar is proportionate to size of predictor subgroup.
See Chapter 2 for complete definitions of Groups 1,2, and 3.
See Appendix C for further information and for data underlying
figures.

toms did appear, and these differences are somewhat predictive of dropping out and college entrance.

Figure 5-4 presents the relationship between somatic symptoms and educational attainment. About 10 percent of our respondents said that "Sometimes" or more often they were bothered by such things as nervousness, headaches, loss of appetite, trouble sleeping, difficulty getting up in the morning and the like. We estimate that about one-third of those individuals dropped out of high school, while only 17 percent entered college. Nearly three-quarters of our sample reported that they only "Seldom" or "Never" experienced most of the somatic symptoms on the checklist. There was relatively little variation in educational attainment within that range of symptoms; estimated dropout rates ranged from 9 to 15 percent, while 46 to 49 percent went on to college.

Social Values

We reported in Chapter 4 that "academic achievement value" measured in tenth grade showed a moderate relationship to later educational attainment. A number of other value dimensions were included in the questionnaire, based largely on items developed by Scott (1965) and Klinger (1961). Building on the theoretical position that values reflect a sense of "oughtness" that one applies to all people, we asked respondents to rate each of a number of statements using a 6-point scale ranging from "a very good thing for people to do" to "a very bad thing for people to do."

Six value dimensions were found to be intercorrelated and also closely related conceptually; accordingly, a composite measure of *social values* was constructed by computing a mean for each respondent based on the following scales:

Honesty
Kindness
Reciprocity
Self-control
Social responsibility
Social skills

The complete listing of items in these scales is provided in Volume I of this series (Bachman, et al., 1967) and some of the responses are discussed in Volume II (Bachman, 1970).

The relationship between the social values measure and educational attainment is displayed in Figure 5-5. The lowest category shown in the figure consists of those who gave a mixture of favorable and unfavorable responses to the items on the value

FIGURE 5-4:   EDUCATIONAL ATTAINMENT RELATED TO
SOMATIC SYMPTOMS

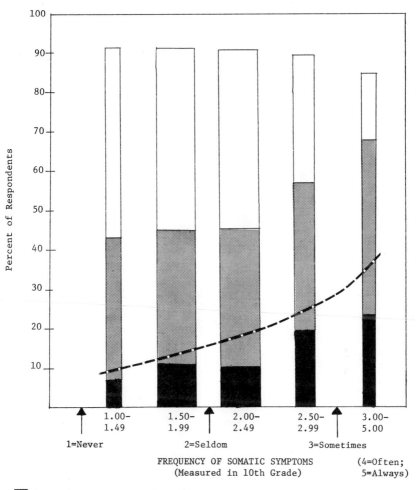

Group 1: High school dropouts
Group 2: Stayins who were not "primarily students" after high school
Group 3: Stayins who were "primarily students" after high school

Dropout rate estimated from total sample (incl. "undiscovered dropouts")

Eta (treating educational attainment as a trichotomous criterion) = .24

NOTES: Width of each bar is proportionate to size of predictor subgroup.
See Chapter 2 for complete definitions of Groups 1, 2, and 3.
See Appendix C for further information and for data underlying
figures.

FIGURE 5-5: EDUCATIONAL ATTAINMENT RELATED TO
            SOCIAL VALUES

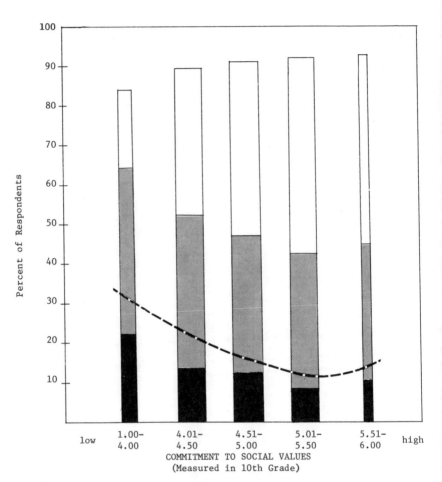

Group 1: High school dropouts
Group 2: Stayins who were <u>not</u> "primarily students" after high school
Group 3: Stayins who <u>were</u> "primarily students" after high school

━━━Dropout rate estimated from <u>total</u> sample (incl. "undiscovered dropouts")

Eta (treating educational attainment as a trichotomous criterion) = .20

NOTES: Width of each bar is proportionate to size of predictor subgroup.
        See Chapter 2 for complete definitions of Groups 1,2, and 3.
        See Appendix C for further information and for data underlying
        figures.

scales. Such individuals often showed disapproval of such things as "Turning the other cheek, and forgiving others when they harm you; Always telling the truth, even though it may hurt oneself or others; Being careful of a borrowed book; Doing a favor for someone who has done one for you; Being well-mannered and behaving properly in social situations; Never losing one's temper, no matter what the reason." An estimated one-third of the tenth-graders at this low end of the social values scale later dropped out of school; only 20 percent went on to college. As we move up the scale of commitment to social values, there is a gradual decrease in the proportion who dropped out and an increase in the proportion who entered college. There is a very slight reversal in that trend at the top category; perhaps this indicates that those who invariably expressed themselves as foursquare behind the socially approved answer were a bit less sophisticated than those who occasionally were willing to approve "Telling a lie to spare someone's feelings" or "Helping a close friend get by a tight situation, even though you may have to stretch the truth a bit to do it." In any event, the main direction of the relationship is clear: educational attainment was higher than average among those who showed fairly strong approval of commonly held social values.

Occupational Attitudes and Aspirations

By the time they enter tenth grade most young men have formed some attitudes and aspirations about the sort of job they would like to hold in a few years. These thoughts are not, of course, unrelated to plans and expectations for completing high school and entering college. Thus it is no surprise to find that occupational attitudes and aspirations are among the dimensions which predict to educational attainment.

Ambitious Job Attitudes. Volume II in this series reports the development of a scale of ambitious job attitudes which gives positive weighting to items reflecting a desire for self-development and "getting ahead" and gives negative weighting to items suggesting an aversion to such things as "working too hard" and assuming responsibilities. Ambitious job attitudes were found to be positively correlated with socioeconomic level, the family relations measure, and intelligence (Bachman, 1970).

The relationship between ambitious job attitudes and educational attainment is presented in Figure 5-6. At the left-hand side of the figure are those who expressed relatively little "ambition" and showed more concern about a job where they could avoid such things as getting dirty, taking a lot of responsibility, and working

FIGURE 5-6:   EDUCATIONAL ATTAINMENT RELATED TO
               AMBITIOUS JOB ATTITUDES

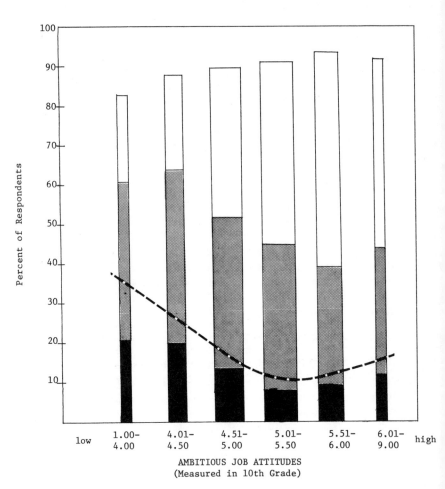

AMBITIOUS JOB ATTITUDES
(Measured in 10th Grade)

■ Group 1: High school dropouts
▒ Group 2: Stayins who were <u>not</u> "primarily students" after high school
□ Group 3: Stayins who <u>were</u> "primarily students" after high school

—▪— Dropout rate estimated from <u>total</u> sample (incl. "undiscovered dropouts")

Eta (treating educational attainment as a trichotomous criterion) = .23

NOTES: Width of each bar is proportionate to size of predictor subgroup.
        See Chapter 2 for complete definitions of Groups 1,2, and 3.
        See Appendix C for further information and for data underlying
        figures.

too hard. We estimate that about one-third of these young men dropped out of school, while only 22 percent went on to college. Toward the right side of the figure are those who expressed less desire to avoid responsibility and hard work, and showed more interest in developing and using skills, earning a good salary, and "getting ahead." The dropout rate was lower among these young men, and the rate of college entrance was high.

It is interesting to note that the same sort of reversal of trend found in Figure 5-5 (social values) appears a bit more strongly in Figure 5-6. Those who showed the very highest levels of "ambition" were not quite so high in educational attainment as those who showed only moderately strong "ambition." This may be another indication that the more sophisticated college-bound respondents tended to avoid the extreme positions on our response scales and/or tended to provide a more complex mixture of answers. (It may also be that our original assignment of items to the ambitious job attitudes scale does not maximize prediction of educational attainment. It is beyond the scope of our present effort to explore alternative combinations and weightings of items, but this represents an interesting possibility for future analyses of our data.)

Occupational Aspirations. A simple and direct measure of occupational aspirations consists of asking the respondent what occupation he hopes to enter. In response to such a question in the interview, about three-quarters of our tenth-grade respondents mentioned some specific occupation or occupational category.[2] Rather than deal with a great variety of specific occupations, our analyses have been concentrated on a continuum representing the *status* of aspired occupation. Our measure of status is the Duncan socioeconomic status index (Reiss, 1961). As we noted in Volume II of this series, the status of aspired occupation showed a good deal of stability throughout the high school years. It was also strongly and consistently related to intelligence, socioeconomic level, and other family background dimensions (Bachman, 1970).

The relationship between tenth-grade occupational aspirations and later educational attainment is presented in Figure 5-7. The effect is particularly strong and clear for college entrance; among

---

[2]We reported in Volume II of this series that 85 percent of our tenth grade respondents mentioned some occupational plans in the interview; however, it was possible to provide Duncan status codings for only 74 percent of the respondents. This does not substantially affect the results and conclusions in Volume II; nevertheless, we regret the oversight in not reporting the two percentages separately in the earlier volume.

FIGURE 5-7:   EDUCATIONAL ATTAINMENT RELATED TO
              STATUS OF ASPIRED OCCUPATION

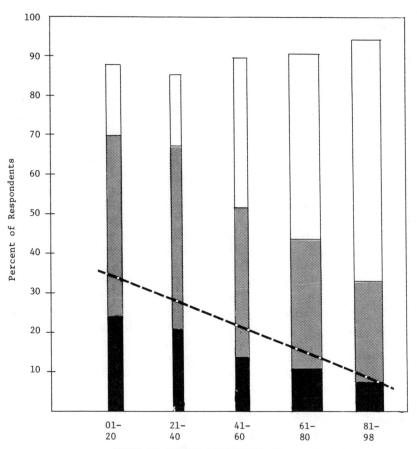

STATUS OF ASPIRED OCCUPATION   (Duncan Scale)
(Measured in 10th Grade)

■ Group 1:   High school dropouts
▨ Group 2:   Stayins who were not "primarily students" after high school
☐ Group 3:   Stayins who were "primarily students" after high school

--- Dropout rate estimated from total sample (incl. "undiscovered dropouts")

Eta (treating educational attainment as a trichotomous criterion) = .30

NOTES: Width of each bar is proportionate to size of predictor subgroup.
         See Chapter 2 for complete definitions of Groups 1,2, and 3.
         See Appendix C for further information and for data underlying
         figures.

those who had the lower status occupational aspirations in tenth grade only 18 percent went on to college, whereas 61 percent of those with high status aspirations entered college. An estimated one-third of those with lowest occupational aspirations became dropouts, whereas only 9 percent dropped out among those with highest aspirations.

The major distinction in occupational aspiration lies between those who went on to college and those who did not. The mean Duncan value for the college-bound was 71; it was 48 for dropouts and 54 for those who ended their education at high school graduation. We reported in Volume II the high correlation (.59) between status of aspired occupation and plans to enter college. It is thus not surprising to find that those with the highest occupational aspirations were in fact most likely to succeed in entering college, especially since high-status occupations usually require a college education.

Impulsiveness and Independence

A number of studies have found that dropouts are more inclined to be impulsive than are stayins (Combs and Cooley, 1968; Lichter, et al., 1962; Kelly, et al., 1964). Two scales in the present study involve impulsiveness or are closely related to it; both do a good job of distinguishing dropouts from stayins.

Independence. The 6-item scale of independence is based on items selected from an inventory developed by Sampson (1960). On a 5-point scale ranging from "Almost always true" to "Never true," a majority of respondents checked each of these items as "Sometimes true" or "Often true" of them:

> I demand freedom and independence above everything.
> I become stubborn when others try to force me to do something.
> I like to be on my own and be my own boss.
> I argue against people who try to boss me around.
> One of my goals in life is to be free of the control of others.
> I go my own way in spite of what others think.

Figure 5-8 relates the independence scale to educational attainment. The sharpest differentiation lies between the dropouts and all others. We estimate that about 37 percent of those highest in independence at the start of tenth-grade dropped out, while at the lower levels of independence the estimated dropout rate ranges from 11 to 16 percent. College entrance was relatively low among those at the top of the independence scale, although this part of the relationship is not so strong as that involving dropping out.

The curvilinearity noted in some other relationships appears

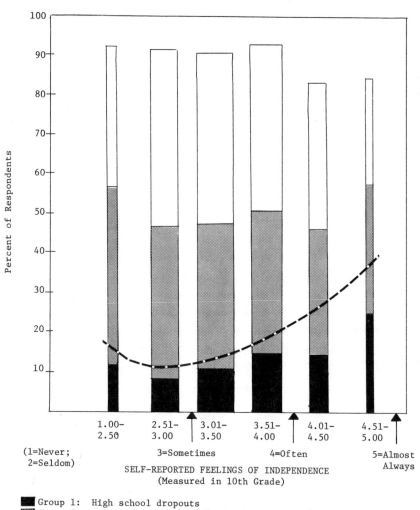

FIGURE 5-8:   EDUCATIONAL ATTAINMENT RELATED TO
              LEVEL OF INDEPENDENCE

Group 1: High school dropouts
Group 2: Stayins who were <u>not</u> "primarily students" after high school
Group 3: Stayins who <u>were</u> "primarily students" after high school
- - - Dropout rate estimated from <u>total</u> sample (incl. "undiscovered dropouts")

Eta (treating educational attainment as a trichotomous criterion) = .12

NOTES: Width of each bar is proportionate to size of predictor subgroup
        See Chapter 2 for complete definitions of Groups 1,2, and 3.
        See Appendix C for further information and for data underlying
        figures.

again here. The "best" amount of independence, in terms of ed-ucational attainment, is not at either extreme on the scale; rather, it lies *near* the lower end. Bearing in mind that the general level of independence was fairly high among our respondents, this means that a boy who said the items listed above were "Sometimes" true of him was most likely to be among those entering college, and least likely to become a dropout. The boy who said the items were "Seldom" true of him was most likely to finish high school but not go on to college. The boy who said the items were "Al-most always true" of him stood the best chance of dropping out.

Impulse to Aggression. Four items were adapted from a scale used by Cobb, et al., (1966) and made applicable to students: "I feel like swearing, I feel like losing my temper at my teachers, I feel like being a little rude to my teachers, I feel like picking a fight with my parents." Each of these statements was endorsed by about 20 percent of the boys, who said they were often or al-most always true; about 28 percent said they were sometimes true; and about half said they were seldom or never true. It might be expected that those most given to aggressive impulses, at least on the teacher-specific items, would be more likely than average to drop out (or be expelled). This expectation is borne out by the data.

Figure 5-9 shows the relationship between the impulse to aggression scale and educational attainment. Here, as was true for the independence scale, the sharpest distinctions appeared be-tween the dropouts and all stayins. There is a steady increase in rate of dropping out as we move from the left side of the scale to the right. For those highest in impulse to aggression, we es-timate the dropout rate was about 30 percent.

Delinquent Behavior

Dropouts often engage in delinquent behaviors. This cor-relation has sometimes been used to support the conclusion that dropping out leads to delinquency (Cervantes, 1965; Hathaway, et al., 1969; Namenwirth, 1969). However, findings from the present study indicate that delinquent behaviors *precede* dropping out of high school.[3]

Our measure of delinquent behaviors was adapted directly from one used by Gold (1966). Volume II in this series includes

---

[3]One interpretation of this relationship was suggested in a personal communication from our colleague Martin Gold: the correlation between delinquent behavior and dropping out may occur because both are conse-quences of academic failure and adjustments to that failure.

FIGURE 5-9:   EDUCATIONAL ATTAINMENT RELATED TO
              IMPULSE TO AGGRESSION

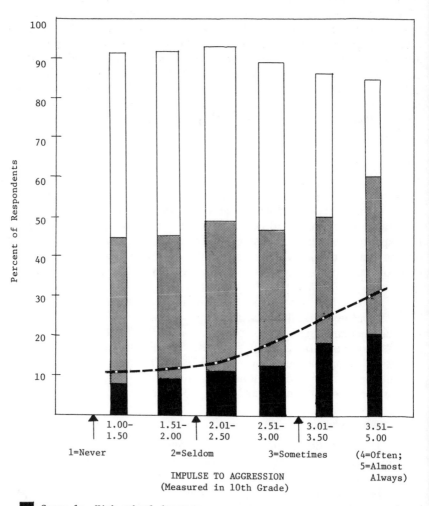

Group 1: High school dropouts
Group 2: Stayins who were <u>not</u> "primarily students" after high school
Group 3: Stayins who <u>were</u> "primarily students" after high school

- - - Dropout rate estimated from <u>total</u> sample (incl. "undiscovered dropouts")

Eta (treating educational attainment as a trichotomous criterion) = .18

NOTES: Width of each bar is proportionate to size of predictor subgroup
         See Chapter 2 for complete definitions of Groups 1,2, and 3.
         See Appendix C for further information and for data underlying
         figures.

a discussion of the measure and some data suggesting validity; a few excerpts from that discussion will be adequate for our present purposes.

> A 26-item checklist was administered as a separate questionnaire, with special instructions that emphasized the complete confidentiality of the information. . . .
> The behaviors covered in the checklist range from rather innocuous things like staying out too late. . .to very serious matters like assault. . . . The items vary not only in their seriousness, but also in their substantive nature. Some deal with disruptive or delinquent behavior in school. . .some focus on interpersonal aggression. . .and some cover acts of theft and vandalism. . . . Each of the above topics has been the basis for a separate sub-scale. . . . Two additional sub-scales reflecting frequency and seriousness of delinquent behavior have been developed, based on the work of Gold (1966) and Sellin and Wolfgang (1964). The sub-scales are based on overlapping sets of items; they are highly correlated with each other and with a total score based on all 26 items.

The total score based on all 26 delinquency items was found to be negatively related to educational attainment. An examination of each sub-scale was then carried out, with the following results.

The sub-scales reflecting frequency (9 items) and seriousness (10 items) of delinquency showed essentially the same patterns of relationships with educational attainment. Across the lower range of delinquency—that within which two-thirds of the sample fell—the rates of dropping out and college entrance remained constant (at roughly 12 to 15 percent and 42 to 46 percent respectively). As delinquency rates rose above that level, estimated dropout rates soared as high as 60 percent and rates of college entrance dropped below 20 percent. In short, it was only when frequency or seriousness of delinquency became rather high that later educational attainment was affected.

The strongest associations between delinquency sub-scales and educational attainment involve the two dimensions that would have been chosen on an *a priori* basis: interpersonal aggression and delinquent behavior in school.

Interpersonal Aggression and Delinquent Behavior in School. The items included in these two sub-scales are displayed in Table 5-1. Our earlier summary of the sub-scales will be useful here:

> Delinquent or disruptive behaviors in school during the preceding three years are admitted by a considerable number of tenth-grade boys. Half of them report getting into a serious fight with another student at least once. There were 40 percent who said they skipped at least one day of school unexcused. About one in four admits having intentionally damaged school property, while 8 percent report having hit a teacher.

TABLE 5-1

ITEMS COMPRISING THE DELINQUENT BEHAVIORS IN SCHOOL AND
INTERPERSONAL AGGRESSION INDEXES

Delinquent Behavior in School Items:

1. How often have you gotten into a serious fight with a student in school?
2. How often have you been suspended or expelled from school?
3. How often have you damaged school property on purpose?
4. How often have you hit a teacher?
5. How often have you smoked in school (against the rules)?
6. How often have you had to bring your parents to school because of something you did?
7. How often have you skipped a day of school without a real excuse?

Interpersonal Aggression Items:

1. How often have you gotten into a serious fight with a student in school?
2. How often have you gotten something by telling a person something bad would happen to him if you did not get what you wanted?
3. How often have you hurt someone badly enough to need bandages or a doctor?
4. How often have you hit a teacher?
5. How often have you hit your father?
6. How often have you taken part in a fight where a bunch of your friends are against another bunch?
7. How often have you hit your mother?
8. How often have you used a knife or gun or some other thing (like a club) to get something from a person?

Hitting a teacher and fighting with students are instances of interpersonal aggression as well as delinquency in school. Other sorts of aggression include the following: 9 percent report having hit their father during the last three years and 6 percent report having hit their mother; 33 percent report participation in group fights; and 6 percent report the use of a weapon to threaten someone.(Bachman, 1970, p. 164)

The sub-scales share two common items, and are highly correlated. The relationships with educational attainment are also very similar for the two sub-scales. Since delinquent behavior in school is the stronger predictor of the two, it will be convenient to concentrate on the relationships for that scale, bearing in mind that essentially the same conclusions hold for the interpersonal aggression sub-scale.

The relationship between educational attainment and delinquent behavior in school is shown in Figure 5-10. The pattern is the strongest shown in this chapter, and equals most of the strong-

FIGURE 5-10: EDUCATIONAL ATTAINMENT RELATED TO
DELINQUENT BEHAVIOR IN SCHOOL

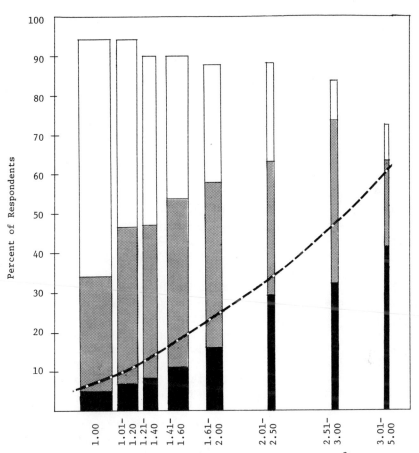

FREQUENCY OF DELINQUENT BEHAVIOR IN SCHOOL[a]
(Measured in 10th Grade)

■ Group 1: High school dropouts
▨ Group 2: Stayins who were <u>not</u> "primarily students" after high school
☐ Group 3: Stayins who <u>were</u> "primarily students" after high school

━ ━ Dropout rate estimated from <u>total</u> sample (incl. "undiscovered dropouts")

Eta (treating educational attainment as a trichotomous criterion) = .37

NOTES: Width of each bar is proportionate to size of predictor subgroup.
See Chapter 2 for complete definitions of Groups 1,2, and 3.
See Appendix C for further information and for data underlying
figures.

─────────────────

[a]See text for description of scale.

est predictors in preceding chapters (the one exception being average classrooms grades for ninth grade). When it comes to predicting dropouts (i.e., ignoring the distinction between stayins who
do and do not go on to college), the measure of delinquent behavior
in school is the most powerful of all our predictors. (We shall
have more to say about this in Chapter 6.) At the low end of the
delinquency sub-scale, only an estimated 6 to 7 percent dropped
out. Among those most delinquent in school an estimated 60 to 65
percent dropped out.

The delinquency sub-scales assigned a score of 1.0 to those
who consistently responded "Never" to the scale items. A score
of 2.0 was assigned to those whose average response was "Once."
Scores could theoretically range as high as 5.00, meaning that an
individual checked "5 or more times" for every item on the sub-
scale; in fact, however, scores on the delinquent behaviors in
school sub-scale seldom exceeded 3.0. The average dropout had
a score of 2.0, which means that he reported engaging in seven
or more delinquent behaviors in school during the last three years
(essentially grades seven through nine). This does not mean that
all the behaviors in the upper part of Table 5-1 were covered
equally. The typical dropout probably skipped more than one day
of school, and got into one or two fights with other students. There
is a good chance that he had to bring a parent to school once because of something he had done, and he probably damaged school
property once or twice. He *may* have been suspended or expelled,
and he *might* have hit a teacher (although most dropouts did not).

It is obvious that some of these things go together. The boy
who hits a teacher stands a better than average chance of getting
himself suspended or expelled. And those individuals who get expelled are likely to become dropouts. But it is important to bear
in mind that all of these self-reported events occurred *prior* to
the tenth-grade data collection that marked the start of the study.
When the data were collected, all the respondents who had been
suspended or expelled in the past had come back and were once
again attending classes.

Delinquent behavior in school was lowest among those destined for college; their average score was 1.3, meaning that they
reported doing just two things on the average from the list in
Table 5-1. Scores were slightly higher among those who went on
to graduate from high school but did not enter college; the average
was 1.5, indicating about three-and-a-half delinquent acts during
grades seven through nine—just half as many as reported by those
who dropped out.

Results from the interpersonal aggression sub-scale are similar to those reported above, although the differences between groups were not quite as strong. The mean interpersonal aggression score for those destined to become dropouts was just under 1.9; for the college-bound the mean was just under 1.4; for those who would end their education with high school graduation the mean was between 1.5 and 1.6.

Multivariate Prediction from Personality and Behavior Measures

Twelve different dimensions of personality and behavior have been presented and discussed in this chapter. They were combined in a Multiple Classification Analysis predicting to educational attainment (the dropout/college entrance dimension); the resulting multiple R was .48, indicating that the 12 predictors could account for about 23 percent of the variance in the criterion.

As in earlier chapters, it was desirable to reduce the total number of predictors. The following 5 variables were considered to be the most promising set (based on strength of relationship with the criterion and degree of intercorrelation with other predictors):

Self-esteem
Somatic symptoms
Ambitious job attitudes
Occupational aspirations
Delinquent behavior in school

These 5 variables used in a Multiple Classification Analysis produced a multiple R of .47, indicating that they could account for about 22 percent of the variance in educational attainment. This is only 1 percent less than the prediction based on all 12 personality and behavior measures, thus indicating that the subset of 5 represents the larger set quite adequately.

This level of prediction is somewhat lower than the multiple R of .59 attained using 9 predictors including family background, test scores, school experiences and attitudes (see Chapter 4). Thus in many ways the most interesting question is whether the measures examined in this chapter have any unique contribution in predicting educational attainment. Stated in terms of analysis, the question is this: if we add the 5 personality and behavior measures to the 9 predictors mentioned above, do we raise the multiple R above .59? A Multiple Classification Analysis using all 14 predictors produced a multiple R of .62, representing an explanation of about 38 percent of the variance in our educational attainment criterion. This indicates that the personality and behavior measures we have been examining in this chapter do indeed have some unique explanatory power—roughly 4 percent of the variance in educational attainment was related to predictors of this sort, above and beyond the prediction from family background, test scores, school performance, and attitudes about school.

Summary

A number of personality and behavior dimensions (in addition to those treated in earlier chapters) were related to educational attainment. Dropout rates were lower, and college entrance more frequent, among those high in needs for self-development and self-utilization, and those who felt some control over their own destinies. Self-esteem was positively related to educational attainment, whereas attainment was lower among those characterized by negative affective states and somatic symptoms. Commitment to social values (honesty, kindness, reciprocity, etc.) was positively related to educational attainment.

Not surprisingly, ambitious job attitudes and high occupational aspirations were most prominent among the college-bound. Among the non-college entrants, the differences between dropouts and high school graduates were in the expected direction (dropouts lower) but not very large.

Individuals very high in the need for independence, and those with strong impulses to aggression, were more likely than average to become dropouts. Also more likely to become dropouts were boys disposed toward delinquent behavior; in particular, a measure of delinquent behavior in school proved to be a very strong predictor of dropping out. College-bound students averaged lowest on these dimensions, but they differed relatively little from the non-college high school graduates; the major distinction in aggressive and delinquent behavior was between dropouts and all others.

Chapter 6
PREDICTING
EDUCATIONAL ATTAINMENT:
SUMMARY AND APPRAISAL

At the end of the preceding chapter we reported a multiple correlation of .62, predicting educational attainment from a combination of family background, ability, school experience, personality, and behavior dimensions. In this chapter we will review and compare the several sorts of predictors we have used in these analyses. We will summarize the evidence bearing on our treatment of educational attainment as a continuum. And, finally, we will discuss our analyses in the context of the conceptual framework first introduced in Volume I of this series.

Review and Comparison of Predictors

Several dozen variables which predict to dropping out of high school and/or college entrance have been discussed in earlier chapters. Among the most important of these are the 14 dimensions summarized in Table 6-1. The table presents means and standard deviations separately for the three analysis groups which comprise our continuum of educational attainment. A comparison of mean scores is also displayed graphically in Figure 6-1.

A word of caution is in order before we explore the data in Table 6-1 and Figure 6-1. A comparison of mean scores is a much more simplified treatment of relationships than that used in earlier chapters. It has the advantage of being compact, and thus permitting a convenient comparison of a number of relationships at once. But it has the disadvantage of oversimplifying, and potentially leading to incorrect or only partially correct conclusions. This problem is not especially severe for the data displayed in Table 6-1, but one or two illustrations will help to establish the limits of these summary data. Table 6-1 indicates that the average dropout has 3.6 siblings, the average respondent who ends his education with high school has 3.2 siblings, while the average college entrant has only 2.4 siblings. Those figures suggest that the

TABLE 6-1

SUMMARY OF PREDICTOR CHARACTERISTICS FOR THREE
LEVELS OF EDUCATIONAL ATTAINMENT

NOTE: Top entries in each row are means (unless otherwise indicated); lower entries are
standard deviations (where appropriate)

Predictor	Group 1	Group 2	Group 3	Total
FAMILY BACKGROUND				
Socioeconomic level	4.60	4.76	5.34	5.00
	.73	.73	.73	.80
Number of siblings	3.60	3.22	2.44	2.93
	2.07	1.93	1.65	1.89
Broken home (% intact)	71%	79%	86%	80%
Parental punitiveness	2.58	2.39	2.21	2.33
	.77	.69	.61	.68
INTELLECTUAL SKILLS				
GATB-J test of vocabulary	14.90	17.25	21.95	19.04
	5.87	5.79	6.12	6.55
Gates reading test	32.89	34.99	38.44	36.25
	7.63	6.01	4.40	6.00
SCHOOL EXPERIENCE AND ATTITUDES				
Grade failure (% having failed a grade)	53%	27%	8%	24%
Classroom grades	C	C+	B-/B	C+/B-
Negative school attitudes	2.26	1.97	1.69	1.89
	.67	.60	.49	.60
PERSONALITY AND BEHAVIOR				
Self-esteem	3.59	3.67	3.86	3.75
	.55	.51	.50	.52
Somatic symptoms	2.36	2.17	2.02	2.13
	.66	.62	.51	.59
Ambitious job attitudes	4.87	4.99	5.24	5.08
	.76	.71	.62	.69
Status of aspired occupation	47.89	54.13	70.93	61.04
	27.62	27.00	21.68	26.49
Delinquent behavior in school	2.00	1.52	1.30	1.49
	.85	.58	.41	.60

smaller the family, the more likely a boy is to complete high school and go on to college. This is true over most of the range of family size. However, it would be a mistake to assume a straight-line relationship and conclude that a boy with no siblings has the best chance of entering college and the lowest likelihood of becoming a high school dropout. The more detailed data presented in Chapter 3 (Figure 3-2) indicate that the rate of college entrance in our sample was highest, and the dropout rate was lowest, among those with *one* sibling, rather than those with no siblings. Some other predictors also fail to show a strictly straight-line relationship with educational attainment. For example, young men who described their parents as highly punitive were later found to be above average in dropout rate, and below average in college entrance. On the other hand, those who rated their parents very low in punitiveness differed little in educational attainment from those near the middle of the parental punitiveness scale (see Figure 3-4). The point of these illustrations is simply this: the data presented in this chapter are useful for summary purposes, but are not appropriate substitutes for the detailed analyses presented in earlier chapters.

With this caution in mind, let us turn to the summary of relationships presented in Figure 6-1. The predictor scales have been arranged in such a way that the dropouts (Group 1) always appear on the left side and the college entrants (Group 3) always appear on the right. Those who ended their education with high school graduation (Group 2) invariably appear somewhere between the other two categories, sometimes closer to the dropouts and other times closer to the college entrants.

Among the family background dimensions, the most important by far is socioeconomic level—most important, at least, when it comes to predicting who will go to college. The difference between Groups 1 and 2, on the other hand, is not particularly large, indicating that SEL is not so important in predicting whether a boy will complete high school. It is worth noting that Combs and Cooley, analyzing data from Project TALENT, found *no* SEL difference between male dropouts and "controls" (high school graduates who did not go on to college), and concluded that ". . .the economic conditions of the home do not appear to be forcing students out of school" (1968, p. 351). Economic conditions seem to have little effect on completion of high school, but they are important predictors of college attendance, and this may have some indirect effect on high school completion. Some young men may view high school as a necessary evil to be tolerated in order to get into college. Those who see college as unattainable because

FIGURE 6-1

PREDICTORS RELATED TO LEVELS OF
EDUCATIONAL ATTAINMENT

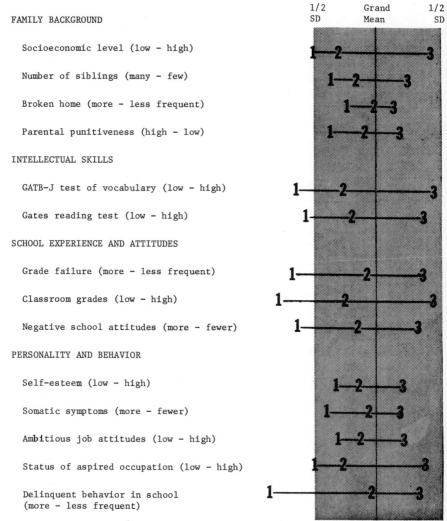

1 Dropouts

2 Graduates; no post-high school education

3 Post high-school education

of economic limitations may thus lack an important incentive for high school graduation. That may be one of the reasons why we do find a difference (albeit only a small one) between dropouts and those who finish high school—perhaps some of those in the latter group had hopes of entering college, particularly in their first years of high school.

All measures reflecting intellectual skills and school performance are prominent as predictors of academic attainment. On the GATB-J vocabulary test, for example, the difference between Groups 1 and 2 is about one-third of a standard deviation (the equivalent of about 5 IQ points in tests of intelligence), while the difference between Groups 2 and 3 is about two-thirds of a standard deviation. The Gates Reading Test shows a similar pattern.

One of the most important predictors of dropping out is past failure—being held back a grade. Over half of those who later dropped out were held back prior to tenth grade; among those in Group 2 just over one-quarter were held back, while only 8 percent of those who went on to post-high school education had been held back. Another dimension of school performance, equally powerful in predicting educational attainment, is the average classroom grade a boy earned during ninth grade. Those who later dropped out averaged just under a "straight C" in ninth grade; those who went on to college had grades on the average between "B" and "B-" during ninth grade; those who ended their education with high school graduation averaged just over "C+". (As we noted in Chapter 4, there is some evidence that self-reports of classroom grades are fairly accurate; however, it seems likely that predictions made from actual grade reports rather than students' recollections would do an even better job of predicting future educational attainment. Indeed, high school grades have consistently been among the best predictors of academic success in college.)

It is not surprising, given the above findings, to see that negative school attitudes are related fairly strongly to educational attainment. Groups 1, 2 and 3 are spaced out fairly evenly (at about one-half standard deviation intervals) along this dimension, suggesting that "commitment to education" or perhaps "tolerance of educational systems" may be thought of as a continuum—one that relates fairly strongly (eta = .33) to our continuum of educational attainment. (It is tempting here, as in the case of classroom grades, to speculate about how large the "real" relationship would turn out to be if our predictor were more valid and more reliable—if we had a better measure of the degree to which youngsters are really "turned off" by school.)

Another strong and obvious predictor of educational attainment, particularly college entrance, is occupational aspiration. Those tenth-graders who aspired to high status occupations (the occupations which require college education) were much more likely than others to go on to college. (Moreover, as we shall see in the following chapter, their high aspirations did not diminish as they went through high school and completed their first year of college.)

Delinquency as a Predictor of Dropping Out. Perhaps the most dramatic predictor of dropping out is delinquent behavior in school. Our analysis in Volume II of this series (Bachman, 1970) found delinquency measures essentially unrelated to intelligence, socioeconomic level, or other family background dimensions except for the measure of family relations. Delinquency did relate to some of the personality dimensions explored in Volume II, but it did not correlate with any of the "hard" or "objective" measures employed in the study. (At that stage of our work it seemed quite possible that the relationships which did appear were really artifacts due to nothing more than questionnaire response patterns— some respondents tend to exaggerate difficulties and misbehaviors while others minimize such things.)

But the relationship shown at the bottom of Figure 6-1 clearly indicates that the delinquency measure does relate to an objective event—dropping out. Indeed, delinquent behavior in school during the junior high school years is our most powerful predictor of dropping out.

Delinquent behavior in school is the only predictor which makes a much sharper differentiation between dropouts and stayins than between college and non-college groups. Most of the predictors space Groups 1, 2 and 3 fairly equally; the others, such as socioeconomic level and occupational aspiration, make the clearest distinction between the college group and the other two groups. But the delinquency measure is far better as a predictor of dropping out than as a predictor of college entrance. Moreover, its prediction of dropping out is largely unique—i.e., it does not overlpa much with other predictors. (This conclusion is based on findings from a Multiple Classification Analysis reported below.)

In short, we have found a number of dimensions that predict to educational attainment. If a boy starting tenth grade is high in academic ability, has done well in junior high school, and has fairly positive attitudes about school, he stands a good chance of graduating from high school and going on to college. If he is lower on these dimensions, his chances of college entrance are dimmed. If, in addition, he has a history of delinquent behavior in school, he stands a much better than average chance of becoming a dropout—sometimes because the school requires him to leave.

Educational Attainment—Is It a Continuum?

We have asserted throughout this monograph that dropping out, high school graduation, and college entrance can usefully be treated as three points along a continuum of educational attainment.[1] Now it is time to "take apart" the continuum of educational attainment and consider a number of dichotomies based on its ingredients. We will look at dropouts versus all stayins (Group 1 versus Groups 2 and 3), dropouts versus non-college stayins (Group 1 versus Group 2, with Group 3 excluded), college entrants versus all others (Group 3 versus Groups 1 and 2), and college entrants versus non-college high school graduates (Group 3 versus Group 2, with Group 1—the dropouts—excluded). In short, we will consider virtually every way of putting together Groups 1, 2 and 3; the results should help us judge the usefulness of treating educational attainment as a continuum.

Table 6-2 presents the results of five Multiple Classification Analyses, predicting different combinations of the educational attainment criterion. The predictors are those we have been discussing above, bracketed in the same way as shown in earlier chapters. The table contains a great deal of information; we will summarize only some of the highlights here, particularly since some of the relationships discernable in this table were already treated in our discussion of Figure 6-1.

1. The eta values and multiple correlation shown in the first column of Table 6-2 are consistently larger than those in any other column. This means that the educational attainment criterion, which treats dropout, high school graduation, and college entrance as three points on a continuum, is more "predictable" than the dichotomous criteria we have developed from the same ingredients. We interpret this finding as support for our conception of educational attainment as a continuum. We also take it as evidence that we have not distorted or masked relationships by our use of this trichotomy as a criterion in Multiple Classification Analysis.

2. The second and third columns in Table 6-2 present separately the two dichotomies which, taken together, comprise an educational attainment continuum; clearly the larger relationships appear in the third column, which distinguishes college entrants

---

[1]We have done more than simply assert it. We have gone so far as to treat this trichotomy as the criterion in a series of Multiple Classification Analyses. This may have proved distressing to those readers who are aware that MCA was designed to use criteria which are either continuous variables or dichotomies. In what follows we will try to demonstrate that our earlier analyses did not seriously abuse the MCA technique.

TABLE 6-2

PREDICTION TO ALTERNATE VERSIONS OF THE
EDUCATIONAL ATTAINMENT CONTINUUM

NOTE: Entries in the main portion of the table are etas
indicating bivariate association between the predictor variable
and the version of the educational attainment criterion shown
in each column. At the bottom of each column are the R and R^2
values (adjusted) derived from the Multiple Classification
Analysis based on all fourteen predictors.

Predictor	Group 1 vs Group 2 vs Group 3	Group 1 vs Group 2	Group 2 vs Group 3	Group 1 vs Group 2 + Group 3	Group 3 vs Group 1 + Group 2
FAMILY BACKGROUND					
Socioeconomic level	.37	.13	.36	.22	.38
Number of siblings	.25	.13	.22	.18	.24
Broken home	.14	.08	.11	.11	.13
Parental punitiveness	.23	.14	.18	.18	.21
INTELLECTUAL SKILLS					
GATB-J test of vocabulary	.40	.18	.35	.25	.39
Gates reading test	.37	.18	.35	.24	.37
SCHOOL EXPERIENCE AND ATTITUDES					
Grade failure	.37	.24	.25	.31	.31
Classroom grades	.42	.25	.36	.31	.40
Negative school attitudes	.33	.20	.25	.25	.30
PERSONALITY AND BEHAVIOR					
Self-esteem	.19	.08	.17	.12	.19
Somatic symptoms	.24	.13	.20	.17	.22
Ambitious job attitudes	.23	.12	.20	.16	.22
Status of aspired occupation	.30	.11	.28	.18	.30
Delinquent behavior in school	.37	.32	.24	.35	.30
	R = .617	R = .436	R = .522	R = .493	R = .568
	R^2 = .381	R^2 = .190	R^2 = .273	R^2 = .243	R^2 = .323

(Group 3) from high school graduates who do not enter college (Group 2). This is partly due to the fact that Groups 2 and 3 are more nearly equal in size than are Groups 1 and 2, but it also reflects the fact that the differences between Groups 2 and 3 are generally larger than those between Groups 1 and 2 (as noted earlier in Figure 6-1). The one exception, of course, involves delinquent behavior in school; this predictor discriminates more sharply between Groups 1 and 2 (eta = .32) than between Groups 2 and 3 (eta = .24).

3. The fourth and fifth columns in Table 6-2 represent "matches" for the second and third columns (respectively). The second and fourth columns represent the dropout versus stayin distinction, but in one case the college entrants are excluded from the analysis. Similarly, the third and fifth columns contrast those who do and do not enter college, but in one case the analysis is limited to high school graduates. For both of these contrasts, dropouts versus stayins and college versus non-college, the prediction is strongest when all respondents are included, and is diminished when the group at the other end of the educational continuum is excluded. We take this finding to be another indication that educational attainment is a continuum, with dropouts and college entrants at opposite poles.

4. We do not intend to place a great deal of emphasis on exact amounts of variance explained in these analyses, since our primary interest is in patterns of relationships rather than their exact strength. Nevertheless, it may be instructive to consider some of the differences in variance explained (multiple R squared) for the several criteria shown in Table 6-2. We can explain roughly 19 percent of the variance in dropping out if we exclude college entrants (column 2); the percentage goes up to 24 when we include college entrants in the analysis (column 4). Similarly, we can explain about 27 percent of the variance in college entrance if we limit our analysis to high school graduates (column 3); but we explain 32 percent if we include everyone in the analysis (column 5). Finally, if we consider the whole continuum of educational attainment, treating dropouts and college entrants as separate categories, we have a criterion in which we can predict 38 percent of the variance (column 1). We view this as still further evidence in favor of treating educational attainment as a continuum.

5. Having presented several observations which support the view that educational attainment can usefully be treated as a continuum, we must recall some of the limitations in that pattern. As we noted in our discussion of Figure 6-1, some predictors seem to work better for the college versus non-college part of

the continuum while at least one (delinquent behavior in school) is better at distinguishing dropouts from stayins. The eta values shown in Table 6-2 provide further evidence that some predictors work better for one or the other part of the continuum.

In summary, we find the balance of the evidence to be in favor of treating educational attainment as a continuum. It is true that some predictors work better for the dropout end of the continuum while others do their best in predicting college entrance. But it is also true that several of the most important predictors, particularly those having to do with school experiences and motivation, arrange our three analysis groups into neatly equal intervals (see Figure 6-1). Perhaps most important to our argument is the fact that along every predictor scale treated in this volume, the analysis groups are ordered 1, 2, 3 or 3, 2, 1—i.e., the rank-ordering of the data always matches our conception of educational attainment as a continuum.

Educational level is frequently treated as a continuum in survey research. Indeed, our own measure of socioeconomic level places parents' education along a five-point continuum (less than high school, some high school, high school graduate, some college, college graduate). Our conclusion here is that one part of the continuum—the point at which high school graduates are distinguished from dropouts—is best studied in the context of the larger continuum.

Educational Attainment as Effect and as Cause: A Conceptual Overview

In Volume I of this monograph series we introduced a conceptual framework in which to view the relationships we were to study (Bachman, et al., 1967, pp. 13-17). That framework is summarized in Figure 6-2 below.

Educational Attainment Treated as a Criterion. Our analysis in the present chapter and the preceding ones has treated dropping out and college entrance as criteria (or, more precisely, as a single criterion of educational attainment). We have looked at various aspects of family environments as causes of educational attainment (Arrow 2 in the framework), and we have considered a variety of person characteristics as predictors of educational attainment (Arrow 1). We have not explored person-environment interactions (Arrow 3, 4 and 5) in our statistical analyses, but it may be argued that certain person characteristics such as limited vocabulary and reading skills represent a poor "fit" between a person and the typical high school environment.

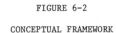

FIGURE 6-2

CONCEPTUAL FRAMEWORK

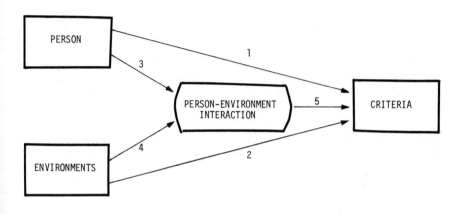

This analysis of the *antecedents* of educational attainment has been of considerable interest in its own right. But even if this were not the case, the analysis would have been necessary prior to an examination of the *consequences* of educational attainment. We turn to that topic next.

Educational Environments Treated as Predictors. At the start of the Youth in Transition study all respondents were in tenth grade, and thus spent considerable portions of their time in the school environment. The high school environment remained an important factor in the life of most of our respondents until the time when they graduated (shortly after the third data collection, in most cases). For some, however, educational environments ceased to be a part of daily life sometime after the first or second data collection. These high school dropouts ceased to experience in a direct day-to-day fashion the advantages—and disadvantages— of the high school environment. Their "criterion behavior"—dropping out—had placed them in a new "predictor category."

As we turn to a consideration of the effects of dropping out and the effects of college entrance, we must keep clearly in mind that we are entering a distinctly different phase of analysis. What was our criterion is now our predictor. And in many respects the reverse is also true—some of the variables which served as predictors will now be treated as criteria. For example, we will examine the effects of dropping out on personality dimensions such as self-esteem and somatic symptoms, and on behavioral dimensions such as delinquency.

One other shift in our style of analysis follows from what has already been said. Up to this point we have looked at a wide range of predictors while concentrating on a single criterion—educational attainment. Now we are going to concentrate on a single set of predictive categories (reflecting educational attainment) and see how they relate to a wide range of criteria—in most cases criteria measured at several points in time.

In treating such person dimensions as criteria we will concentrate on *shifts* that occur across the time spanned by our longitudinal design. We already know, for example, that tenth-graders who later become dropouts tend to be below average in self-esteem; now we want to know what happens to self-esteem *after* dropping out—does it fall still lower, or stage a recovery, or remain at roughly the same level? In the next chapter we try to answer this question and a number of others like it.

Summary

In our review we have found a number of dimensions that predict to educational attainment. If a boy starting tenth grade is high in academic ability, has done well in junior high school, and has fairly positive attitudes about school, he stands a good chance of graduating from high school and going on to college—especially if his family background includes fairly high socioeconomic level. If he is lower along these dimensions, he is less likely to enter college. If, in addition, he has a history of delinquent behavior in school, he stands a much better than average chance of becoming a dropout.

A series of Multiple Classification Analyses compared a number of two-way classifications of dropouts versus graduates, college versus non-college entrants, etc. The results support our view that it is fruitful to treat educational attainment as a continuum, and that the distinction between high school graduates and dropouts is best studied in the context of the larger continuum.

The chapter closes by noting that we have ended the phase of our analysis in which educational attainment has been the *criterion*, and are now entering a phase in which different educational environments are treated as *predictors*. In the chapter that follows we will be using our longitudinal design to search for *changes* attributable to dropping out and/or entering college.

Chapter 7
EFFECTS OF DROPPING OUT:
PERSONALITY AND BEHAVIOR

At the start of this volume we distinguished between dropping out as a *symptom* of problems, and dropping out as a *problem* in its own right—a cause of other difficulties. We argued that any analysis which makes an "after the fact" comparison of dropouts and stayins will not be able to separate the causes of dropping out from the effects of dropping out.

In Chapters 3 through 6 we applied our longitudinal design to one-half of the analysis of dropping out—a study of the causes. We looked at young men entering tenth grade and asked about their family backgrounds and past school experiences, measured their abilities and some dimensions of personality, and found a number of things which enabled us to distinguish in advance those boys who were most likely to become dropouts. (We also found that the same dimensions were good predictors of college entrance—those least likely to drop out were also most likely to enter college.) In short, we found that dropouts were different before they dropped out; dropping out is thus a symptom of earlier and more pervasive problems and limitations.

This general conclusion is scarcely surprising. It has long been recognized that youngsters from disadvantaged homes, and those who are doing poorly in school, are dropout-prone. The more important question has to do with the further effects of dropping out. Does a young man compound his disadvantages when he decides to drop out of school? What then happens to his self-esteem, his "mental health," his commitment to society's values? Does his self-esteem plunge as he finds himself in a less socially-approved role? Does his rate of delinquency, already well above average, go still higher?

To answer such questions requires a different application of our longitudinal design, one which looks at the same dimensions of personality and behavior at several points in time—both before and after dropping out. In this chapter we present many such applications. We will look at more than a score of personality

111

and behavior dimensions, measured over a period of nearly four years. We will ask how dropouts changed on these dimensions; and we will ask whether changes among dropouts were substantially different from changes among students who continued their education to the end of high school, and those who went on to college.

We will not attempt to describe the many dimensions reported in this chapter, except to note that most were measured at all four data collections, and most used indexes based on several questionnaire items. Many of the dimensions treated here were discussed in Chapter 5, and a few in Chapter 4; others not discussed in earlier chapters were described in Volumes I and II in this series (Bachman, et al., 1967; Bachman, 1970).

Self-Esteem and Affective States

Self-esteem. What does dropping out do to a boy's self-esteem? It seemed appropriate to begin our summary of the effects of dropping out by trying to deal with this rather popular question. Of course, we can provide only a partial answer to the question, since our measurement of self-esteem is limited to that obtainable through paper-and-pencil questionnaire procedures. Nevertheless, the measure has shown relationships to family background characteristics (Bachman, 1970); moreover, we found in Chapter 5 that boys who later dropped out showed below average self-esteem in tenth grade, while those headed for college were above average. Thus there is reason to think that our measure of self-esteem has at least some degree of validity.

Figure 7-1 presents mean self-esteem scores across time for Group 1 (dropouts), Group 2 (those who end their education with high school graduation), and Group 3 (those who continue on to post-high school education). The figure shows at a glance three important facts about self-esteem during the high school years:

1. College-bound young men were consistently above average in self-esteem. Among the non-college-bound, there was very little difference between dropouts and stayins.

2. There was an upward trend in self-esteem for all groups. The shift was nearly one-half of a standard deviation for the non-college groups, and about one-fifth of a standard deviation for the college entrants.

3. Most important, there is no evidence that dropping out has a negative impact on self-esteem; dropouts and non-college stayins were nearly identical in self-esteem at the start of tenth grade, and their relative positions were unchanged after nearly four years. (In fact, the temptation is to argue that these groups

FIGURE 7-1:   CROSS-TIME SELF-ESTEEM SCORES FOR
              THREE LEVELS OF EDUCATION

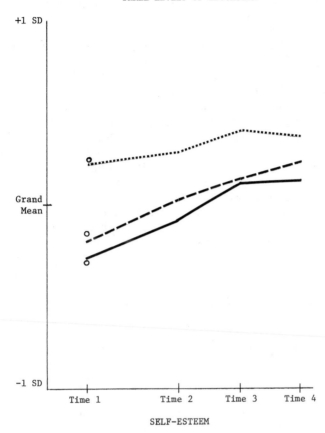

SELF-ESTEEM

━━━━━Group 1:   High school dropouts
•━━•Group 2:   Stayins who were <u>not</u> "primarily students" after high school.
••••••••Group 3:   Stayins who <u>were</u> "primarily students" after high school.

Notes: Lines connect means for only those participating in <u>all</u> data collections.
         Circles indicate means based on all Time 1 respondents, regardless of
             further participation, who could be classified into analysis groups.
         Ordinate is scaled to show Time 1 grand mean ± 1 standard deviation.
         See Chapter 2 for complete definitions of Groups 1, 2, and 3.
         See Appendix C for further information and for data underlying figures.

showed greater gains in self-esteem than did the college entrants.
We have not made that argument because of the possibility of a
"ceiling effect" operating for the college group.[1])

A Few Notes on Methodology. Having drawn the above conclusions from Figure 7-1, let us digress briefly to explain some
details of the figure, and some notes on the methodology to be
followed throughout this chapter. First of all, it should be noted
that the horizontal axis in the figure represents time; the time
between the first and second data collections was 18 months,
whereas roughly 12 to 13 months elapsed between later data collections (thus accounting for the uneven intervals on the horizontal axis). Second, the verticle axis represents the criterion dimension under study—in this case self-esteem. Third, the three
lines in the figure represent the mean scores across time for our
three analysis groups. More precisely, the lines represent mean
scores based on only those members of each analysis group who
continued as participants in the study throughout all four data collections. (Table 2-2 presents the numbers of cases in each group
which meet this criterion.)

That final point deserves elaboration. In designing this
phase of our analysis we were faced with a choice: we could
base our mean scores on all respondents available at any point in
time, or we could limit ourselves to the subgroup of respondents
for whom data were available at all four points in time. This
problem of attrition was most severe in the case of high school
dropouts; of the 286 Time 1 participants later identified as dropouts, only 157 remained as participants in the study at Time 4.
Had we included all 286 in our Time 1 mean scores, and then
found that Time 4 mean scores (based on 157) were different, we
would not have been able to distinguish between changes in the
composition of the group and genuine changes within individuals.
Clearly it was necessary to limit our cross-time analyses to those
respondents who continued their participation until the end of the
study.

The decision summarized above was made as a part of our
pre-conceived analysis plan, and we continue to feel that it is the
proper choice in such situations. But now, after the fact, it is of
interest to ask whether our results would have been much different if we had taken the alternative course of action and included

---

[1]This illustrates a general problem in the interpretation of changes
across time. A shift of one-half standard deviation at one place on a
scale may not mean the same as an equal shift at a different place, especially if one shift occurs near the limit of the scale.

all available respondents at each point in time. The data have been examined for all relationships reported in this chapter, and without exception we can state that our findings would have been virtually unchanged if we had included all available respondents. The three circles in Figure 7-1 indicate the mean values based on all respondents at Time 1; they clearly fall very close to the mean scores based on only those who participated through Time 4.

In the figures shown on the following pages the same sort of circles will be used to indicate the mean Time 1 scores for all respondents. The correspondence is not in all cases as close as that displayed in Figure 7-1, but the general conclusion holds: the 157 dropouts who remained in the study at Time 4 were very similar at Time 1 to the 129 dropouts who did not continue their participation in the study. This conclusion is most encouraging, for it means that we are in a fairly good position to make generalizations based on our sample of dropouts, in spite of our panel losses.[2]

One other methodological note should be included here. In Volume I of this series (Bachman, et al., 1967, pp. 37-38) we discussed the problem of repeated interviewing effects (sometimes referred to as the "Hawthorne effect"), and we outlined a procedure for obtaining data from a "control group" sample selected in the fall of 1966 from some of the same schools used in the original study. More than one hundred "control" respondents were interviewed for the first time at Time 4, and their answers were compared with answers from regular Youth in Transition panel members who came from the same schools. The detailed results of these analyses will be reported elsewhere, but the basic finding can be stated quite simply: the "control" respondents and their matches from the same schools were virtually identical; all differences were trivial and well within the limits expected by chance. We can conclude, therefore, that the patterns of change reported in this chapter are not distorted by repeated interviewing effects.

We have come to the end of our methodological digression and are ready to return to the substance of this chapter. Our problem now is to present a considerable amount of data clearly and concisely. The format used in Figure 7-1 compresses a good deal of information into a single chart and represents an efficient

---

[2]Of course, it is possible that the dropouts who did not continue in the study started out the same as the other dropouts, but afterward experienced different patterns of change. That is a possibility and we cannot reject it. But we can say that the interpretation we have chosen is much more parsimonious.

means of displaying complex relationships which are sometimes difficult to summarize in words. Accordingly, we will reply heavily on this sort of display, in a smaller and somewhat abbreviated version. (The data underlying Figure 7-1 and the other figures in this chapter are presented in detail in Appendix C; the information reported includes number of cases, means, standard deviation, and eta values.)

Affective States. Four measures of affective states are displayed in Figure 7-2. The first, a summary measure of negative affective states, indicates modest initial differences between the three groups and very little difference between them by the last data collection (see Part A of Figure 7-2). A similar pattern appears for a measure of happiness (Part B of Figure 7-2)—little difference initially and even less difference by the end of the study.

The measure of somatic symptoms (Part C of Figure 7-2) shows larger initial differences between analysis groups, but very little evidence of change across time. Those who entered higher education (Group 3) had consistently low levels of somatic symptoms. Along this dimension the dropouts (Group 1) ended the study just about where they began—about two-thirds of a standard deviation higher than the college entrants. Those who graduated from high school but did not go on for further education (Group 2) showed a slight decrease in somatic symptoms—16 percent of a standard deviation.

The scale we have labelled "impulse to aggression" shows a bit more change than the others (see Part D of Figure 7-2). Part of that apparent change can be traced to a change of wording in two of the four items which comprise the scale. The items "I feel like losing my temper at my teachers" and "I feel like being a little rude to my teachers" were inappropriate for those not in school, so at Times 2, 3 and 4 these items were changed for all respondents, and "people" was substituted for "my teachers."[3] It is interesting to note that 24 percent of our respondents at Time 1 said they "often" or "almost always" felt like losing their tempers at "teachers," but only half that many at Time 2 expressed similar feelings about the broader category of "people." Needless

---

[3]Obviously it would have been better if our initial question had used "people" rather than "my teachers," but in this case we failed to anticipate the difficulties that would be posed by the specific wording. We had several other occasions throughout our longitudinal study to be reminded of the value of stating questionnaire items in ways that avoid unnecessary limitations.

FIGURE 7-2:   CROSS-TIME AFFECTIVE STATES FOR
THREE LEVELS OF EDUCATION

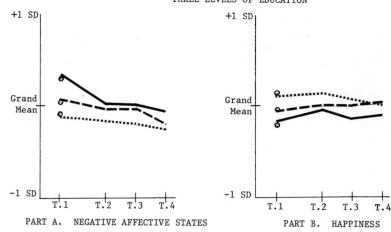

PART A.   NEGATIVE AFFECTIVE STATES

PART B.   HAPPINESS

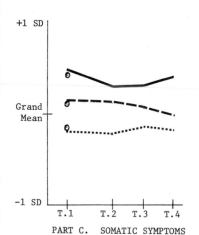

PART C.   SOMATIC SYMPTOMS

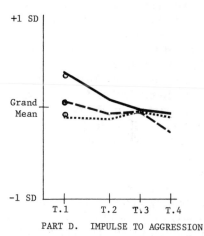

PART D.   IMPULSE TO AGGRESSION

───── Group 1: High school dropouts
── ── Group 2: Stayins who were <u>not</u> "primarily students" after high school.
········ Group 3: Stayins who <u>were</u> "primarily students" after high school.

Notes: Lines connect means for only those participating in <u>all</u> data collections.
Circles indicate means based on all Time 1 respondents, regardless of
further participation, who could be classified into analysis groups.
Ordinates are scaled to show Time 1 grand mean ± 1 standard deviation.
See Chapter 2 for complete definitions of Groups 1,2, and 3.
See Appendix C for further information and for data underlying figures.

to say, the dropouts were heavily represented among those most likely to feel rude and ill-tempered toward teachers, and this accounts for most of the differences between Groups 1, 2 and 3 at Time 1. From Time 2 through Time 4 there was little overall change in impulse to aggression; scores remained stable for the college-bound (Group 3), while the other two groups showed slight decreases.

On the whole, the measures of affective states summarized in Figure 7-2 show more stability than change. Those differences which appeared between analysis groups were, if anything, a bit larger at the start of the study than at the end. As in our analysis of self-esteem, we find no consistent evidence that dropping out of high school had a negative impact on affective states.

Needs for Self-Development and Self-Utilization

The cross-time trends in the needs for self-development and self-utilization are shown in Figure 7-3. Self-development need scores (Part A of Figure 7-3) were very stable for dropouts (Group 1). College entrants (Group 3) showed a very slight decline at Time 4, while the non-college high school graduates (Group 2) showed a small increase; however, these changes amount to less than one-fifth of a standard deviation. On the whole, the picture is one of rather little change.

Need for self-utilization was also fairly stable across time (see Part B of Figure 7-3). There was a moderate tendency for scores to drop at Time 4; for the college students (Group 3) the drop was about one-quarter of a standard deviation, the dropouts (Group 1) showed slightly less change, and Group 2 showed virtually no change.

We find scant evidence in these data that dropping out substantially reduces needs for self-development and self-utilization. If any group showed consistent change, it was the college entrants— and even there the shifts were very modest indeed.

Values and Attitudes

Does dropping out or going to college lead to changes in young men's values and attitudes? The picture is far from clear; we see some evidence of change, but the patterns are varied and difficult to interpret.

Social and Academic Values. Figure 7-4 presents the change patterns for the composite measure of social values discussed in Chapter 5, and the academic achievement value scale discussed in Chapter 4. Both of these dimensions follow a pattern that has been

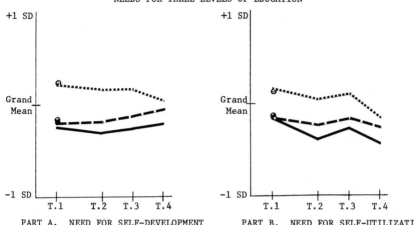

FIGURE 7-3: CROSS-TIME SELF-DEVELOPMENT AND SELF-UTILIZATION
NEEDS FOR THREE LEVELS OF EDUCATION

PART A. NEED FOR SELF-DEVELOPMENT   PART B. NEED FOR SELF-UTILIZATION

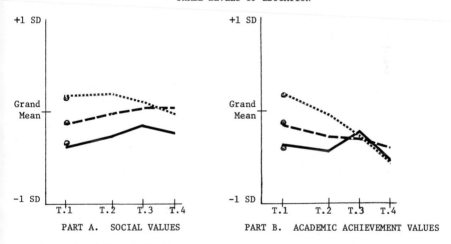

FIGURE 7-4: CROSS-TIME VALUE SCORES FOR
THREE LEVELS OF EDUCATION

PART A. SOCIAL VALUES   PART B. ACADEMIC ACHIEVEMENT VALUES

—————— Group 1: High school dropouts
— — — Group 2: Stayins who were <u>not</u> "primarily students" after high school.
•••••••• Group 3: Stayins who <u>were</u> "primarily students" after high school

Notes: Lines connect means for only those participating in <u>all</u> data collections.
Circles indicate means based on all Time 1 respondents, regardless of
further participation, who could be classified into analysis groups.
Ordinates are scaled to show Time 1 grand mean $\pm$ 1 standard deviation.
See Chapter 2 for complete definitions of Groups 1, 2, and 3.
See Appendix C for further information and for data underlying figures.

seen before in this chapter (and will be seen again)—the differences between analysis groups were largest at the start of tenth grade. Along both value dimensions, the college-bound were highest at the start of the study, while those who would later become dropouts were lowest.

Along the social values dimension, the college entrants showed a small drop over time, whereas the non-college groups—both dropouts and stayins—showed a very slight increase.

The changes in Part B of Figure 7-4 are somewhat more dramatic. Dropouts (Group 1) began and ended a bit lower than the non-college stayins (Group 2); and both groups showed a modest overall decline in academic achievement value. The college entrants showed a much larger drop, and most of the change occurred before they left high school. Apparently those bound for college began tenth grade with a very strong commitment to "study hard to get good grades. . .achieve academic honors. . .get the top grade-point average in the group." For at least some students, this enthusiasm was eroded, and they were less willing to endorse such activities as "very good things for people to do." It is a matter of no small interest that among the college-bound—those who were probably striving hardest—the value of such efforts came more and more into question. (Incidentally, the measures of positive school attitudes, discussed briefly in Chapter 4, showed a similar erosion over time, especially among those bound for college.)

Most of the important changes noted here involved Group 3, those who went on to college. It must be stressed, however, that these changes cannot be viewed entirely—or even primarily—as the *result* of going to college. Much of the changing, particularly in academic achievement values, took place before high school graduation.

Ambitious Job Attitudes. We noted in Chapter 5 that our measure of ambitious job attitudes, administered at the start of tenth grade, showed a moderate tendency to predict dropping out and college entrance. That relationship found at Time 1 diminished considerably by Time 2, as Part A of Figure 7-5 indicates; by Times 3 and 4 the distinctions were still smaller. The scores for dropouts (Group 1) increased somewhat over time, but still remained lower than those of stayins (Groups 2 and 3). Those who completed high school but did not continue into college (Group 2) showed the same sort of increase over time as did the dropouts. The job attitudes scores of those headed for college (Group 3) remained fairly stable.

Internal Control of One's Fate. The change pattern for the Rotter (1966) measure of internal control is presented in Part B

FIGURE 7-5: CROSS-TIME ATTITUDE SCORES FOR
THREE LEVELS OF EDUCATION

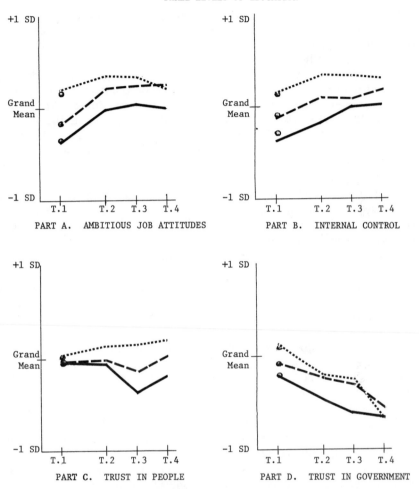

PART A. AMBITIOUS JOB ATTITUDES

PART B. INTERNAL CONTROL

PART C. TRUST IN PEOPLE

PART D. TRUST IN GOVERNMENT

━━━━Group 1: High school dropouts
━ ━ ━Group 2: Stayins who were not "primarily students" after high school
••••••••Group 3: Stayins who were "primarily students" after high school

Notes: Lines connect means for only those participating in all data collections.
Circles indicate means based on all Time 1 respondents, regardless of
    further participation, who could be classified into analysis groups.
Ordinates are scaled to show Time 1 grand mean ± 1 standard deviation.
See Chapter 2 for complete definitions of Groups 1, 2, and 3.
See Appendix C for further information and for data underlying figures.

of Figure 7-5. Once again we see a relationship that was strong-est at the start of the study, and then gradually diminished over the next several years. The dropouts were consistently lowest in internal control, and the college entrants were highest; however, the differences between the groups were half as large at Time 4 (after the dropping out and college entrance had occurred) as they were at Time 1 (when all were together starting tenth grade).

Attitudes of Trust. Two measures of trust, *trust in people* and *trust in the government*, were reported in Volume II of this series (Bachman, 1970, pp. 150-154). As we noted in the earlier volume, it is hard to define, much less measure, such attitudinal dimensions as faith in one's fellow man or trust in social insti-tutions. Thus we feel more cautious than usual in presenting the following data.

Part C of Figure 7-5 displays, for the first time in this chapter, a dimension along which our three analysis groups *di-verged* somewhat from Time 1 through Time 4. Feelings of trust in people showed a very slight increase over time among those headed for college, while those who dropped out apparently exper-ienced a slight reduction in such feelings of trust. The differences are not large, but they are interesting since they represent one of the very few instances in which dropping out seems associated with changes that might be termed "negative."[4]

A second measure of trust, trust in the government, is shown in Part D of Figure 7-5. Several things should be noted in this figure. First, and most important, trust in government scores showed a substantial decline from Time 1 (1966) to Time 4 (1970); average scores for all respondents dropped more than two-thirds of a standard deviation. This overall change should not be attrib-uted solely to some process of maturation during the late teens; data collected from adults during roughly the same period show a sim-ilar decline in trust in government (Bachman and vanDuinen, 1971). The second conclusion to be drawn from the figure is that the de-cline in trust was greatest among those who entered college. Fin-ally, the figure shows a tendency for the several analysis groups

---

[4]The following eta values were obtained when we used the classifi-cation into analysis Groups 1, 2 and 3 as a "predictor" of trust in people scores: Time 1 eta = .04, Time 2 eta = .08, Time 3 eta = .16, Time 4 eta = .11. Precise significance tests are not possible, given our cluster-ed sample; however, we estimate that a value of eta as large as .10 is likely to occur by chance less than 5 times in 100, and perhaps as sel-dom as one time in 100. (Similar eta statistics corresponding to all fig-ures in this chapter are included in the tabular data in Appendix C.)

to *converge* as we move from Time 1 to Time 4; the college-bound began the study slightly above average in trust, but at the end of the study all groups were about the same in their (somewhat lower) levels of trust. (For a more detailed discussion of these findings, see Bachman and vanDuinen, 1971.)

Summarizing this section on values and attitudes, we have see only one small instance (the trust in people measure) in which there is any indication that dropping out might lead to more "negative" attitudes. It has more often been the case that the values and attitudes of the college-bound students in our sample became less "positive" and perhaps more bitter or cynical. On the whole the differences between groups in this section, like those in the preceding sections, have been rather modest.

Delinquent Behaviors

Now we turn to an area where the differences between dropouts and stayins are not modest. We found in Chapter 5 that measures of delinquent behavior make relatively good predictors of dropping out. Now we want to deal with a question raised at the start of the present chapter: given that delinquent boys are more likely to drop out, is it also true that dropouts become still more delinquent after they actually quit school?

The data presented in Figure 7-6 provide an answer. Along all four dimensions presented in the figure the results are clear—dropouts remained considerably more delinquent than stayins, but there is *no* evidence whatever that dropping out *increased* their rate of delinquency. It is interesting to note that all of the delinquency scales except interpersonal aggression remained at roughly the same level across time. This represents a problem, to some extent, since the delinquency scores at Time 1 were based on self-reports of delinquent events "during the past 3 years" whereas the reports at Times 2 and 3 were based on events "during the past 18 months" and the reports at Time 4 were based on "the past year." The fact that the total amount of delinquency reported for the 3 years preceding tenth grade is just about equal to the total amount reported for the following 18 months could reflect a gradual rise in delinquency prior to tenth grade and a stable rate after that time. A more likely explanation, in our view, is that delinquent events are best remembered and reported for a shorter interval than 3 years—perhaps only 1 year. In any event, our intention here is not to argue that levels of delinquency are entirely stable over the high school years; the crucial point is that the rate of self-reported delinquency among dropouts showed no *relative*

FIGURE 7-6:   CROSS-TIME DELINQUENCY SCORES FOR
THREE LEVELS OF EDUCATION

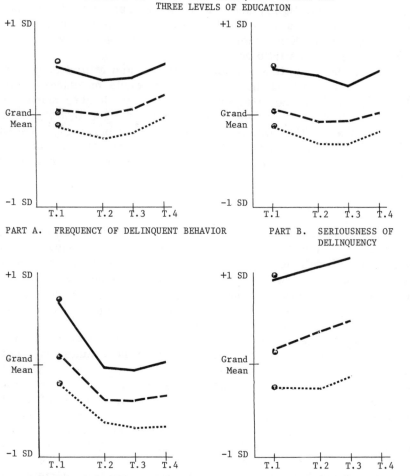

PART A.   FREQUENCY OF DELINQUENT BEHAVIOR

PART B.   SERIOUSNESS OF
DELINQUENCY

PART C.   INTERPERSONAL AGGRESSION

PART D.   DELINQUENT BEHAVIOR IN SCH

─────── Group 1:   High school dropouts
━ ━ ━ Group 2:   Stayins who were not "primarily students" after high school
•••••••• Group 3:   Stayins who were "primarily students" after high school

Notes: Lines connect means for only those participating in all data collectio
Circles indicate means based on all Time 1 respondents, regardless of
further participation, who could be classified into analysis groups.
Ordinates are scaled to show Time 1 grand mean ± 1 standard deviation.
See Chapter 2 for complete definitions of Groups 1, 2, and 3.
See Appendix C for further information and for data underlying figures

increase after they dropped out of school—they started tenth grade high in delinquency and they continued that way.[5]

The scores on interpersonal aggression (Part C of Figure 7-6) show an overall drop from Time 1 to Time 2 for all groups. This might reflect the shorter time interval at Time 2 (as discussed above), but it may also indicate simply that boys cut down on gang fighting and fighting in school by the time they start tenth grade; certainly it is the case that fighting, in school or outside, becomes a more serious matter as boys become older, and this could account for the change in aggression scores.

Delinquent behavior in school (Part D of Figure 7-6) shows the largest differences between groups, consistent with our findings reported in Chapter 5. The difference between groups remained almost identical from Time 1 through Time 3 (the items were not measured at Time 4). It may seem surprising that dropouts would have such a high average score on school-related delinquency at Time 3; however, most of them were in school sometime during the 18 months preceding Time 3, and when asked to think back they must have been able to recall quite a number of delinquent behaviors that happened shortly before they dropped out.

Several additional delinquency scales showed findings identical to those reported here—tenth graders who later dropped out of school began the study high in delinquency and continued that way. All of these findings are consistent with the oft-asserted position that dropouts tend to be above average in delinquency; but the data do *not* square with the interpretation that dropping out is the *cause* of delinquency, and there is no basis in our findings to believe that keeping boys in school by one means or another would make much of a difference in their level of delinquent behavior.

Measures of Knowledge

Two measures of current level of information were included in the study design and repeated at all four data collections. The more important of the two is a 25-item test of job information; Volume II in this series describes the job information test and its rather strong correlation with tests of intelligence and verbal skills (Bachman, 1970). Part A of Figure 7-7 shows the changes in job

---

[5]The use of several different time intervals for retrospective self-reports on delinquent behavior is an unfortunate flaw in our measurement of this important dimension. There is no point in recounting the sequence of events which led to the use of different time intervals; it is sufficient to say that based on the greater wisdom of hindsight we should have picked a one-year interval for all retrospective reports of delinquency.

information scores for the three analysis groups. All three groups increased in job information, and the ordering of the three groups was about the same at the end of the study as in the beginning. But differences among groups did increase slightly over the course of time; the dropouts (Group 1) showed a gain of 1.4 points, whereas those in Group 2 showed a gain of 2.2 points and those in Group 3 showed a gain of 2.6 points. This greater gain on the part of Group 3 is particularly noteworthy, since it occurred in spite of a possible "ceiling effect." The average final score for Group 3 was 20.4 correct answers out of a possible 25, which indicates that many of the respondents were close to the upper limit.

The one other measure of information included in repeated data collections was a very brief test of "political knowledge". The test consisted of asking a respondent to name the President of the United States, the Secretary of Defense, the Secretary of State, and the two U. S. Senators from his own state. Part B of Figure 7-7 shows the changes in "political knowledge" for the three analysis groups. The important point to note is that the trend lines are very nearly parallel, and at both the beginning and the end of the study the dropouts scored a bit below average and the college entrants scored a little above average. (The overall decline in scores resulted from turnover in the positions of Secretary of State and Secretary of Defense; ability to name Senators improved somewhat over the course of the study, but this was offset by the poorer performance in naming the Secretaries.)

What can we conclude from these two measures of knowledge? We are hesitant to draw any firm conclusions, since these measures are rather limited and deal with only two quite specific areas of knowledge. The Youth in Transition project was not intended to measure changes in performance in "right answer" tests, so the instrumentation is inadequate for that purpose. The data from the Job Information Test provide some hint that dropouts learned a bit less about a variety of occupations; however, the effect is small and can only be viewed as suggestive. The more general conclusion to be drawn from these findings is consistent with the rest of this chapter: the pattern of differences between dropouts and stayins, and between those who did and did not enter college, was clearly evident by the time the young men entered tenth grade.

Occupational and Educational Aspirations

Our earlier analyses of aspirations (Bachman, 1970) found that occupational aspirations and college plans are highly correlated; in addition, Chapter 5 of this volume reported the strong

FIGURE 7-7: CROSS-TIME TEST SCORES FOR
THREE LEVELS OF EDUCATION

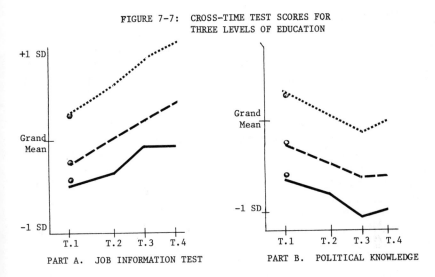

PART A.   JOB INFORMATION TEST   PART B.   POLITICAL KNOWLEDGE

FIGURE 7-8: CROSS-TIME ASPIRATIONS FOR
THREE LEVELS OF EDUCATION

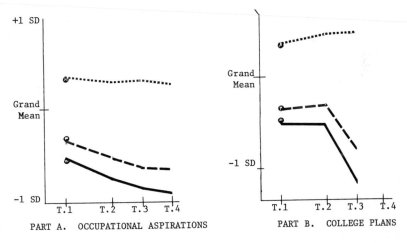

PART A.   OCCUPATIONAL ASPIRATIONS   PART B.   COLLEGE PLANS

━━━ Group 1: High school dropouts
━ ━ ━ Group 2: Stayins who were not "primarily students" after high school
••••••• Group 3: Stayins who were "primarily students" after high school

Notes: Lines connect means for only those participating in all data collections.
        Circles indicate means based on all Time 1 respondents, regardless of
           further participation, who could be classified into analysis groups.
        Ordinates are scaled to show Time 1 grand mean ± 1 standard deviation.
        See Chapter 2 for complete definitions of Groups 1, 2, and 3.
        See Appendix C for further information and for data underlying figures.

association between occupational plans in tenth grade and later educational attainments. Now we want to see how occupational and educational aspirations changed over time for those who ended their education before high school graduation, those who graduated from high school but did not continue their studies, and those who went on to college.

The data are presented in the two parts of Figure 7-8. Part A indicates that those who went on to post-high school education were consistently high in their occupational aspirations; moreover, their high aspirations showed virtually no decline over the nearly four-year span of the study. The others, both dropouts (Group 1) and stayins (Group 2), showed a moderate decline in occupational aspiration over the same period of time, with dropouts consistently averaging somewhat lower than stayins. (The decline is *not* due to a general downward shift among most respondents in these groups; rather, it is due almost entirely to a special subset identified later in this section.)

Part B of Figure 7-8 shows the changes in college plans among those who actually did and did not succeed in entering post-high school education. Eighty percent of those in Group 3 were planning on college when they started tenth grade, and that figure grew to 90 percent by the time of high school graduation. (It should be noted that some respondents in Group 3 went on to technical and vocational programs may not have viewed these programs as "college," and this probably accounts for many of the 10 percent in Group 3 who did not indicate at the time of high school graduation that they planned to enter college.) Of those who graduated from high school but did not continue directly to further education (Group 2), almost half began high school with hopes of entering college. Their hopes remained high through the end of eleventh grade, but by the end of their senior year only one-quarter hoped to enter college. (And, of course, some of those hopes were quite realistic, especially among young men who planned to enter college after completing a term in military service.) About one-third of the dropouts (Group 1) started tenth grade planning to go on to college; by the time when they would have been graduating from high school, the number still expecting to enter college had dropped to almost zero.

In short, Part B of Figure 7-8 shows one of the largest, but also one of the most obvious and predictable, changes to result from dropping out of high school—dropping out causes a young man to give up any plans of college he may have had.

Drop in Occupational Aspirations Linked to College Plans.
We noted above that many of those who did not continue into col-

lege (i.e., many of those in Groups 1 and 2) began tenth grade
with the idea that they *would* go to college. We also noted a drop
in occupational aspirations among the non-college groups. These
two kinds of changes are very closely linked; indeed, the drop in
occupational aspirations is limited almost entirely to those who in
tenth grade were planning to go on to college, but did not succeed
in doing so.

Figure 7-9 presents trends in occupational aspiration separately for those who said at the start of tenth grade that they
planned to enter college, and those who did not express such plans.
At the start of tenth grade, occupational aspirations were consistent with educational plans—those planning for college had consistently higher occupational aspirations than those who did not have
college plans. Within each of these categories, however, there
were already differences between those who would eventually become college students and those who would not.

By the end of the high school years (Time 3) occupational
aspirations were consistent with educational realities. Those who
in tenth grade planned to enter college but failed to do so by the
end of the study (categories 1-I and 2-I) showed a marked decline
in status of aspired occupation; nevertheless, they retained somewhat higher occupational aspirations than their counterparts who
had not initially planned to enter college (categories 1-II and 2-II).
Those who did not state college plans when they were in tenth
grade but later did become college students (category 3-II) showed
a substantial increase in status of aspired occupation.

Those respondents whose college plans in tenth grade matched their later outcomes (categories 1-II, 2-II, and 3-I) showed
great consistency in *average* occupational aspiration. (Individuals,
of course, showed variations from time to time, with some changing their aspirations to higher status occupations and others mov-
ing in the opposite direction. The stable pattern noted above is
simply the absence of any predominant upward or downward shift.)

We do not want to give the impression that relatively stable
occupational aspirations are *caused* by stable educational plans
and attainments, or that changes in educational plans determine
changes in occupational aspirations. Surely the two kinds of aspiration, occupational and educational, are closely interconnected,
so that a change in either one is likely to have important implications for the other.

What, then, can we conclude from the data in Figure 7-9?
Two important findings are dominant, in our view, and are con-
sistent with the major themes in this chapter and earlier ones.
First, among those respondents who have relatively consistent ed-

FIGURE 7-9

TRENDS IN OCCUPATIONAL ASPIRATIONS
(SEPARATELY FOR THOSE WHO DID AND DID NOT
HAVE COLLEGE PLANS IN TENTH GRADE)

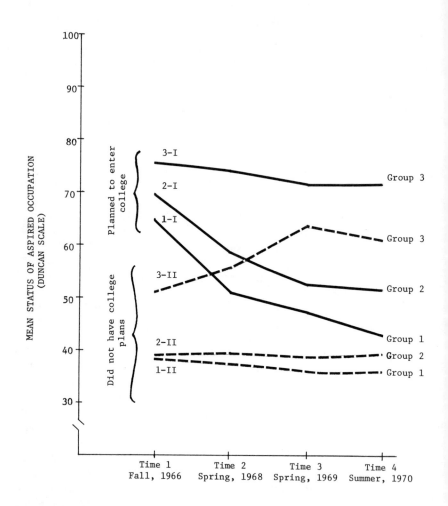

Group 1:   High school dropouts

Group 2:   Stayins who were not "primarily students" after high school

Group 3:   Stayins who were "primarily students" after high school

ucational plans and attainments (and these are clearly in the majority), occupational aspirations show the same sort of relative stability we have seen along so many other dimensions in this chapter. To put it another way, dropping out of high school or ending one's education at high school graduation does not lead to a drop in occupational aspiration unless there has also been a drop in educational aspiration.

The second major conclusion is that occupational aspirations differ far more between college and non-college respondents than between dropouts and stayins. This is consistent with our findings in earlier chapters that the primary dividing line in educational attainment is not a matter of whether one graduates from high school or drops out, but whether one continues into post-high school education.

Dropouts at Work or Unemployed

The original design of the Youth in Transition study placed considerable emphasis on a comparison of employed versus unemployed dropouts (Bachman, et al., 1967). Our expectation was that unemployed dropouts would be in a less "favorable" environment than employed dropouts or boys who remained in school, and that consequently there would be greater loss of self-esteem, increases in delinquency, and the like among the unemployed dropouts.

We did not follow that original design for several reasons. One practical consideration was that the dropout group at the end of the study was rather small, and we hesitated to subdivide it into the employed and unemployed. Furthermore, our analyses for dropouts taken as a whole showed little evidence of systematic changes, especially changes which differentiated dropouts from other respondents.

Nevertheless, we did undertake some exploratory analyses to see whether there were differences between employed and unemployed dropouts. We examined employment data for dropouts at Time 3 (when the other members of our panel were about to graduate from high school) and isolated 57 dropouts who were carrying a full work-load (forty or more hours per week) and another 36 dropouts who were out of work. There were other dropouts who did not fit neatly into either of these categories, but we felt that the two groups we isolated would provide a good starting point to see whether the experience of being unemployed led to important changes along the dimensions we had been measuring.

We compared the two groups in terms of self-esteem and delinquency, two dimensions which we thought might show the ef-

fects of unemployment. We found the unemployed dropouts about
one-half standard deviation apart from the employed dropouts along
both dimensions. But the question arises: were these differences
in personality and behavior the result of different employment experiences or were they among the causes? Does being unemployed
cause a dropout to have lower self-esteem and higher rates of delinquency, or is it the case that dropouts who are low in self-
esteem and high in delinquency are least likely to be employed?

An examination of the self-esteem and delinquency scores
across all four data collections in the longitudinal design provides
a clear answer to the question raised above. Those dropouts who
were unemployed at Time 3 had *consistently* lower self-esteem
and higher delinquency rates when compared to dropouts who were
fully employed at Time 3. From fall of 1966 to early summer of
1970 the two groups were different, and the differences at the
start of the study were just about as large as the differences at
the end. In short, we find once again that differences which might
at first blush seem to indicate the effects of different social environments were actually among the factors which determined who
entered (and remained in) the various social environments.

The analyses of employed versus unemployed dropouts were
based on small numbers of respondents, and for this reason we
have not presented our findings in any detail. Nor do we wish to
place great emphasis on the differences which appeared between
employed and unemployed dropouts; we suspect that similar differences may exist between high school graduates who were employed and unemployed at the time of final data collection, but it
is beyond the scope of our present purposes to examine such differences. The primary purpose for reporting this brief analysis
of employed and unemployed dropouts is to indicate that our general conclusions about the impact of dropping out are applicable
to both those in work roles and those experiencing unemployment:
the differences we find between individuals at or near the end of
our longitudinal study were also present when these individuals
were starting tenth grade; therefore, the differences should not be
interpreted as showing the *effects* of dropping out.

Attitudes on Public Issues

In the final stages of the Youth in Transition project a number of questions were included dealing with public issues, national
problems, and the like. Questionnaire indexes along two sorts of
dimensions were included at both Time 3 and Time 4, thus providing an indication of attitude change, particularly any change at-

tributable to the first year of college. The two dimensions measured are racial attitudes and attitudes about the war in Vietnam.
Both of these dimensions, as well as a number of other national
issues, were discussed in some detail by Bachman and vanDuinen
(1971), thus only a summary of the findings need be presented
here.

Racial Attitudes. Three scales of racial attitudes were used
in the study; all items were adapted from the work of Campbell
and Schuman (1968). The first scale dealt with whether the government should take a strong role to insure equal treatment for
all races, especially in schooling and employment. The second
scale dealt with perceptions of racial discrimination in jobs, housing, and schooling. The third scale dealt with social distance between races—willingness to have a supervisor of a different race,
neighbor of a different race, and children's playmates of a different race. Bachman and vanDuinen analyzed the responses of
whites only; their findings are presented in the following summary
and in Figure 7-10:

> Support for government action to insure equal rights showed a
> slight increase between 1969 and 1970 for all three educational sub-
> groups (Part A). The results also show that college students were
> most supportive of government action both before and after they en-
> tered college, and dropouts were least supportive. The differences
> among educational subgroups in perceptions of discrimination are
> shown in Part B. College-bound students perceived more discrim-
> ination than others at the time they graduated (1969), and their per-
> ceptions of discrimination increased during their first year of col-
> lege. High school graduates who did not go on to college started
> out (in 1969) perceiving a bit less discrimination than those bound
> for college, and a year later their perceptions of discrimination had
> dropped very slightly. The dropouts had the lowest perceptions of
> discrimination in 1969, and they perceived still less a year later.
> The results also show that college students were most willing to
> have personal contacts with blacks, and dropouts were least willing
> (Part C)—a pattern similar to that shown for government role. Over-
> all, the willingness to have personal contacts with blacks increased
> from 1969 to 1970; however, the change on the part of non-college
> high school graduates was very slight (Bachman and vanDuinen,
> 1971, p. 42).

In short, the white students in post-high school education
were consistently the most "liberal" on racial attitudes, while the
white dropouts were least so. Most of these differences were apparent at Time 3, the time of high school graduation, so we cannot conclude that the more liberal attitudes of college students
were primarily the result of attitude changes during their fresh-
man year.

FIGURE 7-10

RACE ATTITUDES RELATED TO EDUCATIONAL ATTAINMENT

PART A

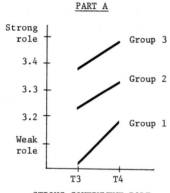

WHITES **ONLY**

Spring, 1969 (Time 3)--
    Senior year of
        high school

Summer, 1970 (Time 4)--
    One year later

STRONG GOVERNMENT ROLE

(Approximate standard
deviation, both times = .64)

PART B

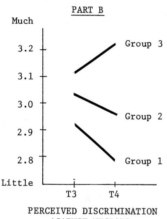

PERCEIVED DISCRIMINATION
AGAINST NEGROES

(Approximate standard
deviation, both times = .72)

PART C

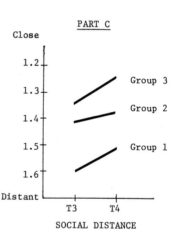

SOCIAL DISTANCE

(Approximate standard
deviation, both times = .55)

NOTES:

Group 1: High school dropouts

Group 2: Stayins who were not "primarily students" after high school

Group 3: Stayins who were "primarily students" after high school

Vietnam Dissent. A six-item index of attitudes toward the war in Vietnam has been labelled the "Vietnam Dissent" index (see Johnston and Bachman, 1970, or Bachman and vanDuinen, 1971, for a description of the items). When the scale was first administered in spring of 1969, dissent was slightly above average for both the dropouts and the college-bound. A readministration of the scale in summer of 1970 found virtually no change among those who ended their education with high school graduation, and very little change among the dropouts. Those who had spent the year in post-high school education, however, showed a substantial increase in Vietnam dissent—about 40 percent of a standard deviation.

Attitude Change Among College Students. The increased dissent over Vietnam found among those in post-high school education seems to form a pattern with other findings mentioned at several points throughout this chapter. Compared with high school graduates who did not continue their education, the college students showed a decline in academic achievement values, and their endorsement of other social values slipped a bit; their emphasis on self-development and job ambition, high at the start of tenth grade, also showed a slight decline; their trust in government dropped sharply. This pattern may reflect a growing realism, greater sophistication in question answering, or perhaps cynicism; quite likely it is a mixture of these and other things. If we had found such a pattern among dropouts we might have taken it as indicative of the damage caused by the dropout experience. But these changes toward greater disenchantment and disillusionment appeared among the most gifted and the most advantaged; they appeared among the college-bound, both before and after they left high school. This is perhaps a disconcerting note on which to leave the topic of attitude change among college students, but leave it we must. There is surely room for further analysis of these data, but such analyses lie outside the scope of the present volume.

Summary and Conclusion

Quite a number of figures have been presented in this chapter to show the trends across time in measures of self-esteem, values and attitudes, aspirations, knowledge, and delinquent behavior. Most of these data do not indicate large and significant changes during the high school years. Quite the contrary, the figures in this chapter show relatively little in the way of *changes* that can be used to distinguish dropouts from non-dropouts. There are exceptions, of course, and we have noted them. But the fact remains that in most cases the figures demonstrate "non-changes" and we have presented the data in some detail so that the reader could "see for himself."

This does not mean that our measures were unable to make useful distinctions among subgroups. A number of measures discriminated between dropouts and stayins, college and non-college groups—but these distinctions generally were just as sharp and clear at the start of tenth grade as they were later after the dropping out or college entering occurred. In some cases the measures showed a degree of change—self-esteem, for example, increased a bit during the high school years—but such changes usually involved *parallel* movement of the several groups we have been examining.

We began this chapter by asking whether dropping out makes things much worse for a young man by lowering self-esteem, impairing his "mental health" and commitment to society's values, and raising his rate of delinquency. We have examined a good deal of data, and the conclusion seems clear: we see ample evidence that dropouts began high school somewhat disadvantaged along most of these dimensions, but we find nothing to support the view that dropping out caused them further harm.

The personality and behavior dimensions examined in this chapter do not indicate that dropping out is a cause of *additional* disadvantage, but we have omitted one important area. We have yet to consider the employment outcomes for dropouts versus high school graduates. We turn our attention to this issue in the next chapter.

Chapter 8
EFFECTS OF DROPPING OUT: OCCUPATIONAL ATTAINMENTS

In the last chapter we presented evidence that dropping out of high school has little or no measurable effect on dimensions of personality and behavior. To put it another way, it does not appear that dropping out causes (further) loss of self-esteem, heightens delinquency, corrupts values, or otherwise leads to undesirable changes in young men.

But there is another powerful argument used in the campaign to prevent dropping out—the economic argument. Dropouts are less likely to find jobs, we are told; and the work they do find will offer poor pay, low status, and unpleasant working conditions. This argument usually places little emphasis on what is actually taught and learned during the final years of high school, but focuses instead on the high school diploma as a necessary *credential*.

In this chapter we will examine some evidence bearing on the economic argument against dropping out. We will begin by examining rates of employment and unemployment for dropouts versus high school graduates. Then we will compare weekly incomes and occupational status. Finally, we will examine levels of job satisfaction and a number of job characteristics.

Our intention is not to provide accurate descriptions of "the average dropout" or "the average high school graduate" in terms of employment experiences; limitations in sample size and response rates rule out such descriptions.[1] Instead, our purpose is to provide a fairly clear comparison and contrast of dropouts and graduates, in order to get some indication of whether the high school diploma really does matter in the world of work. For that reason we will be somewhat selective in defining analysis groups. Rather than covering the full range of experiences of dropouts and grad-

---

[1]Such descriptions of the average dropout and graduate are reported periodically by the Bureau of Labor Statistics, based on data provided by the Census Bureau's Current Population Survey. See Young (1971) and Hayghe (1970) for recent reports.

uates, we will concentrate on the world of civilian employment. In addition, we will focus on full-time (or nearly full-time) employment, and set some upper and lower limits on weekly income levels. These and other restrictions, described in the following sections, serve to exclude some "special cases" which might prove interesting as case studies, but would tend to blur and distort our comparison of dropouts and graduates.

Analysis Groups

The final data collection in the Youth in Transition project took place in June and July of 1970. During the six-month period prior to that data collection, many of our respondents were primarily students in colleges and universities and technical schools, some were in military service, quite a number were employed in various occupations, and a few were unemployed. An additional handful of respondents spent the first months of 1970 in high school; some had "fallen behind" in their progress toward graduation, others had dropped out and later returned to school.

By the early summer of 1970, many of those who had spent the preceding winter as students had found jobs. Most had taken summer jobs, but some (such as those newly graduated from high school or a one-year technical program) were in brand-new "permanent" jobs. In conducting a comparison of the employment experiences of dropouts versus high school graduates, we felt it would be confusing to include those individuals who had just left the role of student and were in the first weeks of a new job or still looking for one. Accordingly, we have limited our analyses in this chapter to those Time 4 respondents who were *not* primarily students in the first months of 1970. This means that we will not be considering the large group of respondents in post-high school education (Analysis Group 3), nor will we be looking at those few who were still working toward their high school diplomas in 1970.

High School Graduates Versus Dropouts without Diplomas. In Chapter 2 we identified two dropout groups, those who dropped out of or interrupted the usual school program but later attained high school diplomas (Subgroup 1a) and those who, at the time of the data collection in 1970, had not received diplomas (Subgroup 1b). In Chapters 3 through 7 we treated both dropout subgroups together, on the grounds that they had much in common that set them apart from other respondents. In the present chapter, however, the presence or absence of a high school diploma is of central importance; therefore, it is no longer appropriate to combine the two dropout subgroups. At the same time, we do not feel comfortable about combining the small group of "dropouts with diplomas" with the much larger group who completed high school in the usual manner. Instead, we will simply limit our analysis in this chapter to the two groups which present the clearest contrast—those who completed high school "on schedule" but did not continue their education beyond that point (Analysis Group 2) and those who dropped out and did not (as of mid-1970) have diplomas (Analysis Subgroup 1b). (The "dropouts with diplomas"—Analysis Subgroup 1a—are discussed in Appendix D.)

Civilian Work Force. With only a handful of exceptions, those Time 4 participants who were not primarily students during the first half of 1970 could be classified into one of three categories: those in military service, those in civilian jobs, and those who were unemployed (including those who were waiting to start new jobs and those who had been "laid off" from earlier jobs). Military service differs from the civilian employment market in many ways, particularly where questions of employment versus unemployment are concerned. Accordingly, we will limit our consideration of employment to those respondents in the civilian work force.

Sample Limitations: Some Words of Caution. At this point in our analysis we are dealing with only those respondents who participated in the final data collection. In earlier chapters we found that dropouts who continued their participation in the study were quite similar in initial characteristics to other dropouts who did not continue in the data collections (but who were identified by themselves or relatives or school records as being dropouts). We found the same kind of similarity in other analysis groups, and concluded that "within each analysis category there is little difference in background and ability between those who continued their participation through Time 4 and those who did not" (Chapter 2). And in Chapter 7 we saw that the personality and behavior scores at early data collections were also, within each analysis category, similar for those who continued their participation in the study and those who did not.

The findings summarized above suggest that we are in a fairly good position to make generalizations based on the Time 4 participants; but now we must add a note of caution. In the present chapter we are looking at dimensions that may be systematically related to a respondent's opportunity to continue participation in data collections. For example, we may underrepresent those young men who moved to geographically different areas in order to find employment. Thus, we do *not* assume that our Time

4 data constitute a bias-free sampling of the employment experiences of young men a year (or more) out of high school.

A second, but related, caution has to do with our ability to
draw conclusions about causation. We found in Chapter 7 that
dropouts were different from stayins (and particularly college entrants) along a number of dimensions, but that most of these differences were every bit as evident as the start of tenth grade as
later on after the dropping out occurred. We thus felt confident
in concluding that dropping out was a *symptom* rather than the
cause of these differences, since the differences preceded the
dropping out. This sort of analysis is not possible in the area of
employment experience, since post-high school employment could
not be measured for most respondents until the Time 4 data collection. Thus if we find different employment experiences for
dropouts versus high school graduates, we will still have to decide
whether the differences were caused by dropping out and the lack
of a diploma, or by those more basic factors which led to dropping
out. Of course, to the degree that we have measured the factors
that give rise to dropping out, we will be able to control them
statistically. But as Chapter 6 indicated, we can do only a modest job when it comes to predicting dropping out—especially when
we limit our consideration to those not going on to post-high
school education. So the problem remains with us to a large extent, and we may have to resort to some judgments or educated
guesses about any employment-related differences we find between
dropouts and stayins.

Rates of Employment

Any definition of "employment" requires that a somewhat
arbitrary dividing line be drawn. There is no problem in decid-
ing that someone working 40 hours per week is employed—and
fully employed by current standards. But how should we classify
a young man who is not a student and who works only 10 hours
a week in a grocery store? Is he similar to the youth who is
working full-time, or is his experience closer to that of the entirely unemployed?

We decided for purposes of this chapter to consider a respondent fully employed if he reported working 30 or more hours
per week at the time he was interviewed (June or July of 1970).
We chose this particular boundary for two reasons: first, we consider 30 hours to be fairly close to the typical 40-hour work
week; and second, we found that only a few respondents reported
working less than 30 hours per week.

More Graduates Fully Employed. A total of 87 dropouts without diplomas and 434 high school graduates remained among the Time 4 respondents after the several restrictions outlined in the preceding section (i.e., when we limited our consideration to the non-student civilian work force, and when we omitted the small number of "dropouts with diplomas"). Among the dropouts, a total of 71 percent were employed 30 hours or more per week. Among the high school graduates, the comparable figure was 87 percent. (An additional 5 percent of both dropouts and graduates were employed for less than 30 hours per week.) In short, employment was substantially lower among dropouts.[2]

This finding required us to deal with the question of causation raised earlier: we wanted to learn whether the lower employment rate among dropouts was a direct result of their dropping out, or a result of prior conditions—perhaps the same ones which led them to drop out of school.

A first step in answering this question involved predicting employment using the background, ability, personality, and behavior dimensions which we earlier used to predict dropping out. Preliminary analyses of the 14 dimensions summarized in Chapter 6 indicated that our most "efficient" prediction would involve just three predictor dimensions: socioeconomic level, the GATB-J test of vocabulary, and the Gates test of reading skill.[3] A Multiple

---

[2]These figures are roughly consistent with data reported by the Bureau of Labor Statistics for civilian non-institutional males aged 18 and 19. In October of 1969, about 84 percent of the high school graduates not enrolled in college were employed, while the comparable figure for dropouts was about 75 percent (based on Hayghe, 1970, p. 38). In October of 1970, the occupational situation had grown more bleak; again considering males aged 18 and 19, about 80 percent of high school graduates not enrolled in college were employed, while for dropouts the figure was about 65 percent (based on Young, 1971, p. 34). It should be noted that in both reports cited above two distinct classifications are applied to those not employed: the term "unemployed" is reserved for those not working who are looking for work, whereas those neither employed nor actively looking for work are defined as not being members of the civilian labor force. Dropouts are consistently higher in both categories of non-employment, i.e., a relatively high percentage of dropouts are considered outside of the civilian labor force, and of those included in the labor force a relatively high percentage are classified as "unemployed." In the present study we have not found it useful to distinguish between the two categories of non-employed young men; accordingly, our use of the term "unemployed" will apply to all those not working irrespective of whether they are actively seeking work.

[3]The use of just three predictors was "efficient" in the sense that using more than three predictors did not add enough new information to offset the additional "noise" or loss of degrees of freedom which resulted from having more predictor categories.

Classification Analysis using these three variables to predict full employment yielded a multiple correlation coefficient of .22, with R-squared equal to .049, adjusted for degrees of freedom. This means that we can account for 4.9 percent of the variance in employment when we take account of socioeconomic level and test scores.

How well do we predict employment simply by knowing whether a young man is a dropout or a high school graduate? The value of Eta for this relationship is .19, and Eta-squared is .037, indicating that we can account for 3.7 percent of the variance in employment by distinguishing dropouts from graduates.

The next step required a Multiple Classification Analysis combining the dropout-graduate variable with socioeconomic level and test scores as predictors of employment. The resulting multiple correlation coefficient is .250, with R-squared equal to .063. In other words, by using dropout data plus family background and ability, we were able to account for 6.3 percent of the variance in employment, and this level of prediction is a bit better than we are able to do when using dropout data alone, or background and ability data alone.

Now let us consider the relationship between background and ability, dropping out, and employment using the intervening variable model introduced in Chapters 3 and 4. The upper part of Figure 8-1 presents the relationship schematically. The lower portion of the figure indicates how the explained variance is assigned. It must be stressed that *we present these figures primarily for their heuristic value*, not because we feel that they fully represent the actual relationships between background, ability, dropping out, and employment. The model in Figure 8-1 indicates that some of the effects of family background and ability are unique or independent of whether a young man drops out (Arrow C), and some effects of background and ability overlap with dropping out (Arrow B). The unique contribution of dropping out, the portion which does not overlap with family background and ability measures, is somewhat smaller than the other effects (Arrow A).

We conclude from this analysis that dropping out may contribute to unemployment, but it makes a smaller contribution than family background and ability. Even this conclusion may overrepresent the importance of dropping out as a cause of unemployment, for there is an inequality between our ability to measure dropping out and our ability to measure accurately and completely the *causes* of dropping out. We can do a rather good job of measuring whether a young man has dropped out or graduated—especially when we simply exclude from analysis those whom we cannot

FIGURE 8-1

MODEL ILLUSTRATING THE EFFECTS OF FAMILY SOCIOECONOMIC
LEVEL, ACADEMIC ABILITY, AND DROPPING OUT UPON EMPLOYMENT

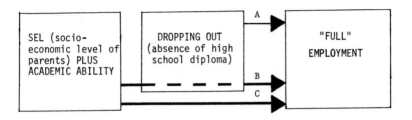

NOTE: This analysis deals with very small
relationships. The figures are presented
primarily for their heuristic value.

Arrow A: Effects of dropping out that are independent of SEL plus
academic ability

Arrow B: Joint or "overlapping" effects of SEL plus academic ability
and dropping out, which we interpret as the effects of SEL
plus academic ability operating through dropping out as an
intervening variable

Arrow C: Effects of SEL plus academic ability that are independent
of dropping out

Arrows A+B: Total effects of dropping out

Arrows B+C: Total effects of SEL plus academic ability

Arrows A+B+C: Total effects of SEL plus academic ability and dropping out

Given the data presented in the text, we can fill in the model as follows:

$$A+B+C = 6.3\% \text{ of variance in "full employment}$$
$$\text{(adjusted for degrees of freedom)}$$

$$A+B = 3.7\%$$

$$B+C = 4.9\%$$

Therefore:

$$A = 1.4\%$$

$$B = 2.3\%$$

$$C = 2.6\%$$

fit clearly into one or the other category. But our measures of socioeconomic level are far from perfect, and our brief tests of vocabulary and reading skill leave much to be desired. If our measures of background and ability were as accurate as our distinctions between dropouts and graduates, we might expect background and ability to be much more impressive as predictors, and we might find still less unique prediction from dropping out to unemployment. Yet even if we had perfect measures of socioeconomic level and flawless tests of vocabulary and reading skill, there remain other causes of dropping out, some of which we did not even attempt to measure. Just as family background and ability relate to both dropping out and unemployment, so may these other causes of dropping out also contribute to unemployment.

In sum, we conclude that dropping out probably makes it more difficult to obtain employment; however, the more important causes of unemployment are those pervasive differences in background and ability which precede and help determine the act of dropping out. To put it another way, dropping out may *contribute* to unemployment, but it is also a conveniently-measured *symptom* of more basic causes of unemployment.

Income and Status

According to the anti-dropout commercials, dropouts earn less than high school graduates. In this section we check this assumption for dropouts and graduates working 30 or more hours per week in civilian jobs.

Weekly Income. A total of 62 dropouts and 379 graduates in our sample were working 30 or more hours per week at the time when they were interviewed. The mean of weekly incomes reported by all dropouts was $136, while that for all graduates was $119. An examination of frequency distributions for dropouts and graduates revealed that some of the apparent difference between the two groups was due to a few respondents reporting very high (or low) incomes.[4] When the analysis was limited to 54 dropouts and 351 graduates who reported incomes between $50 and $199 per week, the mean for dropouts was $119 and that for graduates was $112.

This finding of slightly higher incomes for dropouts corresponds very closely to Project TALENT data indicating that annual

---

[4]There is reason to question some of the very high weekly incomes reported by a few respondents; they may have resulted from a misunderstanding of the interview question.

salaries for dropouts averaged about 4 percent higher than those of graduates who did not continue their education after leaving high school. The TALENT authors suggested that the difference was due to greater seniority for the dropouts—they had simply been working longer than the graduates (Combs and Cooley, 1968). We examined this possible explanation for our own findings by looking at mean dropout and graduate earnings for those who started their jobs prior to 1969, during 1969, or during 1970. A total of six different time periods was considered, as shown in Table 8-1.

TABLE 8-1

MEAN DROPOUT AND GRADUATE EARNINGS CLASSIFIED BY
LENGTH OF TIME ON THE JOB

NOTE: Main entries are weekly earnings at time of interview; parenthetical entries are unweighted N's.

	Date When Respondent Started Job					
	1968 and earlier	January through April, 1969	May through August, 1969	September through December, 1969	January through April, 1970	May, 1970 and later
Dropouts	$130. (9)	$131. (5)	$145. (6)	$113. (12)	$99. (14)	$125. (8)
Graduates	$116. (23)	$125. (8)	$114 (92)	$113. (72)	$114. (94)	$103. (57)

The data in Table 8-1 indicate that among those who had held their jobs less than a year (since September, 1969), there was no consistent difference in weekly earnings between dropouts and graduates. For those who had held their jobs longer, dropouts had slightly higher weekly incomes on the average.

Another possible explanation for the slightly higher dropout earnings involves the number of hours worked per week—dropouts might gravitate toward the kind of jobs that involve overtime work, especially during the summer months, and this could have caused the difference in weekly earnings between dropouts and graduates. An examination of the interview data ruled out this hypothesis; there were virtually no differences between dropouts and graduates in numbers of hours worked per week.

There is a danger that the above analyses of weekly income will be misinterpreted. The average pay difference between dropouts and graduates is not at all large; indeed, it is not large enough to be considered statistically significant.[5] The real point of this analysis is that *dropout incomes in our sample were not found to be lower than the incomes of high school graduates.* And this is, of course, not at all consistent with the anti-dropout commercials.

Occupational Status. The Duncan status coding for the occupations of dropouts and graduates produced little evidence of differences between the two groups, but what differences there were appeared to favor the graduates. Looking at all fully-employed respondents, the mean Duncan status code for dropouts was 22.3 and that for graduates was 24.9; when the analysis was restricted to those reporting weekly incomes between $50 and $199, the mean for dropouts was 21.5 and that for graduates was 25.6.

This status difference, like the difference in income levels between dropouts and graduates, is not large enough to be statistically trustworthy; nevertheless, it is interesting, partly because it runs in the opposite direction from the difference in income. It begins to appear that the dropouts in our sample were employed in slightly lower status occupations, but ones which paid fairly well. Now let us consider how satisfied they were with their jobs.

Job Characteristics and Job Satisfaction

Early in the interview segment dealing with current jobs, the respondents were asked a general question concerning job satisfaction. Table 8-2 summarizes the question, the response scale, and the answers given by dropouts and graduates. Over two-thirds of both dropouts and graduates said that they were "quite satisfied" or "very satisfied" with their work experience on their present job. The differences between the two distributions are not large enough to meet criteria of statistical significance; the small differences which do appear are in the direction of greater satisfaction among dropouts.

A fairly large number of items in the paper-and-pencil questionnaire dealt with specific characteristics of jobs. On the whole, the responses to these items were not very different for dropouts versus graduates. Some of the items dealing with job characteristics are presented in Table 8-3. Some of the response distributions are of interest even when they show no difference at all

---

[5]A recent report based on a longitudinal study by Parnes and his colleagues at Ohio State University found a slight difference in the opposite direction: dropout earnings averaged $2.98 per hour in 1968 while non-college high school graduates averaged $3.18 (Kohen and Parnes, 1971, p. 75).

TABLE 8-2

GENERAL RATING OF JOB SATISFACTION

"All things considered, how satisfied are you with your
work experience on your present job?"

	Dropouts	Graduates
Very satisfied	40%	35%
Quite satisfied	37	33
Somewhat satisfied	16	17
Not very satisfied	4	10
Not at all satisfied	1	4
(Missing data)	(2)	(0)
	100%	100%

between dropouts and graduates. Other items do show some differences that are worth noting. But we must add that any differences in this section must be viewed as suggestive rather than
conclusive; given the limits of sample size in this phase of analysis, we cannot claim that distinctions between dropouts and graduates are statistically trustworthy.

Both dropouts and graduates viewed their jobs as steady
(item 2 in Table 8-3) and as providing good pay (item 9). On the
other hand, neither tended to describe their jobs as being clean
(item 5) or as having a lot of "class" in the eyes of their friends
(item 10). The dropouts were a bit more likely than the graduates
to view their jobs as providing good opportunities for learning
(items 3 and 13), skill utilization (item 11), and advancement
(item 6); but the dropouts were also more likely to say that their
jobs did not require them to "take a lot of responsibility" (item
7) or "work too hard" (item 4). Both groups rated their jobs high
in terms of having "nice friendly people to work with," but the
graduates averaged higher on this dimension than the dropouts.

In sum, the picture presented in Table 8-3 is somewhat
mixed. The differences in job ratings between dropouts and graduates were not large, nor did they consistently show one group to
be more satisfied than the other. Once again, if we had to judge
one group as showing slightly greater job satisfaction than the
other, we would select the dropouts. The clearer and more important conclusion, however, is that *dropouts in our sample do
not show lower job satisfaction than graduates.*

TABLE 8-3

RATING OF JOB CHARACTERISTICS:
DROPOUTS COMPARED WITH GRADUATES

> NOTE: Table entries are percentages. Top row of each set presents data for dropouts; bottom row of each set presents data for graduates.

How true is this for your present job?

	Very true	Pretty true	A little true	Not at all true	Missing data
1. There's no one to boss me on the work	18	25	29	22	5
	9	21	26	38	6
2. It is steady, no chance of being laid off	40	32	16	8	6
	38	32	16	8	6
3. I can learn new things, learn new skills	34	33	16	9	8
	31	25	29	9	6
4. I don't have to work too hard	15	45	25	11	5
	12	37	32	14	6
5. It is a clean job, where I don't get dirty.	16	17	33	29	5
	12	15	29	37	6
6. It has good chances for getting ahead	30	32	25	8	5
	28	25	26	16	6
7. I don't have to take a lot of responsibility.	17	22	32	22	7
	7	28	37	23	6
8. It leaves me a lot of free time to do what I want to do	9	36	26	24	5
	6	26	38	24	6
9. The pay is good	32	38	17	8	5
	22	35	24	14	6
10. It is a job that my friends think a lot of -- has class	5	21	46	22	5
	7	19	36	33	6
11. It uses my skill and abilities -- lets me do the things I can do best.	18	37	25	15	5
	18	23	30	23	6
12. There are nice friendly people to work with	28	47	15	5	5
	12	27	28	27	6
13. It doesn't make me learn a lot of new things.	13	11	41	30	5
	12	27	28	27	6

TABLE 8-4

PERCEIVED RELEVANCE OF HIGH SCHOOL TO SUCCESS IN PRESENT JOB

Percentage Frequencies

	Dropouts	Graduates
What I have learned in high school helps me to do a better job		
Very true	13	16
Somewhat true	41	48
Not at all true	41	30
Missing data.	5	6
I could do my present job just as well without any high school education		
Very true	45	29
Somewhat true	28	35
Not at all true	21	29
Missing data.	6	7
Did anyone in the high school you attended help you to get your present job?		
No	84	81
Yes, I got a little help from people at school. .	7	10
Yes, I got a lot of help from people at school. .	0	3
Missing data.	9	6

Perceived Relevance of High School Training to Job Success.
Part of the popular argument against dropping out is that what
one learns in high school will be helpful in the world of work
after high school. A few of the questions about job characteristics dealt with this issue as perceived by the respondents, and
they are summarized in Table 8-4. As the results in the table
indicate, the dropouts gave rather little credit to the high school
for helping them do well on their jobs; only 7 percent said they
had gotten any help at all from people in school in getting their
jobs, and 45 percent claimed they could do their job just as well
without any high school education. Perhaps this sort of response
is to be expected from dropouts, on the grounds that they would

be motivated to rationalize or try to avoid what Festinger (1957) has termed "cognitive dissonance." But the same argument of avoiding cognitive dissonance would suggest that *graduates* should rate their school experience as important in contributing to their job success. In fact, however, the responses of graduates were not very different from those of the dropouts. Only 13 percent reported help from school in getting their jobs, and 29 percent indicated that high school education was irrelevant for their job performance. Apparently a good many young graduates, as well as dropouts, found themselves in jobs which they considered unrelated to things that are learned in high school.

Summary and Evaluation

Most of the dimensions we have examined in this chapter failed to show statistically signficant differences between dropouts and graduates. Ordinarily we tend to view the lack of significant differences between groups as a rather disappointing finding in research, but this is not an ordinary situation. It was expected that employed dropouts would earn less than graduates and be less satisfied with their jobs; but this is not what we found. The small differences which did appear along these dimensions tended to be in favor of the dropouts as often as not. So we are left with the conclusion that dropouts seemed just about as happy and well-off in their jobs as high school graduates without further training.

But the other finding in this chapter is that unemployment was higher among dropouts than graduates, and this certainly is consistent with one part of the economic argument against dropping out. However, when we ask whether the higher rates of unemployment result directly from dropping out and the lack of a diploma, the issue becomes more complicated. We found that test scores and family socioeconomic level were a bit more important than the high school diploma as predictors of unemployment; and low test scores and disadvantaged family backgrounds were among the important factors leading to dropping out. Thus it seems likely that much of the unemployment difference between dropouts and graduates was due to these earlier and more pervasive differences; those things which caused some young men to drop out of school also made it difficult for them to get and hold jobs. But it seems likely that dropping out and the lack of a diploma added to these difficulties, particularly given the nationwide campaign to discourage dropping out and to urge dropouts to return to school.

We noted earlier the Project TALENT finding reported by Combs and Cooley (1968) that dropouts in their sample earned

slightly more than non-college high school graduates, a finding
very similar to our own. But the Project TALENT results in the
area of unemployment do not match ours:

> In 1964, the employment rates of dropouts and controls were
> quite similar. Ninety percent of the dropouts who did not continue
> their education after leaving high school were employed, 87 percent
> full-time, three percent part-time. Of the controls with no further
> training, 89 percent had full-time jobs and two percent part-time.
> (Combs and Cooley, 1968, p. 352)

How do we account for this difference in the results of two nationwide studies of dropouts? First, we must note that there are
surely differences between the employment market for young men
in 1964 and that in 1970. In addition, there are differences in
research design and procedures between Project TALENT and
Youth in Transition. Perhaps these are sufficient reasons for the
difference in findings. Yet still another difference is worth noting:
between the start and the end of the 1960's we have seen an in-
creasingly vigorous campaign against dropping out. Perhaps the
differences between the TALENT findings and our own data on
dropout unemployment reflect, at least to some degree, a measure of the "success" of that campaign as a self-fulfilling prophecy.

In concluding their dropout article based on the Project
TALENT data, Combs and Cooley made the following observations:

> One of the reasons for undertaking this dropout investigation
> was to try to develop data about dropouts for use in high-school
> guidance. It was hoped that the results would reveal that the non-
> college high school graduate (the control) was much better off than
> the high school dropout as far as future employment and earnings
> are concerned. Large differences in this area might help to dis-
> suade some students from leaving high school before graduation.
> Although there are other cultural advantages in continued education,
> such practical data would probably have a more direct impact on
> potential dropouts.
>
> Unfortunately, the results were not consistent with these ex-
> pectations. Not only were the male dropouts earning as much as
> the controls, but they had been earning it longer. Thus, economi-
> cally, the dropout was certainly at an advantage over the student who
> stayed to graduate. Of course, it must be remembered that when
> the follow-up data were collected, the dropouts were only about 19
> years old. Many of the consequences of leaving high school prior
> to graduation may not become apparent until later life. (1968, pp.
> 361-362)

On the whole, our findings are like the TALENT results in
suggesting that the economic disadvantages of dropping out may
not be so severe after all. Of course, our data are also based

on young men about 19 years old; thus the above qualification about possible later consequences of dropping out must be applied to the findings presented in this chapter.

It was *hoped* that the TALENT findings would provide solid data to support the campaign against dropping out. But the results did not work out that way, as the authors clearly acknowledged. The campaign has gone on, nevertheless, and with a good deal of success. As we shall see in the next chapter, many dropouts have been persuaded by the economic argument and have reached the conclusion that they made a great mistake in leaving high school. It is ironic that most of our findings, like those from Project TALENT, fail to support that conclusion.

Chapter 9

DROPOUTS SPEAK FOR THEMSELVES

The preceding chapters of this volume have analyzed some of the "causes" and "effects" of dropping out of high school. We have seen that combinations of family background characteristics, ability, school experience, personality, and behavior measures can predict educational attainment fairly well. Among the most potent predictors have been family socioeconomic level, tests of vocabulary and reading skills, grade failure before tenth grade, grades in school, negative school attitudes, and delinquent behavior in school. We have seen also that when the educational attainment continuum is used as a predictor (rather than as a criterion), there are infrequent—and for the most part very undramatic—measurable cross-time changes in outcomes. Young men in the three analysis groups along the continuum (dropouts, high school graduates without further education, and college entrants) differed on several dimensions at the start of the study, but the differences (particularly between the first two groups) remained very similar across time, indicating that additional effects as a result of dropping out of high school are almost negligible.

This rather systematic presentation of the causes and effects of educational attainment follows familiar research reporting procedures, and provides a concise way of organizing and discussing massive amounts of information. Nevertheless, there is something which is jeopardized if we deal only in terms of predictors, criteria, means, and standard deviations. What we risk losing is a sense of the feelings of the respondents themselves. For instance, we have assigned dropouts to "Group 1" on our educational attainment continuum—but we have not examined how it feels to belong in that category. What does a high school dropout think about being a high school dropout? The answers to this sort of question require the personal perspective of those who have experienced dropping out. Putting terms such as predictors and criteria aside for the moment, it adds to our understanding of dropouts to discover *their* views of why they left high school, and what the effects have been. We can get a better grasp of their feelings (as they know them) by "listening" to what the dropouts said as they spoke for themselves.

This, then, will be a chapter quite unlike earlier ones. It is based upon strictly univariate data, with no attempt to relate the words of the dropouts statistically to other dimensions, either as predictors or as criteria. We will make occasional references to analysis results from earlier chapters, but our primary objective is to describe how young men expressed themselves as they sat in an interview session in the early summer of 1970 and talked about why they left high school, and how leaving school affected their lives.

Two Types of Dropouts. Data for two analysis subgroups will be described in this chapter. These are Subgroup 1a (dropouts with diplomas) and Subgroup 1b (dropouts without diplomas). The reader may recall that these two subgroups were combined as "high school dropouts" (Group 1) for analyses of prediction to educational attainment (Chapters 1-6) and for analyses of personality outcomes (Chapter 7). This was reasonable, since of course those in both subgroups experienced the act of dropping out. When educational attainment was used as a predictor of occupational outcomes (Chapter 8), we limited our consideration of dropouts to those without diplomas (Subgroup 1b).

In the present chapter it seems appropriate that both subgroups again be included in the discussion, although we have chosen to present the data for the two subgroups separately and in parallel form. A number of questions are relevant only for those dropouts who did not (at the time of the fourth data collection) have a diploma, and so in those cases our findings are based only on Subgroup 1b.[1]

Reasons for Dropping Out of High School

Why young men decide to leave the high school environment without earning a diploma is one of the most significant facets to be understood about the dropout experience. Our study of predictors to dropping out (Chapters 1-6) has revealed much in the way of answers to such a question; young men's personal perceptions of the conditions under which they left school can add more.

---

[1]The response distributions to be presented for the two subgroups are from questions in a special five-page "Dropout Segment" of the Time 4 (1970) interview.

The distributions of responses to questions about reasons for leaving high school appear in Table 9-1.[2]

We can see reminders of earlier chapters in the distribution of responses in Table 9-1. The set of code categories headed "School Reasons" got a higher total frequency of responses than any other; and nearly all of the "Authority Reasons" reflected problems with school authorities. This is consistent with our findings in Chapter 4 that average grades, grade failure, and negative school attitudes serve as strong predictors of dropping out of high school. The following quotations from respondents exemplify the kinds of answers coded as "School Reasons" for leaving high school.[3]

> "I was mostly just discouraged because I wasn't passing."
> "I just quit. I failed in some subjects so I got disgusted. I had no reason to want to go back."
> "I just quit. I was failing in three subjects."
> "Well, I flunked history in 12th grade. I just didn't go back, as I got a job. I wasn't doing too well in school anyway, so I became disgusted."
> "I was failing, so I quit school. I was working and didn't have time to study. I wasn't interested in it either."
> "I was bored. I had the grades but was just bored. It was the teachers—didn't make it interesting enough."
> "School in general. It didn't teach me true things. It didn't teach me how to cope with society once I got out of school doors."

"Work and Financial Reasons" were mentioned fairly often. This is particularly true when one considers that some responses coded under the first "Family Reasons" category or under the third "Personal Reasons" category might also have been classified under "Work and Financial Reasons."

In their most extreme form, such reasons might be worded in terms like those used by one respondent who said, "I had to work to help my family survive," or another who reported he left

---

[2]The format of the response distribution tables in this chapter is extremely straightforward. At the top of the table is the question as it was asked for each subgroup. Below on the left are the code categories used in classifying respondents' answers. Only those code categories which received a frequency of at least two are included. The columns on the right-hand side of the page provide the response pattern for each of the subgroups (1a and 1b) for which the question was appropriate. The frequencies are given as unweighted N's. It would be misleading to percentagize, since the sizes of the subgroups are not only small (1a=32; 1b=125), but also very different from one another.

[3]The following are exact quotations from respondents. Throughout the remainder of this chapter, all responses enclosed in quotation marks are, likewise, lifted verbatim from interview booklets.

TABLE 9-1

REASONS FOR LEAVING SCHOOL

Interview items:

(For subgroup 1a, dropouts with diplomas) Why did you finish your school work
this way rather than going straight through high school?

(For subgroup 1b, dropouts without diplomas) How did you happen to leave high
school?

	Frequencies	
Code category*	Subgroup 1a N=32	Subgroup 1b N=125
FAMILY REASONS		
Parents (family) need the money; the respondent dropped out to help his family financially	2	8
The respondent was ill	2	6
Other family reasons		2
TOTAL FAMILY REASONS	4	16
PERSONAL REASONS		
The respondent felt grown up; the respondent felt as though he was too good for school; he felt he was a "big shot"; he thought it was smart to drop out		2
The respondent preferred to be doing other things (except work); he wanted freedom and leisure		4
The respondent had to get married; he got married; the respondent had to support his family		8
Other personal reasons	4	10
TOTAL PERSONAL REASONS	4	24
WORK AND FINANCIAL REASONS		
The respondent had to go to work; he needed money	1	4
The respondent wanted to work; he was more interested in work than in school; he would rather be out working	1	10
Other financial or work reasons	1	2
TOTAL WORK AND FINANCIAL REASONS	3	16

---

*Only categories with frequencies of two or more are presented.

TABLE 9-1
Continued

Code Category	Subgroup 1a N=32	Subgroup 1b N=125
SCHOOL REASONS		
The respondent had trouble learning; he got too many poor grades; subject failure; the respondent got discouraged by low grades; he got behind in his schoolwork; non-promotion	4	11
The respondent felt school didn't teach anything valuable; he felt school was not useful; the respondent wasn't learning anything		5
The respondent "didn't like school in general"; he didn't care about school or learning; respondent not interested in school or found school boring	5	12
The respondent was absent too much; he played "hooky" or cut classes		3
Other school reasons or problems	5	5
TOTAL SCHOOL REASONS	14	36
AUTHORITY REASONS		
The respondent got in trouble with teachers and/or administrators and/or counselors	1	4
The respondent couldn't get along with teachers; the respondent disliked the teachers		7
Authorities were too strict; they tried to boss the respondent around too much; school rules were too strict		3
The respondent got expelled; the respondent didn't drop out by choice; the respondent was suspended	3	7
Other authority reasons		3
TOTAL AUTHORITY REASONS	4	24
OTHER REASONS		
The resondent could get a diploma some other way (night school, state delinquency test, etc.)	1	1
The respondent just never returned after suspension		2
Other	1	
TOTAL OTHER REASONS	2	3
Missing data	1	6

school because, "My father got in financial troubles. I quit to help him out or he might have gone to jail." And one respondent typified several others when he said, "I got a job. I got married and had to support my wife. I needed to make some money."

Responses of the "Work and Financial Reasons" sort might be construed as confirmation of our socioeconomic level measure as a predictor of dropping out (see Chapter 3). Of course, all responses coded into these kinds of categories were not of the type hinting at low socioeconomic level; some were matters of preference:

> "I never liked to go to school. I wanted to work for money."
> "I started working on Saturdays and the money looked so good that I wanted more of it, so I stopped school."
> "Well, I left because I wanted to work and I felt that what I was learning in school wouldn't be worth one-half as much as on-the-job training."

And some young men expressed views which combined dissatisfaction with certain aspects of school and interest in a job:

> "I got fed up. After ten weeks of school they tried to get me to take an extra course, which would have meant quitting my job."
> "I went in the Fall of 1968 and asked for work-study program. Coordinator couldn't work it out. I was to come back second semester, but then I had a job so I didn't return."
> "I expected to graduate in June, 1969. I was informed right before graduation that I lacked one credit and couldn't graduate. I didn't drop out of school. I asked if I could get a tutor so I could get that one credit and they told me I would have to come back to school to get it. I would like to get my diploma if I could arrange it so that I wouldn't have to lose so much time off my job."

The "Authority Reasons" were mentioned quite frequently also. This is consistent with our finding in Chapter 5 that "Delinquent Behavior in School" is an important predictor to dropping out. "A bunch of the teachers and I didn't get along. I guess it was my fault. My grades were so bad I couldn't make it. I stayed out one day without an excuse and the teachers thought it was so awful they couldn't let me forget it."

It is interesting, however, that there appears to be some "coloring" of responses. Categories such as "The respondent couldn't get along with teachers; R disliked the teachers" and "Authorities were too strict; they tried to boss the respondent around too much; school rules were too strict" were used almost as often as these categories: "The respondent got in trouble with teachers and/or administrators and/or counselors" and "The respondent got expelled; the respondent didn't drop out by choice;

the respondent was suspended." Yet it is these latter two categories which capture the essence of the "Delinquent Behavior in School" measure which proved so important as a predictor. (After all, reports of delinquent behavior in school would get coded into these latter two categories.) One can't help but wonder if the personal interview situation (rather than a self-administered questionnaire which is the basis for the "Delinquent Behavior in School" measure) prompted some rather defensive respondents to describe the conditions of dropping out in a way which indicated that they were not able to put up with teachers and rules, rather than that teachers and rules couldn't put up with them. For example, respondents said such things as, "They wanted me to do too much of what they wanted and none of what I wanted," and "I just got tired of it. I didn't like most of the teachers. Most of them didn't care what you did."

And finally, some young men described situations which were intermediate between being asked to leave school because of some inappropriate behavior and choosing to leave because of dislike for rules and regulations. These young men talked of the unfortunate circumstance which has come to be known as "high school pushout":

> "They said I could drop out or they'd drop me out. They said I was a rebel. I wore my hair long."
> "I didn't get along with the counselor. He didn't like me at all. He started hammering me to get rid of me."

Attitudes Regarding Dropping Out

Once a young man has dropped out of high school, it seems likely that he would develop a fairly strong attitude about that choice of action. And the sort of attitudes which emerge may vary widely. Table 9-2 presents frequency distributions for responses to an open-ended question about the non-diploma-holders' feelings about having left school. We see that about 60% of the dropouts expressed negative reactions (in their first-mentioned answer). One young man put it rather creatively: "Without a high school diploma, it's like a car without tires. It's very important— I realize my mistake." And the majority of these negative feelings about not having earned a diploma were linked to job market problems. (The next section of this chapter deals more specifically with employment effects of dropping out.)

That many dropouts felt so negative about their decision to leave school is perhaps unfortunate—especially since our analyses in earlier chapters (7 and 8) indicate little basis in fact for such

TABLE 9-2

ATTITUDES OF DROPOUTS REGARDING DROPPING OUT

Interview item:

(Question asked only of subgroup 1b, dropouts without diplomas) How do you feel
about having dropped out of high school? Are there any ways in which you regret
having dropped out of high school? Are there some ways in which you feel that
dropping out was a really good idea for you?

	Frequencies	
Code category	First Mention	Second Mention
NEGATIVE FEELINGS		
I think it was a mistake; I shouldn't have dropped out (unspecified further)	51	2
I'm unhappy because people don't seem to respect me; other people's attitudes about it bother me	3	2
I've had trouble getting a (good) job because I don't have a diploma; employers have turned me down because I don't have a diploma	16	7
Other ways the respondent regrets dropping out	1	3
POSITIVE FEELINGS		
I think it was the best thing for me to do (unspecified further)	6	
I am glad I left because I'm more independent now	3	1
I can get a diploma some other way that will be better for me than continuing high school	2	
Dropping out when I did resulted in my getting a good job	3	3
Other ways the respondent is happy about having dropped out	1	2
OTHER		
It makes absolutely no difference to the respondent; the respondent has no feelings one way or the other about having dropped out	12	
No, the respondent doesn't have any regrets or any good feelings	5	
Reason for dropping out was sickness, accident, etc. (i.e., respondent had no choice)	2	
Other regret about dropping out	1	1
Other feeling favorable to dropping out	2	2
Missing data	17	102

negative feelings. It is not surprising, however, that the attitudes summarized in Table 9-2 were so negative. We discussed in Chapter 1 the widespread anti-dropout campaign which has stressed the importance of having a high school diploma. The "message" apparently got through to young men the age of our panel, and (particularly with an interviewer sitting there!) they may well have felt compelled to express negative feelings. There does indeed seem to be a degree of "cognitive dissonance" involved for a dropout to say he's made a mistake; but perhaps there is a much higher dissonance level to be tolerated by expressing positive attitudes about a behavior which society so consistently discourages.

It is interesting to note a few of the dropouts' positive reactions regarding leaving high school. Most of them alluded to the satisfactions of leaving the very sheltered and confined atmosphere which the high school represents to many young men.

> "It gave me a chance to become more mature in my thinking."
> "Made me able to be my own boss."
> "It gave me more experience with life, working, and making a living; it gave this to me early."
> "I'll get my military service over with sooner."

Employment Effects

Because of the authors' strong interest in employment possibilities and conditions for dropouts versus non-dropouts, dropouts without diplomas were asked a specific question about any hindrances they faced in the job market. Table 9-3 presents the response distribution for this item.

It is notable that 50% of the dropouts said that the lack of a diploma had not been a hindrance as far as jobs are concerned. "Employers always ask, but I have no trouble getting a job," said one respondent. Other comments representative of these 50% who claimed that dropping out presented no problem are:

> "As far as jobs are concerned, you don't need an education."
> "I have a better job than most graduates have right now."

These kinds of comments are consistent with the findings of Project TALENT and the present project which suggest that perhaps a high school diploma does not make a major economic difference. Chapter 8 of this volume reported a higher unemployment rate among dropouts than among non-dropouts; it was suggested, at the same time, that this higher rate of unemployment might have been primarily the result *not* of having dropped out, but rather of the

TABLE 9-3

DROPPING OUT: EFFECTS ON JOBS AND JOB-HUNTING

Interview item:

(Question asked only of subgroup 1b, dropouts without diplomas) Does the fact
of not having a high school diploma seem to hinder you as far as jobs are
concerned?   In what ways?

Code category	Frequencies
I've had trouble getting a (good) job because I don't have a diploma; employers have turned me down because I don't have a diploma	37
Other job-related feelings disfavorable to dropping out	4
Dropping out when I did resulted in my getting a good job	2
Other job-related feelings favorable to dropping out	1
No hindrance; no	62
Missing data	19

differences in background and ability which precede and help determine dropping out.   The fact that half of the dropouts claimed
the lack of a diploma was not in and of itself a hindrance seems
to support such a conclusion.

About 33% of the dropouts described the lack of a diploma
as a definite hindrance in their job-hunting.   Whether these young
men were using this condition as a rationalization for other more
basic causes of unemployment, or whether the diploma really was
critical as a credential, cannot be established with any certainty.
But the comments below clearly indicate that the *perception* of the
lack of a diploma as a hindrance was quite pervasive:

> "Can't find a job—they all ask if you got a diploma."
> "You don't have as much a chance at jobs.   The first thing they ask
> is, 'Do you have a high school diploma?'"
> "A lot of places won't hire you on a job if you haven't got a high
> school diploma."
> "Well, when you go for a job, they make you fill out a lot of papers.
> When they read you didn't finish high school, they don't talk to you
> any more."
> "I had a good job lined up and passed all the tests.   But they asked
> for a diploma and I couldn't produce one."

One young respondent, however, seemed to express both sides
of the issue at hand.   He said, in response to the question about
employment problems he faced because he had no high school diploma, "A diploma means more as far as getting a job, but it

doesn't mean anything but that you went to high school. It doesn't mean how you'll do on your job." The first part of this respondent's statement acknowledges the current importance of the diploma as a "credential," and reflects the sentiments of the many young dropouts who find getting a job difficult. But the latter part of his statement questions the legitimacy of encouraging—indeed demanding—that young people obtain a high school diploma for purely economic reasons.

Expectations to Earn a Diploma

Table 9-4 summarizes the responses of dropouts when asked if they expected to get a diploma eventually. Close to 75% of the dropouts had such expectations, and they reported various means by which they hoped to accomplish this. The most frequently given answer as a way of earning a diploma was "night school," perhaps suggesting an interest in maintaining a job while working towards high school graduation.

Those dropouts who expressed an interest in eventually obtaining a diploma were asked why they felt this way; Table 9-5 summarizes their answers. The dominant reason given by the dropouts in reply to a question asking why they want a diploma was that it would enable them to get a better job. A couple of young men, however, stated that employment opportunities were clearly *not* the source of motivation to attain a diploma. They

TABLE 9-4

EXPECTATIONS OF EVER EARNING A HIGH SCHOOL DIPLOMA

Interview item:

(Question asked only of subgroup 1b, dropouts without diplomas) Do you expect to ever get a high school diploma? How will you get a diploma?

Code category	Frequencies
The respondent doesn't expect to ever get a diploma	20
The respondent expects to get his diploma:	
by passing state examinations	23
by attending "night school" or some other sort of special public school	37
by earning a diploma or equivalent certificate in military service	18
by attending vocational/trade/business school	5
by other means	9
Missing data	13

TABLE 9-5

REASONS WHY DROPOUTS WANT TO ATTAIN
A DIPLOMA EVENTUALLY

Interview item:

(Question asked only of subgroup 1b, dropouts without diplomas) Why do you want
to get a diploma?

Code category	Frequencies
GENERAL REASONS	
To finish my education (unspecified further)	14
FINANCIAL OR JOB-RELATED REASONS	
More education will enable me to get a better job	45
To learn a trade	4
Other financial or job-related reasons	5
ATTITUDE REASONS	
I am bored doing what I am now doing; I have decided I am more interested in school; I would like school better now; I miss school	2
I want to graduate and go to college; want to graduate	10
Other attitude reasons	5
PRESSURE REASONS	
Respondent is being pressured by other people (including parents) to get his diploma	2
OTHER	5
Missing data	33

touched very specifically on the issue of occupational outcomes
being determined by whether or not one enters college, not whether
or not one earns a high school diploma. When asked whether dropping out had proven to be a hindrance as far as jobs are concerned,
these two respondents said:

> "Yes, There's not many jobs that take you unless you have at *least*
> a high school diploma. Most want college."
> "No, I feel it's the lack of a college education that causes that prob-
> lem."

Role-Sending from Others

As well as having to develop his own attitudes about having
left the usual education stream, the dropout must also deal some-
how with the feelings of other people. One of the questions near
the end of the "Dropout Segment" of the interview asked about the
nature of others' reactions. Table 9-6 presents the responses.

One thing to be kept in mind when looking at the data in

Table 9-6 is that they represent dropouts' perceptions of other people's feelings. Without gathering data from fathers, mothers, siblings, and friends, we have no way of evaluating the reality of these perceptions. But of course it may be argued that perceived realities are the more important determinants of dropouts' attitudes and behaviors anyway.

It is clear from Table 9-6 that most dropouts felt that their parents were definitely adverse to the choice to leave school. Siblings and friends were less often perceived as concerned, but seldom considered to be pleased.

If most friends and relatives were not happy about a boy dropping out, it stands to reason that many would have encouraged getting a diploma. The data in Table 9-7 confirm this: close to three-quarters of the dropouts who answered the question reported some role-sending to get a diploma. The strongest encouragement was clearly from parents.

TABLE 9-6

OTHER PEOPLE'S FEELINGS ABOUT THE RESPONDENT'S
HAVING DROPPED OUT OF HIGH SCHOOL

Interview item:

(Question asked only of subgroup 1b, dropouts without diplomas) How do the following people feel about your having dropped out of high school: father, mother, brothers and sisters, friends?

Frequencies

Code category	Father	Mother	Siblings	Friends
This person feels positive about the respondent's having dropped out ("feels happy about it"; "likes it")	4	4	2	5
This person is neutral about the respondent's having dropped out ("doesn't care"; "doesn't mind")	17	11	30	28
This person feels negative about the respondent's having dropped out ("feels unhappy about it"; "doesn't like it")	65	81	38	32
Variation of feelings among siblings/friends (some feel one way, some the other way)			3	9
This person says "it's up to you"	2	3	3	1
Missing data	37	26	49	50

TABLE 9-7

ENCOURAGEMENT TO GET A HIGH SCHOOL DIPLOMA

Interview item:

(Question asked only of subgroup 1b, dropouts without diplomas) Are any of these
people trying to encourage you to get your diploma? Which ones?

Code category	Frequencies	
	First Mention	Second Mention
No one is encouraging the respondent to get a diploma	28	
Father is encouraging the respondent to get a diploma	13	2
Mother is encouraging the respondent to get a diploma	14	11
Brother(s) and/or sister(s) is/are encouraging the respondent to get a diploma	4	9
Friends are encouraging the respondent to get a diploma	13	13
Other relatives are encouraging the respondent to get a diploma	5	4
Everyone; all of these people are encouraging the respondent to get a diploma	7	
Other person (non-relative) is encouraging the respondent to get a diploma	2	
Parents (both) are encouraging the respondent to get a diploma	21	3
Missing data	18	83

Summary

We have tried in this chapter to see what dropouts had to
say about being dropouts. Through presentation of response distributions for selected interview items and through direct quotations from actual dropouts, we have seen a bit about how these
young men viewed their situation.

For the most part, the picture was not a bright one. Dropouts expressed dissatisfactions with high school and preferences
to do things other than attend classes. However, the majority of
these young men felt—and with much corroboration from others—
that they had made a bad choice by leaving school without a diploma. In particular, the dropouts described disadvantages which
they felt in the job market. Almost three-quarters of the dropout
respondents expected to earn a diploma eventually—perhaps this
is the most convincing evidence that they were not entirely happy
with their status as dropouts.

This state in which so many dropouts find themselves is indeed a conflicted one. The problem might be at least partially remedied, however, if the current anti-dropout campaign were "toned down," particularly the assertion that dropping out leads to economic disaster. Evidence from previous chapters indicates that dropping out is not an act with such totally negative results. Perhaps, therefore, we should stop condemning dropouts and thus reduce the feelings of failure and the lack of support from others which so many of the young men quoted in this chapter have described.

Chapter 10
DROPPING OUT IS A SYMPTOM:
SUMMARY, CONCLUSIONS,
IMPLICATIONS

Dropping out of high school is overrated as a *problem* in its own right—it is far more appropriately viewed as the end result or *symptom* of other problems which have their origin much earlier in life. The difficulties experienced by the dropouts we studied—the low aspirations and accomplishments, and even the limitations in self-esteem and self-concept--were already present or predictable by the start of tenth grade, and there is little evidence that dropping out made matters worse.

A related conclusion is that educational attainment is a continuum, with high school dropouts at one end of the scale and college entrants at the other end. "Dropout statistics" can be terribly misleading if they simply contrast dropouts with all those having a high school diploma. Along most of the dimensions we have examined, the largest distinctions are associated with college entrance rather than high school graduation.

The statements above were not views which guided this research effort from the start; rather, they represent our conclusions based on the evidence presented in considerable detail in earlier chapters. In this final chapter we review and discuss that evidence briefly, and consider some implications. Our style here is less technical than in earlier chapters, and perhaps somewhat more argumentative, for our findings lead us to advocate substantial changes in attitudes and policies toward "the dropout problem."[1]

How Solid Is Our Evidence?

Our conclusion that dropping out is primarily a symptom rather than a basic problem may be surprising and perhaps also disconcerting. Certainly it runs counter to the conclusions of

---

[1]Those wishing a step-by-step summary of our analyses and findings may wish also to review the summaries at the ends of the chapters.

some (but not all) other researchers, as well as the "anti-dropout
campaign" being waged on radio and television. Thus it seems
appropriate that we look back over the research design which led
us to this view, and ask whether our evidence really is solid.

The "Before-and-After" Type of Research Design. The Youth
in Transition study was designed specifically to measure changes
over time—especially changes that result from dropping out of
high school. In order to assess such changes, it is necessary to
follow a group of respondents for some extended period and collect the same kinds of data from them at several points in time.
In our case, the respondents were a nationally representative sample of young men; they completed literally scores of interview
items and questionnaire scales at each of four data collections
spaced over a period of nearly four years.

This type of design is conceptually simple and straightforward, and uniquely well-suited to the job of distinguishing causes
from effects. Unfortunately, it is also time-consuming, expensive,
difficult to administer, and thus quite rare.

The more typical source of dropout data is the "after-only"
design in which those who have already dropped out are compared
with those who remained in school. In some instances the stayins
are "matched" to the dropouts in terms of family socioeconomic
level, test scores, and other characteristics. Nevertheless, we
can be sure that the groups were far from perfectly matched--
some prior differences existed which led certain individuals to
drop out while others remained in school. This leaves us for-
ever in doubt about the results of an "after-only" study, because
what might appear to be *results* of dropping out could actually be
among the *causes.*

Our own findings, like the typical "after-only" study, found
that dropouts were different in some respects from stayins—especially those who entered college. For example, the average level
of delinquency reported by dropouts was much higher than that for
stayins. But which came first, the dropping out or the high level
of delinquency?

Because ours was a "before-and-after" design, we were able
to show that in nearly every case a difference which turned up at
the end of the study was present and equally strong at the start—
before the dropping out occurred. Again taking delinquency as our
example, we found that dropouts were above average in delinquency
throughout the entire study, and there is no indication that this
delinquency increased as a result of dropping out (see Figure 7-6).

Dropping Out Is a Symptom of Other Problems

What are the underlying problems signified by dropping out? Stated in most general terms, the problems involve a serious mismatch between some individuals and the typical high school environment. More specifically, dropping out is symptomatic of certain background and ability characteristics, school experiences, and traits of personality and behavior. Let us review some of these dimensions.

Family Background Factors. Most important among family background factors that predict to dropping out is socioeconomic level (SEL); the lower the family SEL, the more likely a boy is to become a dropout. It is worth noting that two of the six ingredients in our composite measure of SEL are father's and mother's education, and a good many parents (about 40 percent) had not finished high school. Thus it appears that if a boy is the son of dropouts, he stands a better than average chance of becoming a dropout himself.

Dropping out is also more frequent among boys from large families and those from broken homes. These relationships are reduced but not eliminated when SEL is controlled statistically.

One other family background characteristic is worth noting in this review. Dropping out occurs more frequently among those boys reporting a high level of parental punitiveness. Since the punitiveness measure was obtained in tenth grade, before the dropping out occurred, it is tempting to argue that parental punitiveness is among the direct causes of dropping out. This may indeed be true, but it is not the only plausible explanation for the relationship. It would be naive to suppose that punitive action by parents is not influenced by the behavior of their children. And some of the behavior patterns which provide the best predictions of dropping out—such things as poor school performance and high levels of delinquency—are the very kinds of behavior likely to produce a punitive reaction from parents. Perhaps it would be best to say that parental punitiveness is part of the mix of forces that precede dropping out, and it may often be both a reaction and a contributing factor.

Ability Limitations. It is no surprise to find that those boys who later became dropouts tended to score below average on the tests of intelligence and academic ability that were administered at the start of the study. What may be surprising is that the differences are really not very large (about the equivalent of five IQ points, on the average) between dropouts and those stayins who did not go on to college. The much larger differences appear between those boys who later went to college and all those who did not.

Past School Failure. Two of the most important predictors of dropping out are poor classroom grades and being held back. We estimate the dropout rate to be about 40 percent among those boys who have failed a grade in school, in contrast to 10 percent among those never held back.

Would dropout rates go down if teachers simply refrained from giving low grades or holding back students who are having difficulty? This is a complex issue, and one that cannot be resolved within the limits of our present design. The poor grades and failures may simply be indicators of a more fundamental inability (or unwillingness) to do well in an academic setting; if so, removing those symptoms might do little to change the underlying realities—including dropout rates. On the other hand, there is a large measure of visibility involved in poor grades and especially in being held back; it may be that such events have a tendency to function as self-fulfilling prophecies—with both the student and his teachers coming to feel that "he just isn't cut out for school work." In addition, the failure experiences in school may lead to feelings of shame and eventually precipitate "fight" and/or "flight" reactions—reactions such as rebellious behavior in school and dropping out.

We have merely touched on what is surely a basic issue in educational philosophy—the damage that may be caused by early experiences of failure. Other longitudinal studies, ones that start with youngsters at the beginning of elementary school or even earlier, might help to resolve such issues.

Rebellious and Delinquent Behavior. We have already noted that boys who become dropouts are more likely to have a background of delinquency. The study included several measures of rebellious behavior in school, and delinquent behavior both in school and outside of school. The results consistently indicate that the boy who is likely to drop out is above average in rebellious and delinquent behavior. Moreover, this is the one set of dimensions on which the dropouts really stand apart from all other respondents. (Along many other dimensions, the distinction between dropouts and stayins is less important than the distinction between those who do and do not enter college.)

How shall we account for the fact that delinquent boys are much more likely to become dropouts? One rather obvious explanation is that boys who manifest rebellious and delinquent behavior in school are likely to be expelled or be invited to leave "for the good of the school." As some of the anecdotal evidence in Chapter 9 indicates, a number of dropouts could also be called "push-outs." But others leave in the absence of such coercion, and sometimes they leave in spite of pressures from parents and teachers to remain in school. Perhaps for some of these boys, dropping out is itself a form of rebellious or delinquent behavior — just one more instance of doing what authority figures tell them not to do. Whatever the causal dynamics, it is clear that an established pattern of rebellious and delinquent behavior is often a precursor of dropping out.

Other Differences Between Dropouts and Stayins. Are there other "personality" characteristics which distinguish those boys most likely to become high school dropouts? A number of relevant dimensions were examined; the results, while not as strong as some reported above, suggest that the potential dropout is (a) lower than average in self-esteem, needs for self-development, commitment to social values, and feelings of personal efficacy; and (b) higher than average in somatic symptoms and negative affective states. The potential dropout is also lower than average in occupational aspiration.

All of the findings summarized thus far fit the stereotype of the dropout as a "loser" — a young man who is delinquent, low in self-esteem, lacking in ambition, and unable to control his own destiny. But there are two cautions to be kept in mind: First, the dropout was a "loser" long before he dropped out — dropping out is the symptom, not the cause. Second, a number of these differences which appear "on the average" are not really very large; there is a substantial range of overlap between dropouts and stayins — especially those stayins who do not go on to college.

Educational Attainment Is a Continuum

Each of the dimensions described above predicts not only dropping out but also college entrance If those lowest in socioeconomic level and academic ability are most likely to become dropouts, those at the highest levels are most likely to enter college. A glance at Figure 6-1 will confirm that dropouts are consistently at one end of a scale while college entrants are at the other.

We take this pattern of findings as confirmation of our view that educational attainment is best studied as a continuum. Further support is provided by a series of multivariate analyses reported in Chapter 6. A three-level continuum of educational attainment, with dropouts at one end and college entrants at the other, proved to be more "predictable" as a criterion than any two-way classification of dropouts versus stayins or college versus non-college.

These findings make sense conceptually. As we argued in Chapter 1, those who feel willing to invest their energy in education as a key to later success are not only less likely to be high school dropouts, but also more likely to extend their education beyond high school. Likewise, those who find education intrinsically satisfying are least likely to drop out and most likely to enter college.

In short, there are both conceptual and empirical reasons for treating educational attainment as a continuum. Moreover, it makes a great difference in any study of dropouts whether the comparison or "control" subjects include all stayins, or only those stayins who did not go on to post-high school education. Why should this matter? Because in most respects dropouts are not so very different from those who end their education with high school graduation; it is more often the ones who go on to college who really stand apart. And this relates directly to our current campaign to persuade young men (and young women) to stay in high school.

The basic thrust of the "anti-dropout campaign" seems to be this: Stay in school long enough to get your high school diploma—your chances of "making it" will be much better. But if the really important educational threshold is college entrance rather than high school graduation, then the "stick it out until the end of high school" approach is highly deceptive. One could argue, of course, that graduating from high school is a prerequisite for college entrance, and the "finish high school" message is a necessary first step. In our view that argument misses the point in at least two ways. First, the idea of college usually is not even mentioned in anti-dropout commercials. Yet it would seem foolish to persuade a potential dropout to stick it out just to the end of high school and then fail to tell him that he *really* ought to be gearing up for college. Second, even if potential dropouts were clearly shown that college is the real issue, their limitations in ability, past school performance, and attitudes toward school make them very poor prospects for a successful college experience. There are exceptions to this general pattern, and some high school dropouts later go on to do very well in higher education. But these are indeed the exceptions, and it seems unwise to build our policy around them.

Does Dropping Out Really Change Anything?

We said at the start of this volume that an effort to persuade individuals to stay in (or return to) high school must be based on the proposition that things get worse for individuals who drop out—and that this happens *as a consequence of dropping out*. In Chapters 7 and 8 we presented a good deal of evidence bearing on this issue. Some findings were clearer and more conclusive than others, but the overall impression to be gained from the data is that dropping out does not change things a great deal—at least not in ways that are apparent by the time a young man reaches the age of 19 or 20.

Changes in Personality and Behavior. In Chapter 7 we examined more than a score of personality and behavior dimensions, measured over a period of nearly four years. We found changes along some dimensions. For example, self-esteem showed some upward trend for all educational subgroups (see Figure 7-1). But the self-esteem increases were actually a bit larger than average among dropouts and those high school graduates who did not enter college—hardly evidence that dropping out has harmful effects on self-esteem. Along a few other dimensions the changes could best be described as a convergence—a blurring of distinctions that were clearer back at the start of tenth grade. For example, along a scale of social values the college entrants showed a slight drop over time, while the non-college groups—both dropouts and stay-ins—showed a very small increase; the college entrants were still a bit higher than the others at the end of the study, but the differences had grown smaller.

We have noted several instances of modest change, but the more fundamental conclusion from Chapter 7 is that there are very few changes of any consequence and virtually none that would support the argument that dropping out damages a young man's "mental health" and his commitment to society's values. This conclusion is based on a wide variety of scales including self-esteem, feelings of personal efficacy (internal control), negative affective states, somatic symptoms, aggressive impulses, needs for self-development and self-utilization, social and academic values, attitudes about government and public issues, delinquent behaviors, and occupational aspirations.

Employed Versus Unemployed Dropouts. An examination of employed versus unemployed dropouts, while based on only a limited number of cases, led to essentially the same sort of conclusion as did our other findings. We found self-esteem lower and delinquent behavior higher among the unemployed dropouts when compared with dropouts who were working. But which is cause and which is effect? Did the unemployment lead to the lower self-esteem and higher delinquency, or is it the case that young men with patterns of delinquent behavior and low self-esteem are less likely to find and keep jobs? Of course, these two lines of causation are not mutually exclusive, and it could be the case that both are at work in a kind of vicious cycle. But our longitudinal data suggest that this is not the most likely explanation. We found that differences which were evident at the end of the study had been there all along, and were just about as large at the beginning (when all were students in tenth grade) as they were at the end. Thus it seems clear that the low self-esteem and high rates of delinquency came first, and should not be viewed as the unfortunate *results* of dropping out and being unemployed.

Are these Measures Valid? Most of the measures of personality and behavior dimensions showed little systematic change over time. We have taken the view that this indicates a good deal of stability in these characteristics. But an alternative interpretation might be that the measures are simply no good--that they do not show changes because they are not measuring what they are supposed to measure. This argument would be plausible if we had found no relationships at all using our measures. But the fact of the matter is that we did find consistent and theoretically sensible differences between dropouts and stayins, and between those who did and did not enter college. In our view these differences constitute further evidence for the "construct validity" of our measures, because they show the kinds of differences that would be predicted in advance. It is not that our measures failed to "work"—they simply failed to indicate that dropping out *changes* a boy in any very fundamental way.

Of course, most of our measures were not specifically designed to reflect changes. Although the *research design* was developed to show changes and to separate causes and effects, the *measures* were in most cases ones which had been developed to tap more-or-less stable personality characteristics or behavior patterns. An alternate approach might have been to try to develop measures for the specific purpose of reflecting change, with items selected for their instability rather than their stability. This was not a feasible alternative in the Youth in Transition study; given the wide range of measures included and the limited time and resources available for instrument development and validation, we chose the course of using established measures whenever possible. But even if it had been possible to develop measures of less stable or more changeable personality characteristics, it is not clear that this would have been appropriate for our purposes. After all, one cannot have it both ways. If a major environmental shift such as dropping out of school is supposed to produce real changes in self-esteem and delinquent behavior, and if these changes really do matter in the long run, then such changes ought to manifest themselves in the more basic dimensions of personality and behavior, not simply superficial ones. In retrospect, the use of fairly stable measures in the Youth in Transition study seemed appropriate, particularly for this study of dropouts. Once we were able to identify those who dropped out, we found that our measures were successful in revealing many of the differences we had been led to expect; what was less expected was the finding that those differences were relatively stable ones which were evident long before dropping out occurred.

Occupational Attainments of Dropouts

In many ways the heart of the argument against dropping out is that those without a high school diploma are less likely to get jobs, and the jobs they do succeed in getting are relatively unattractive and poorly paid. This economic argument places heaviest stress on the value of the high school diploma as a *credential*—an admission card into the world of work.

Our findings on occupational attainments of dropouts versus high school graduates are presented in Chapter 8, and reviewed briefly below. First a brief note on methodology is in order. We argued earlier in this chapter that a "before-and-after" type of longitudinal design is well suited to measuring change and separating cause from effect. That argument holds true when it is possible to make repeated measures of the same dimension. It was meaningful to measure dimensions such as self-esteem and delinquent behavior at all four data collections in our study, and this enabled us to examine whether dropout-stayin differences were already evident before the dropping out actually occurred. But this form of analysis is not workable when we focus our attention on employment. While some of our respondents held part-time jobs at the start of tenth grade when we first interviewed them, we cannot make a clear comparison between such jobs and later full-time post-high school work. At the second and third data collections some dropouts were holding jobs, but their jobs could not be compared meaningfully with the part-time jobs held by some of the stayins. The only sensible time for comparing employment experiences of dropouts and stayins is after the stayins have completed high school—in our case, the fourth and last data collection.

And this means that we have in many respects an "after-only" type of research design when it comes to studying employment experiences. Thus when we find differences between dropouts and stayins, we will still have to ask whether dropping out was truly the cause of the difference, or only another symptom.

Rates of Employment. Limiting our analysis to those in civilian life, we found that among dropouts without diplomas a total of 71 percent were employed 30 hours or more per week (at the time of the final interview); the comparable figure was 87 percent for high school graduates (i.e., those who were not primarily engaged in post-high school education). This finding would surely appear to justify the anti-dropout commercials which claim that "your chances of being unemployed are doubled if you quit school before graduating."

But let us take a closer look at that claim. The clear implication is that the dropping out causes the higher rate of unemployment. But when we consider that dropouts achieve relatively low scores on tests of intelligence and intellectual skills, and when we further note that the dropouts come predominantly from lower socioeconomic levels, we must ask: Is dropping out the cause of greater unemployment, or is it primarily a symptom of other more basic factors that cause unemployment. A partial answer to that question can be obtained by considering the extent to which we can predict unemployment using our measures of family background and ability. The results of this analysis indicate that we can do a better job of predicting unemployment using background and ability measures than by using dropout data, but we can make the best predictions if we use both kinds of information. As we stated in Chapter 8, we conclude that dropping out probably makes it more difficult to obtain employment; however, the more important causes of unemployment are those pervasive differences in background and ability which precede and help determine the act of dropping out.

Thus while unemployment rates may be twice as high among dropouts as among stayins, it is very misleading to claim that the act of dropping out will double a young man's chances of being unemployed. That difference in unemployment rates is caused primarily by family background and ability factors, and these things are not changed when a young man drops out of school.

Levels of Income and Job Satisfaction. When employed dropouts were compared with employed high school graduates, we found their weekly income levels to be nearly identical. (Actually, the small and statistically untrustworthy difference which did appear was in favor of the dropouts, who earned a few dollars more per week than the high school graduates.) One might attribute the lack of an income advantage on the part of high school graduates to seniority differences—they had been on the job for a shorter time than the dropouts. But even after we matched dropouts and graduates according to length of time on the present job, we still found no advantage on the part of the graduates. We cannot, of course, answer the argument that the *long-range* earnings of graduates will be higher—at least not without further follow-ups of the Youth in Transition respondents. But we can say that in the short run there is little justification for the assertion that dropouts who do get jobs will earn less than their counterparts who finished high school.

There is also little justification for the view that dropouts get less satisfying jobs. Three-quarters of the dropouts rated themselves "quite satisfied" or "very satisfied" with their jobs, while two-thirds of the graduates expressed similar levels of satisfaction. Additional ratings of job characteristics, reported in Chapter 8, showed little in the way of consistent differences between dropouts and graduates; certainly it was not the case that dropouts showed less job satisfaction than graduates.

Implications of This Research

Dropouts, like unemployed workers or highway fatalities, make wonderful "statistics." It is hard to measure learning very well, and even harder to measure such nebulous concepts as self-esteem and/or self-development. By comparison, it is a simple matter to measure dropping out; and statistics on dropout rates can be communicated easily to voters, school board members, legislators, and (as we saw in Chapter 1) leaders in the national administration. Thus the temptation is to treat dropping out as if it were a problem in its own right—something to be reduced and eventually eliminated. Everyone agrees that highway fatalities are tragic and should be reduced. Is it not the same for dropping out of school?

We have argued that it is not the same, for dropping out is not primarily a problem in its own right, but rather a symptom of other problems or limitations. Treating a symptom may be easier—and in the short run perhaps more satisfying—than treating the underlying problems. Nevertheless, it may in this instance do more harm than good for two reasons. First, the treatment has some unpleasant side effects, as we shall try to point out in a moment. Second, treating the symptom may distract us from the more basic problems.

Curbing the "Anti-Dropout Campaign." Over the past decade it has been a part of the national educational policy to try to prevent dropping out of high school, and that policy has been reflected in what we have called the "anti-dropout campaign." In our view that campaign ought to be sharply curtailed, for at least three reasons:

1. There is little evidence to support many of the claims of the anti-dropout campaign, and what evidence there is has sometimes been badly abused in order to make it more convincing. The "after-only" comparison of dropouts and stayins (sometimes *all* stayins, including those who go on to college) can be terribly misleading, for the implication is clear that if the potential dropout only stays in school then he can be just like the rest of the graduates. In fact, it simply is not so; by the time he reaches tenth or eleventh grade the potential dropout usually has basic problems and limitations that will not be "cured" by another year or two of high school.

2. Meanwhile, the campaign is giving dropouts a bad name. Most dropouts have become convinced that their action was probably a mistake, and that eventually they had better complete work for a diploma. They feel that their parents, and often other people whose opinions matter, disapprove of their dropout status. We speculated in Chapter 1 that the anti-dropout campaign may have some features of a self-fulfilling prophecy; one of the side-effects of downgrading the status of dropouts may be to encourage employers to make the diploma a requirement when it need not be.

3. The anti-dropout campaign can have the effect of eroding credibility. No doubt some young men are persuaded or partly persuaded by it; but one wonders how many others see through the oversimplifications and become still more skeptical and "turned off" by what they perceive as propaganda. This is not simply a matter affecting potential dropouts; nearly everyone is exposed to the television campaign, and many of our brightest and most perceptive young people may view it as one more instance of heavy-handed manipulation by "the establishment."

We cited in Chapter 8 a report of dropout research that was undertaken to provide data for use in high school guidance. The summary comments by the authors are so relevant to the present discussion that we will repeat them briefly here:

> It was hoped that the results would reveal that the non-college high school graduate (the control) was much better off than the high school dropout as far as future employment and earnings are concerned. Large differences in this area might help to dissuade some students from leaving high school before graduation. . . .

> Unfortunately, the results were not consistent with these expectations. Not only were the male dropouts earning as much as the controls, but they had been earning it longer. . . . (Combs and Cooley, 1968, pp. 361-362)

It had been *hoped* that the dropouts would look bad so that the evidence might be used to *dissuade* other potential dropouts, but *unfortunately* the data did not come out that way. To the authors' credit, they reported their unexpected findings in a clear and straightforward manner. Nevertheless the anti-dropout campaign continues unabated, leaving us with a nagging question: Why should we sponsor research on "the dropout problem" if we have already made up our minds about the matter, and if we are going to campaign against dropping out no matter how the research comes out?

The Need for Early Intervention. We said at the outset of this chapter that dropping out is a symptom which signifies a mismatch between certain individuals and the typical high school environment. In principle, the mismatch could be resolved by (a) changing the individuals so that they are better able to fit into the high school environment, (b) changing the high school environment, or (c) changing both. We think there is room for change on both sides.

Among the important elements in the mismatch between potential dropouts and the high school environment are individual limitations in academic ability, past scholastic failure, and patterns of delinquent behavior. These are not problems that are likely to be resolved in high school, and simply persuading a young man to remain through the last year or two of school is not going to make much of a difference along these dimensions. But early intervention, in elementary school and perhaps much earlier, may overcome many of the problems which are deeply ingrained by the time an individual is ready to drop out of high school.

Twelve Years of Schooling—Is It Ideal for Everyone? Even if we hope eventually to reduce or eliminate experiences of early school failure and other problems which are presently associated with dropping out, it is still worth asking whether our current approach to high school education is ideal. Is it clear that we should prescribe twelve or more years of uninterrupted schooling for virtually all young people in the United States? The campaign against dropping out seems based on the assumption that everyone needs at least twelve years of formal education. But the research reported here has led us to question that assumption. We have found that some young men can manage reasonably well on the

basis of ten or eleven years of education. Perhaps others would
do so if they were not branded as "dropouts."

Certainly there are alternatives to a twelve-year diploma;
perhaps one based on ten years would be sufficient. Young people
wishing to enter college might spend the years equivalent to grades
eleven and twelve in publicly supported college preparatory acad-
emies. Others might enter one-year or two-year vocational training or work-study programs; some such programs could be publicly operated, and some might be privately operated in conjunc-
tion with a system of publicly-supported tuition vouchers. Still
other young people might choose to go directly into the world of
work after their tenth-grade graduation—some to return to part-
time or full-time education after a year or two or three. The
recent growth of community colleges with their wide-ranging course
offerings, flexible time schedules, generous enrollment policies
and low tuition rates suggests that there is a growing need for
this sort of educational freedom of opportunity.

In a world of rapidly changing technology with its emphasis
on continuing education and periodic retraining, there is less and
less reason to maintain the traditionally sharp boundary between
the role of student and the later role of worker. Shortening the
prescribed minimum period for full-time uninterrupted schooling
might be a positive step toward new patterns of lifetime education
in which individuals can choose for themselves among a wide
range of "educational life-styles." If such changes would reduce
the credential value attached to high school diplomas, all the better. One of the unfortunate side effects of the anti-dropout campaign has been the tendency to confuse education with credentials;
any step in the opposite direction could have a salutary effect on
our whole educational establishment.

The above notions are speculations triggered by some of our
findings; we are not presenting them as thoroughly researched pro-
posals. Our purpose is simply to illustrate that there are potentially viable alternatives to the traditional twelve-year program
of study which we now urge upon practically every teenager. The
basic point, in our view, is that such alternatives should be given
serious consideration.

Concluding Comments

We began this research with the recognition that a number
of very different outcomes were possible. We might have found
predominantly "bad" effects from dropping out, and then we would
have concluded that vigorous efforts to discourage dropping out
are warranted. But this is not what we found.

At the other extreme, we might have found mostly "good" effects from dropping out, leading to the conclusion that dropping out should be encouraged among those having difficulty in high school. But this is not what we found either, and thus we must stress that *we are not encouraging young men to drop out of school.*

Our findings indicate that dropping out is neither especially "good" nor "bad." We find it to be a symptom, rather than a cause of new troubles or a cure for old ones.

We have stated these conclusions based on the evidence presently available. At the same time we recognize the limitations of a study which follows young men only until the age of 19 or 20. We are hopeful that further follow-ups of the Youth in Transition respondents will be possible, thus permitting an assessment of dropouts and stayins in their mid-twenties and perhaps still later.

Meanwhile, however, we must work with the findings at hand. Given those findings, we propose the following: (a) The anti-dropout campaign should be sharply curtailed. (b) Greater emphasis should be placed on early school and pre-school interventions. (c) The range of educational options for young people aged 16 to 18 should be broadened, and serious consideration should be given to reducing the number of years necessary for attaining a high school diploma.

APPENDICES

Appendix A
ESTIMATES OF SAMPLING ERROR *

As reported in Bachman, et al., (1967, pp. 21-24, 123-129), the sample for this study was selected in three stages. Stage one consisted of the Survey Research Center's national sample of counties and metropolitan areas selected from each of 88 strata. Stage two involved selecting one school from each such county or metropolitan area. (In one area several attempts were unsuccessful in locating a school willing to participate; therefore, it was necessary to omit this area and proceed with 87 schools.) Finally, stage three consisted of randomly selecting about 25 boys from each school.**

Given this type of clustered and stratified sample design, it is not appropriate to apply the standard, simple random sampling formulas to obtain estimates of sampling errors. The use of these formulas will almost always understate the actual sampling errors.

One measure of this understatement is the design effect (DEFF). For each sample estimate, the design effect is the square of the ratio of actual standard error to the expected standard error of the estimate from a simple random sample of the same size.

$$\text{DEFF (sample estimate)} = \left(\frac{\text{actual standard error of the estimate}}{\text{expected standard error of the estimate if the sample were simple random of the same size}} \right)^2$$

For most of the <u>simple means</u> in this monograph, our estimates suggest that design effects will be under 3.

We recommend that an assumed value of DEFF = 2.8 be used in computing standard errors for the proportions (p) presented in chapters 3 - 6. Estimate s.e.(p) by

$$\text{s.e.(p)} = \sqrt{\frac{\text{DEFF } p(1-p)}{N}} = 1.7 \sqrt{\frac{p(1-p)}{N}}$$

Although the clustered nature of the data collection (sampling) introduces correlation between observations, we feel that the sampling error of a difference between two proportions p_1 and p_2, based on subclass sizes of N_1 and N_2 respectively, may be

---

*This appendix was written by Martin Frankel, Sampling Section, Survey Research Center.

**We are grateful to Leslie Kish and Irene Hess for developing the sampling procedure used in this study.

conservatively estimated as

$$s.e.(p_1-p_2) = \sqrt{DEFF \left[\frac{p_1(1-p_1)}{N_1} + \frac{p_2(1-p_2)}{N_2} \right]} =$$

$$1.5 \sqrt{\frac{p_1(1-p_1)}{N_1} + \frac{p_2(1-p_2)}{N_2}} .$$

Even when design effects for simple means are rather large, there exists a good deal of evidence to indicate that design effects for more complex statistics (e.g., regression and MCA coefficients, correlation coefficients, MCA Etas and Betas) are significantly lower (Kish and Frankel, 1970; Frankel, 1971).

The table below presents what we feel are conservative estimates of the standard errors for the MCA Etas of chapters 3 - 6 (but not chapter 8). These standard errors are based on a sample size N=1996 and a Design Effect (DEFF)=2.3 using the approximation

$$S.E. (ETA) = \sqrt{\frac{DEFF(1-ETA^2)^2}{N}} .$$

Value of ETA	S.E. (ETA)
<.10	.034
.15	.033
.20	.033
.30	.031
.40	.028
.50	.025
.60	.022
.70	.017
.80	.012

The user is cautioned against using these standard errors for computing "exact" significance levels, confidence (or credible) intervals. These standard errors as well as the necessary normal distributional assumptions are approximations. For further discussion of some of the issues raised in this appendix, see Kish (1967), Kish and Frankel (1970), Frankel (1971).

Appendix B
ADDITIONAL ANALYSES OF ABILITY AND BACKGROUND FACTORS RELATED TO EDUCATIONAL ATTAINMENT

The purpose of this appendix is to present analyses of the educational attainment criterion using exactly the same procedures and predictors as in Volume II of the Youth in Transition series (Bachman, 1970). Educational attainment was not available as a criterion dimension when Volume II was written. The tables here thus represent a sort of extension of Volume II, and will be of interest primarily to those who have examined that volume and wish to be able to interpret our educational attainment data in precisely comparable terms.

Table B-1 presents predictions to educational attainment treated as an equal-interval continuum (with Group 1 assigned a score of "1", Group 2 a score of "2", and Group 3 a score of "3"). (Chapter 6 contains data and discussion supporting this treatment of educational attainment as if it were an equal-interval scale.) Table B-2 shows predictions to dropping out versus staying in, excluding those who entered post-high school education. Table B-3 shows predictions to another "portion" of the educational attainment continuum -- the contrast between graduates who do and do not continue into post-high school education. Table B-4 predicts dropping out with all stayins (Groups 2 and 3) combined.

Table B-1 shows the strongest relationships, indicating that the equal-interval treatment of educational attainment provides the most "predictable" criterion of those considered here. Relationships in Table B-3 are next strongest, thereby demonstrating that the distinction between those who do and do not go on to college is the dominant factor in the educational attainment continuum.

Readers of Volume II may wish to compare Tables B-1 and B-3 with the multiple classification analysis predicting to college plans (Bachman, 1970, p.177). With only one exception (community size), the predictions to actual post-high school education were a bit larger than our earlier predictions to tenth-graders' plans for college. This is consistent with the view expressed in Volume II that family background effects remain strong throughout the high school years.

189

TABLE B-1

MULTIPLE CLASSIFICATION ANALYSIS OF BACKGROUND FACTORS
PREDICTING TO EDUCATIONAL ATTAINMENT CONTINUUM

	PREDICTING FROM EACH CHARACTERISTIC SEPARATELY		PREDICTING FROM QUICK TEST AND 8 BACKGROUND CHARACTERISTICS SIMULTANEOUSLY	
BACKGROUND PREDICTORS:	Eta	Eta^2	Beta	$Beta^2$
Socioeconomic level	.37	.140	.26	.069
Number of siblings	.25	.065	.12	.014
Broken home	.14	.020	.07	.005
Family relations	.23	.052	.16	.024
Religious preference	.21	.043	.09	.009
Family political preference	.11	.013	.08	.006
Community size	.10	.010	.06	.004
Race (Five-category)	.15	.021	.10	.009
Quick test of intelligence	.31	.095	.18	.031

$$R = .470$$
$$R^2 = .221$$

Percent
Variance
Explained = 24.0

Eta is the correlation ratio unadjusted.
Beta is the correlation ratio adjusted for effects of other
    predictors.
R is the multiple correlation coefficient corrected for degrees of
    freedom.
R^2 indicates the proportion of variance in the dependent variable
    explained by all predictors together after correcting for degrees
    of freedom.
The Percent Variance Explained is the percentage of variance in the
    dependent variable explained by all predictors together with no
    correction for degrees of freedom.

TABLE B-2

MULTIPLE CLASSIFICATION ANALYSIS OF BACKGROUND FACTORS
PREDICTING TO DROPOUTS (GROUP 1) VERSUS
NON-COLLEGE STAYINS (GROUP 2)

	PREDICTING FROM EACH CHARACTERISTIC SEPARATELY		PREDICTING FROM QUICK TEST AND 8 BACKGROUND CHARACTERISTICS SIMULTANEOUSLY	
BACKGROUND PREDICTORS:	Eta	Eta^2	Beta	$Beta^2$
Socioeconomic level	.13	.018	.08	.007
Number of siblings	.13	.017	.11	.011
Broken home	.08	.007	.06	.003
Family relations	.12	.015	.12	.014
Religious preference	.12	.014	.09	.009
Family political preference	.08	.007	.08	.006
Community size	.07	.006	.09	.008
Race (Five-category)	.14	.019	.11	.012
Quick test of intelligence	.11	.012	.09	.008

$$R = .200$$
$$R^2 = .040$$

Percent
Variance
Explained = 8.3

Eta is the correlation ratio unadjusted.
Beta is the correlation ratio adjusted for effects of other
  predictors.
R is the multiple correlation coefficient corrected for degrees of
  freedom.
R^2 indicates the proportion of variance in the dependent variable
  explained by all predictors together after correcting for degrees
  of freedom.
The Percent Variance Explained is the percentage of variance in the
  dependent variable explained by all predictors together with no
  correction for degrees of freedom.

TABLE B-3

MULTIPLE CLASSIFICATION ANALYSIS OF BACKGROUND FACTORS
PREDICTING TO COLLEGE ENTRANTS (GROUP 3) VERSUS
NON-COLLEGE STAYINS (GROUP 2)

BACKGROUND PREDICTORS:	PREDICTING FROM EACH CHARACTERISTIC SEPARATELY		PREDICTING FROM QUICK TEST AND 8 BACKGROUND CHARACTERISTICS SIMULTANEOUSLY	
	Eta	Eta^2	Beta	Beta^2
Socioeconomic level	.36	.129	.27	.071
Number of siblings	.22	.050	.10	.010
Broken home	.11	.011	.05	.003
Family relations	.19	.034	.12	.014
Religious preference	.19	.035	.09	.008
Family political preference	.09	.007	.07	.005
Community size	.12	.014	.04	.002
Race (Five-category)	.11	.012	.10	.010
Quick test of intelligence	.29	.084	.17	.031

$$R = .428$$
$$R^2 = .183$$

Percent
Variance
Explained = 20.6

Eta is the correlation ratio unadjusted.
Beta is the correlation ratio adjusted for effects of other
    predictors.
R is the multiple correlation coefficient corrected for degrees of
    freedom.
R^2 indicates the proportion of variance in the dependent variable
    explained by all predictors together after correcting for degrees
    of freedom.
The Percent Variance Explained is the percentage of variance in the
    dependent variable explained by all predictors together with no
    correction for degrees of freedom.

TABLE B-4

MULTIPLE CLASSIFICATION ANALYSIS OF BACKGROUND FACTORS
PREDICTING TO DROPOUTS (GROUP 1) VERSUS
ALL STAYINS (GROUPS 2+3)

	PREDICTING FROM EACH CHARACTERISTIC SEPARATELY		PREDICTING FROM QUICK TEST AND 8 BACKGROUND CHARACTERISTICS SIMULTANEOUSLY	
BACKGROUND PREDICTORS:	Eta	Eta^2	Beta	$Beta^2$
Socioeconomic level	.22	.048	.15	.022
Number of siblings	.18	.031	.10	.011
Broken home	.11	.012	.06	.004
Family relations	.16	.026	.12	.015
Religious preference	.14	.019	.08	.006
Family political preference	.09	.008	.07	.005
Community size	.06	.004	.07	.005
Race (Five-category)	.14	.019	.10	.010
Quick test of intelligence	.19	.035	.12	.014

R = .302
R^2 = .091

Percent
Variance
Explained = 11.3

Eta is the correlation ratio unadjusted.
Beta is the correlation ratio adjusted for effects of other
   predictors.
R is the multiple correlation coefficient corrected for degrees of
   freedom.
R^2 indicates the proportion of variance in the dependent variable
   explained by all predictors together after correcting for degrees
   of freedom.
The Percent Variance Explained is the percentage of variance in the
   dependent variable explained by all predictors together with no
   correction for degrees of freedom.

Appendix C

GUIDE TO FIGURES AND SUPPORTING DATA

The purpose of this appendix is two-fold. First, it is intended as a guide and explanation for most of the figures used in this volume. Second, it provides complete tabular data corresponding to the figures (and in some respects going beyond the figures).

Analysis Groups

In all of the data summarized in this appendix, three major analysis groups are used. They are described in detail in Chapter 2, and can be summarized briefly as follows:

Group 1: High school dropouts (including a few dropouts who later attained high school diplomas).

Group 2: High school graduates who were not primarily engaged in post-high school education during the first half of 1970.

Group 3: High school graduates who were primarily engaged in post-high school education during the first half of 1970.

(Some other analytic groups are also included in the tabular portion of this appendix; they are defined in the section of this appendix which deals with estimating dropout rates.)

Format for Figures in Chapters 3,4, and 5

The solid (black) portion of each bar represents Group 1 (dropouts). The height of the solid portion of a bar indicates the percent of respondents in a given predictor category who were classified in Group 1.

The shaded (gray) portion of each bar represents Group 2 (non-dropouts who were not primarily students after high school).

The open (white) portion of each bar represents Group 3 (those primarily students after high school).

The width of each bar is proportionate to the total number of cases classified in each predictor category. (In Figure 3-1, for example, the widest bars are found in the middle categories of socioeconomic level, indicating that most respondents come from middle SEL homes.)

195

The area of each portion of a bar represents the total number of respondents who can be classified according to a given predictor and criterion. This feature can be used to indicate the distribution of each analysis group across a set of predictor categories. (In Figure 3-3, for example, the heights of the solid bars indicate that dropping out occurs more often than average among those in broken homes; nevertheless, a comparison of the total area of each of the solid bars indicates that the majority of dropouts come from intact homes.)

The gap between the top of a bar and the top of a figure represents the percent of respondents in a given predictor category who began the study in 1966 but could not (as of 1970) be classified into one of the three analysis groups. (In Figure 3-3, for example, there are roughly twice as many "missing" or unclassified respondents in the broken home categories as in the intact home category.)

It should be kept in mind that the "missing" respondents in these figures represent that subset of the non-respondents whom we were unable to classify based on other information. Many of our initial sample members who did not stay with the study until its conclusion were nevertheless classifiable using information gained from them or their families or schools.

The dashed line in each figure represents the estimated dropout rate, taking into account the "undiscovered dropouts" -- those who began the study in 1966 and later dropped out of school, but could not be positively identified as dropouts. The procedures for making such estimates are outlined later in this appendix.

The eta statistic presented with each figure represents the correlation between the predictor and the educational attainment criterion, treating the latter as an equal interval scale. In other words, the criterion assigns a score of "1" to dropouts, "2" to graduates who do not continue their education beyond high school, and "3" to those who go on to post-high school education. (Chapter 6 presents data supporting our treatment of educational attainment as a continuum.)

Eta can be interpreted in roughly the same manner as the product-moment correlation (Pearson's r) with one very important exception: eta does not require the relationship to be linear; it is equally appropriate for linear and non-linear relationships. This makes it especially well-suited for categorical predictors such as broken home or grade failure in school.

Our purpose in presenting the eta value for each figure is to provide an overall indication of the strength of relationship involved in the figure, since eta squared is a measure of explained variance.

Tabular Data Corresponding to Figures

As we said in the preceding volume in this series, we hope that the several "gimmicks" used in the figures will not over-shadow the findings they are designed to display. Our intention

has been to present findings in such a way that much of the rich
detail of relationship can be grasped more easily than would be
possible in tabular presentation. For some purposes, of course,
it is useful to know the exact values underlying a graphic display.
Accordingly, the last part of this appendix consists of tabular
data underlying most of our figures.

Tables Corresponding to Chapters 3,4, and 5. Table entries
consist of weighted numbers of cases. (Weighted numbers are about
14 percent larger than the actual numbers of cases.) In addition
to data for each major analysis group, the tables include data for
a number of special groups identified in the section of this
appendix that deals with estimating dropout rate.

Tables Corresponding to Chapter 7. The format for the figures
in Chapter 7 is discussed extensively in the text at the beginning
of that chapter, and needs no further elaborlation; however, the
corresponding tabular data in this appendix require a few introductory notes.

Tabular data are presented for each analysis group (plus a
total of the three groups) at each of the four data collections.
The left-hand side of the table is limited to those respondents
who participated in all four data collections, thereby avoiding
bias due to panel attrition. The right-hand side of the table
includes all available respondents at a given data collection.
Comparison of the two sides of the table can provide an indication
of the degree to which distortion has been produced by panel
attrition.

The data given for each group at each time include mean ($\overline{X}$),
standard deviation (SD), and the number of weighted cases (N Wt'd).

For each time period an eta statistic is also included. The
eta in these tables represents our ability to explain variation in
the criterion score by classifying respondents into the three
analysis groups. Some of this involves a sort of backward
prediction; for example, the eta of .22 in Table C-7-1 indicates
our ability to "explain" self-esteem at the start of tenth grade
by knowing which boys later became dropouts (Group 1), college
entrants (Group 3), and others (Group 2).

We have included the eta statistics in these tables for two
reasons. First, they provide an overall indication of the strength
(or weakness!) of relationships. Second, when compared across time
they provide an indication of whether the differentiation according
to educational attainment is growing stronger or weaker. For
example, the eta values displayed in Table C-7-1 indicate that the
self-esteem differences between Groups 1,2, and 3 actually grow
weaker over time.

Estimating Dropout Rate

As we noted in the text in Chapters 1 and 3, the members of
our sample whom we were able to identify as dropouts (Group 1) tend
to underrepresent the total number of dropouts. This occurs because
we are missing some respondents who can be termed "Undiscovered
Dropouts." What follows is a rationale and procedure for estimating

numbers (or percentages) of undiscovered dropouts.* We begin by
defining several other categories of respondents.

Trackbacks are those respondents who did not continue their
participation in the project beyond the first or second data
collection, but were "tracked back" by interviewers at Time 2 or
Time 3 and classified as dropouts or stayins. (Some tracking back
occurred also at Time 4; however, the tracking back at Times 2 and
3 produced virtually all of our data identifying dropouts. If a
young man participated at Time 3, we were able to classify him as
a dropout or stayin even if we did not succeed in contacting him at
Time 4.)

Trackback Dropouts are those tracked back and identified as
dropouts (and thus included in Group 1).

Trackback Stayins are those tracked back and identified as not
having dropped out. (In nearly all cases they were included in
Group 2.)

Unclassifieds are those respondents who did not continue their
participation until at least the Time 3 data collection and were not
tracked back and classified by interviewers.

Our task now is to estimate how many of the unclassifieds are
undiscovered dropouts. We will not be able to identify which
of the unclassifieds are the ones who dropped out, but it does
seem possible to make an estimate of how many unclassifieds in any
predictor category are likely to be undiscovered dropouts.

In order to proceed further, we must make an assumption: we
assume that, within any predictor category, the proportion of
undiscovered dropouts among the unclassifieds is equal to the
proportion of trackback dropouts among all trackbacks (dropouts
plus stayins). This simply means that we think the group most like
the unclassifieds is probably the trackback group. The trackbacks,
like the unclassifieds, did not (for one reason or another) continue
their participation throughout the project -- the only difference
is that the trackbacks could be classified as dropouts or stayins
by the interviewers. The data support this assertion that the
unclassifieds are like the trackbacks. Along the dimensions
presented in Chapters 3,4, and 5, there is a good deal of similarity
between the two groups. The reader wishing to examine the data may
compare columns 4 and 8 in the Tables C-3-1 through C-5-10 of this
appendix.

The assumption stated above is expressed in the following
equation:

$$\frac{\text{Undiscovered Dropouts}}{\text{All Unclassifieds}} \equiv \frac{\text{Trackback Dropouts}}{\text{All Trackbacks}}$$

---
*
This section of the appendix is just a bit technical; it may be
skipped by those who prefer to "take our word for it" rather than
review the procedure for estimating dropout rate.

From the equation above we can derive the following procedure for estimating Unidentified Dropouts:

$$\text{Undiscovered Dropouts} \ = \ \frac{\text{Trackback Dropouts}}{\text{All Trackbacks}} \left(\text{All Unclassifieds}\right)$$

These estimates were computed separately for each predictor category in each of the figures described earlier in this appendix. In some instances the calculations had to be based on very few cases, thus it seemed desirable to use some degree of smoothing to represent our estimated total dropout rate.

The dashed line in each figure, representing our estimate of the total dropout rate, was produced using the following steps:

1. The estimated number of undiscovered dropouts was computed separately for each category of the predictor variable.

2. Each of the above estimates was added to the corresponding number of respondents in Group 1. (In other words, the undiscovered dropouts were added to the "known dropouts" in each category.)

3. The resulting total number of dropouts in each category was divided by the total number of cases in the category, thereby providing the percent of respondents in each category estimated to be dropouts.

4. The percentages resulting from Step 3 were plotted, and a dashed line was drawn through the points (with some smoothing of the line when necessary).

The reader who wishes to replicate any of these calculations, or perhaps examine alternate methods, will find all of the necessary ingredients in the tabular portion of this appendix.

TABLE C-3-1*

EDUCATIONAL ATTAINMENT RELATED TO
SOCIOECONOMIC LEVEL

S.E.L. Categories	Group 1	Group 2	Group 3	Unclassifieds	Total	Trackback Dropouts	Trackback Stayins	Total Trackbacks
	1	2	3	4	5	6	7	8
1 (low)	38	89	18	22	167	8	7	15
2	83	174	79	50	386	24	19	43
3	99	299	227	63	688	40	30	70
4	55	220	328	46	649	21	34	55
5	21	87	224	33	365	8	14	22
6 (high)	7	23	133	17	180	2	2	4
Missing Data	23	31	17	13	84	10	5	15
Total	326	923	1026	244	2519	113	111	224

TABLE C-3-2*

EDUCATIONAL ATTAINMENT RELATED TO
FAMILY SIZE

Family Size Categories	1	2	3	4	5	6	7	8
0 siblings	16	41	63	19	139	6	7	13
1 sibling	44	150	274	39	507	17	17	34
2 siblings	48	189	270	55	562	19	31	50
3 siblings	62	179	203	40	484	19	18	37
4 siblings	50	130	102	30	312	18	18	36
5 siblings	27	97	51	19	194	7	11	18
6 siblings	39	54	22	11	126	15	5	20
7 siblings or more	40	83	41	31	195	12	4	16
Missing Data	---	---	---	---	---	---	---	---
Total	326	923	1026	244	2519	113	111	224

*Cell entries are weighted N's; see beginning of Appendix C for description of analysis groups.

TABLE C-3-3*

EDUCATIONAL ATTAINMENT RELATED TO
BROKEN HOME

Broken Home Categories	Group 1	Group 2	Group 3	Unclassifieds	Total	Trackback Dropouts	Trackback Stayins	Total Trackbacks
	1	2	3	4	5	6	7	8
Home intact	231	729	883	159	2002	76	99	175
Home broken by death	33	67	67	33	200	10	5	15
Home broken by divorce, etc.	62	127	76	52	317	27	7	34
Missing Data	---	---	---	---	---	---	---	---
Total	326	923	1026	244	2519	113	111	224

TABLE C-3-4*

EDUCATIONAL ATTAINMENT RELATED TO
PARENTAL PUNITIVENESS

Parental Punitiveness Categories	1	2	3	4	5	6	7	8
1 (low)	13	63	58	9	143	2	8	10
2	35	105	174	35	349	7	18	25
3	53	194	294	47	588	18	30	48
4	54	189	224	44	511	19	15	34
5	54	150	152	45	401	24	21	45
6	51	121	68	30	270	21	9	30
7	32	49	33	16	130	8	5	13
8 (high)	20	27	16	12	75	9	1	10
Missing Data	14	25	7	6	52	5	4	9
Total	326	923	1026	244	2519	113	111	224

*Cell entries are weighted N's; see beginning of Appendix C for description of analysis groups.

TABLE C-3-5*

EDUCATIONAL ATTAINMENT RELATED TO
RACE

Race Categories	Group 1 1	Group 2 2	Group 3 3	Unclassifieds 4	Total 5	Trackback Dropouts 6	Trackback Stayins 7	Total Trackbacks 8
All Whites	258	798	933	191	2180	*98*	*105*	*203*
Blacks in inte- grated schools	7	25	31	16	79	---	*3*	*3*
Blacks in nor- thern segre- gated schools	23	21	17	11	72	*4*	*1*	*5*
Blacks in sou- thern segre- gated schools	28	69	30	15	142	*7*	---	*7*
Other racial minorities	10	10	15	11	46	*4*	*2*	*6*
Missing Data	---	---	---	---	---	---	---	---
Total	326	923	1026	244	2519	*113*	*111*	*224*

TABLE C-3-6*

EDUCATIONAL ATTAINMENT RELATED TO
QUICK TEST SCORES

Q.T. Score Categories	1	2	3	4	5	6	7	8
0-91	59	102	32	39	232	*16*	*10*	*26*
92-102	85	210	121	50	466	*22*	*30*	*52*
103-113	112	377	367	85	941	*43*	*42*	*85*
114-124	61	195	367	54	677	*27*	*27*	*54*
125-150	9	39	139	16	203	*5*	*2*	*7*
Missing Data	---	---	---	---	---	---	---	---
Total	326	923	1026	244	2519	*113*	*111*	*224*

*Cell entries are weighted N's; see beginning of Appendix C for description of
analysis groups.

TABLE C-3-7*

EDUCATIONAL ATTAINMENT RELATED TO
VOCABULARY SKILLS (GATB-J TEST)

GATB-J Score Categories	Group 1	Group 2	Group 3	Unclassifieds	Total	Trackback Dropouts	Trackback Stayins	Total Trackbacks
	1	2	3	4	5	6	7	8
0-10	66	112	33	46	257	18	10	28
11-16	122	287	154	72	635	38	34	72
17-21	99	311	295	60	765	44	39	83
22-27	35	180	358	47	620	13	21	34
28-44	2	33	185	19	239	---	7	7
Missing Data	2	---	1	---	3	---	---	---
Total	326	923	1026	244	2519	113	111	224

TABLE C-3-8*

EDUCATIONAL ATTAINMENT RELATED TO
READING SKILLS (GATES TEST)

Gates Reading Test Scores	1	2	3	4	5	6	7	8
0-23	41	48	18	21	128	12	3	15
24-27	20	46	13	23	102	9	3	12
28-31	42	86	30	33	191	8	13	21
32-35	71	229	126	43	469	24	30	54
36-39	89	312	305	65	771	31	36	67
40-43	59	202	534	58	853	29	26	55
Missing Data	4	---	---	1	5	---	---	---
Total	326	923	1026	244	2519	113	111	224

---

*Cell entries are weighted N's; see beginning of Appendix C for description of analysis groups.

TABLE C-4-1[*]

EDUCATIONAL ATTAINMENT RELATED TO
GRADE FAILURE

Grade Failure	Group 1 1	Group 2 2	Group 3 3	Unclassifieds 4	Total 5	Trackback Dropouts 6	Trackback Stayins 7	Total Trackbacks 8
Held back once or more	172	251	83	98	604	*74*	*30*	*104*
Never held back	153	672	943	145	1913	*39*	*81*	*120*
Missing Data	1	---	---	1	2	---	---	---
Total	326	923	1026	244	2519	*113*	*111*	*224*

TABLE C-4-2[*]

EDUCATIONAL ATTAINMENT RELATED TO
AVERAGE GRADES IN NINTH GRADE

Grades	1	2	3	4	5	6	7	8
A	4	21	171	13	209	---	*4*	*4*
B	54	319	523	78	974	*26*	*50*	*76*
C	198	519	313	118	1148	*60*	*51*	*111*
D	64	63	13	26	166	*25*	*6*	*31*
E(F)	4	1	2	1	8	*2*	---	*2*
Missing Data	2	---	4	8	14	---	---	---
Total	326	923	1026	244	2519	*113*	*111*	*224*

[*]Cell entries are weighted N's; see beginning of Appendix C for description of analysis groups.

TABLE C-4-3[*]

EDUCATIONAL ATTAINMENT RELATED TO
SELF-CONCEPT OF SCHOOL ABILITY

Self-Concept of School Ability	Group 1	Group 2	Group 3	Unclassifieds	Total	Trackback Dropouts	Trackback Stayins	Total Trackbacks
	1	2	3	4	5	6	7	8
Far below average	1	---	---	---	1	1	---	1
Below average	11	15	2	4	32	4	1	5
Slightly below average	97	200	72	49	418	32	15	47
Slightly above average	169	537	489	129	1324	56	82	138
Above average	43	165	392	55	655	19	12	31
Far above average	3	5	69	5	82	---	1	1
Missing Data	2	1	2	2	7	1	---	1
Total	326	923	1026	244	2519	113	111	224

TABLE C-4-4[*]

EDUCATIONAL ATTAINMENT RELATED TO
HOURS SPENT ON HOMEWORK

Hours	1	2	3	4	5	6	7	8
0-4 hours	63	114	60	42	279	27	12	39
5-9 hours	123	340	318	82	863	41	36	77
10-14 hours	76	250	337	70	733	18	37	55
15-19 hours	42	123	187	27	379	17	14	31
20-30 hours	16	73	114	17	220	8	8	16
Missing Data	6	23	10	6	45	2	4	6
Total	326	923	1026	244	2519	113	111	224

[*] Cell entries are weighted N's; see beginning of Appendix C for description of analysis groups.

TABLE C-4-5[*]

EDUCATIONAL ATTAINMENT RELATED TO
SELF-RATING OF SCHOOL EFFORT COMPARED WITH OTHERS

Self-Rating of Effort	Group 1 1	Group 2 2	Group 3 3	Unclassifieds 4	Total 5	Trackback Dropouts 6	Trackback Stayins 7	Total Trackbacks 8
Much harder	9	24	19	9	61	---	2	2
Harder	23	82	214	26	345	10	13	23
About average	197	668	685	157	1707	63	85	148
Less hard	82	144	101	48	375	35	11	46
Much less hard	15	4	7	4	30	5	---	5
Missing Data	---	1	---	---	1	---	---	---
Total	326	923	1026	244	2519	113	111	224

TABLE C-4-6[*]

EDUCATIONAL ATTAINMENT RELATED TO
INTEREST IN SCHOOL COURSES

Interest in Courses	1	2	3	4	5	6	7	8
Very exciting and stimulating	22	78	57	19	176	9	7	16
Quite interesting	100	325	484	90	999	31	42	73
Fairly interesting	134	379	389	96	998	43	47	90
Slightly dull	45	112	80	26	263	15	11	26
Very dull	20	26	11	10	67	13	3	16
Missing Data	5	3	5	3	16	2	1	3
Total	326	923	1026	244	2519	113	111	224

---

[*]Cell entries are weighted N's; see beginning of Appendix C for description of analysis groups.

TABLE C-4-7*

EDUCATIONAL ATTAINMENT RELATED TO
NEGATIVE SCHOOL ATTITUDES

Extent of Negative School Attitudes 1=Not at all 2=A little 3=Pretty much 4=Very much	Group 1 1	Group 2 2	Group 3 3	Unclassifieds 4	Total 5	Trackback Dropouts 6	Trackback Stayins 7	Total Trackbacks 8
1.00-1.50	55	257	453	55	820	19	46	65
1.51-2.00	70	293	377	69	809	30	24	54
2.01-2.50	97	189	127	63	476	22	17	39
2.51-3.00	61	117	45	30	253	28	14	42
3.01-4.00	39	45	16	22	122	12	3	15
Missing Data	4	22	8	5	39	2	7	9
Total	326	923	1026	244	2519	113	111	224

TABLE C-4-8*

EDUCATIONAL ATTAINMENT RELATED TO
REBELLIOUS BEHAVIOR IN SCHOOL

Frequency of Rebellious Behavior 1=Never 2=Seldom 3=Sometimes 4=Often 5=Almost always	1	2	3	4	5	6	7	8
1.00-1.50	19	129	187	15	350	6	21	27
1.51-2.00	105	358	490	95	1048	38	56	94
2.01-2.50	82	243	244	62	631	27	20	47
2.51-3.00	81	121	84	40	326	29	7	36
3.01-5.00	36	52	17	30	135	12	2	14
Missing Data	3	20	4	2	29	1	5	6
Total	326	923	1026	244	2519	113	111	224

*Cell entries are weighted N's; see beginning of Appendix C for description of analysis groups.

TABLE C-5-1[*]

EDUCATIONAL ATTAINMENT RELATED TO
NEED FOR SELF-DEVELOPMENT

Need for Self-Development	Group 1	Group 2	Group 3	Unclassifieds	Total	Trackback Dropouts	Trackback Stayins	Total Trackbacks
	1	2	3	4	5	6	7	8
(low) 1.00-3.00	62	147	77	33	319	23	10	33
3.01-3.50	86	306	251	78	721	32	39	71
3.51-4.00	117	299	409	79	904	37	41	78
4.01-4.50	46	134	202	43	425	13	10	23
4.51-5.00 (high)	12	28	82	10	132	5	8	13
Missing Data	3	9	5	1	18	3	3	6
Total	326	923	1026	244	2519	113	111	224

TABLE C-5-2 *

EDUCATIONAL ATTAINMENT RELATED TO
INTERNAL CONTROL

Internal Control	1	2	3	4	5	6	7	8
(low) 1.00-1.40	38	69	78	24	209	11	8	19
1.41-1.60	131	328	264	98	821	44	35	79
1.61-1.80	86	293	317	63	759	34	29	63
1.81-2.00 (high)	59	209	353	53	674	22	33	55
Missing Data	12	24	14	6	56	2	6	8
Total	326	923	1026	244	2519	113	111	224

---

[*] Cell entries are weighted N's; see beginning of Appendix C for description of analysis groups.

TABLE C-5-3*

EDUCATIONAL ATTAINMENT RELATED TO
SELF-ESTEEM

Self-Esteem	Group 1	Group 2	Group 3	Unclassifieds	Total	Trackback Dropouts	Trackback Stayins	Total Trackbacks
	1	2	3	4	5	6	7	8
(low)								
1.00-3.00	47	100	65	20	232	23	10	33
3.01-3.50	104	266	209	60	639	23	28	51
3.51-4.00	106	334	357	103	900	40	35	75
4.01-4.50	54	179	311	48	592	20	26	46
4.51-5.00	11	39	79	13	142	5	10	15
(high)								
Missing Data	4	5	5	---	14	2	2	4
Total	326	923	1026	244	2519	113	111	224

TABLE C-5-4*

Frequency of
Symptoms
1=Never
2=Seldom
3=Sometimes
4=Often
5=Always

EDUCATIONAL ATTAINMENT RELATED TO
SOMATIC SYMPTOMS

	1	2	3	4	5	6	7	8
1.00-1.49	20	107	145	25	297	7	20	27
1.50-1.99	83	255	358	63	759	29	37	66
2.00-2.49	82	277	356	67	782	30	33	63
2.50-2.99	74	146	120	45	385	22	10	32
3.00-5.00	56	109	41	38	244	22	6	28
Missing Data	11	29	6	6	52	3	5	8
Total	326	923	1026	244	2519	113	111	224

---

*Cell entries are weighted N's; see beginning of Appendix C for description of
analysis groups.

TABLE C-5-5[*]

EDUCATIONAL ATTAINMENT RELATED TO
SOCIAL VALUES

Commitment to Social Values	Group 1	Group 2	Group 3	Unclassifieds	Total	Trackback Dropouts	Trackback Stayins	Total Trackbacks
	1	2	3	4	5	6	7	8
(low) 1.00-4.00	66	124	58	47	295	20	11	31
4.01-4.50	78	219	213	59	569	27	21	48
4.51-5.00	105	296	373	69	843	38	31	69
5.01-5.50	48	190	279	48	565	15	35	50
5.51-6.00 (high)	20	65	90	14	189	11	11	22
Missing Data	9	29	13	7	58	2	2	4
Total	326	923	1026	244	2519	113	111	224

TABLE C-5-6[*]

EDUCATIONAL ATTAINMENT RELATED TO
AMBITIOUS JOB ATTITUDES

	1	2	3	4	5	6	7	8
(low) 1.00-4.00	43	81	44	34	202	14	7	21
4.01-4.50	72	158	86	44	360	25	14	39
4.51-5.00	81	213	219	57	570	25	21	46
5.01-5.50	56	242	300	54	652	16	32	48
5.51-6.00	45	146	268	31	490	22	25	47
6.01-9.00 (high)	24	66	97	17	204	10	9	19
Missing Data	5	17	12	7	41	1	3	4
Total	326	923	1026	244	2519	113	111	224

[*]Cell entries are weighted N's; see beginning of Appendix C for description o
analysis groups.

TABLE C-5-7[*]

EDUCATIONAL ATTAINMENT RELATED TO
STATUS OF ASPIRED OCCUPATION

Status of Aspired Occupation (Duncan scale)	Group 1	Group 2	Group 3	Unclassifieds	Total	Trackback Dropouts	Trackback Stayins	Total Trackbacks
	1	2	3	4	5	6	7	8
01-20	70	134	53	34	291	22	11	33
21-40	43	95	36	30	204	15	6	21
41-60	36	102	100	28	266	12	5	17
61-80	67	198	282	56	603	23	28	51
81-98	36	140	332	33	541	17	23	40
Missing Data	74	254	223	63	614	24	38	62
Total	326	923	1026	244	2519	113	111	224

TABLE C-5-8[*]

EDUCATIONAL ATTAINMENT RELATED TO
LEVEL OF INDEPENDENCE

Frequency of Feelings of Independence 1=Never 2=Seldom 3=Sometimes 4=Often 5=Almost always	1	2	3	4	5	6	7	8
1.00-2.50	24	89	69	15	197	6	5	11
2.51-3.00	45	201	232	42	520	13	28	41
3.01-3.50	79	264	311	68	722	24	34	58
3.51-4.00	86	206	241	41	574	27	22	49
4.01-4.50	55	115	132	56	358	21	15	36
4.51-5.00	35	45	37	22	139	22	6	28
Missing Data	2	3	4	---	9	---	1	1
Total	326	923	1026	244	2519	113	111	224

[*]Cell entries are weighted N's; see beginning of Appendix C for description of analysis groups.

TABLE C-5-9[*]

EDUCATIONAL ATTAINMENT RELATED TO
IMPULSE TO AGGRESSION

Impulse to Aggression 1=Never 2=Seldom 3=Sometimes 4=Often 5=Almost always	Group 1 1	Group 2 2	Group 3 3	Unclassifieds 4	Total 5	Trackback Dropouts 6	Trackback Stayins 7	Total Trackbacks 8
1.00-1.50	26	118	151	27	322	8	13	21
1.51-2.00	41	171	219	37	468	13	22	35
2.01-2.50	69	223	261	41	594	30	29	59
2.51-3.00	63	172	212	52	499	16	21	37
3.01-3.50	55	95	106	38	294	16	7	23
3.51-5.00	55	102	64	40	261	18	15	33
Missing Data	17	42	13	9	81	12	4	16
Total	326	923	1026	244	2519	113	111	224

TABLE C-5-10[*]

EDUCATIONAL ATTAINMENT RELATED TO
DELINQUENT BEHAVIOR IN SCHOOL

Frequency of Delinquent Behavior 1=Never 2=Once 3=Twice 4=3-4 Times 5=5 or More Times	1	2	3	4	5	6	7	8
0.00-1.00	31	184	383	35	633	10	31	41
1.01-1.20	26	156	188	24	394	7	24	31
1.21-1.40	24	113	127	30	294	8	9	17
1.41-1.60	46	181	152	40	419	18	14	32
1.61-2.00	53	136	95	43	327	16	18	34
2.01-2.50	44	52	38	18	152	13	9	22
2.51-3.00	39	50	12	20	121	19	4	23
3.01-5.00	37	20	8	25	90	16	---	16
Missing Data	26	31	23	9	89	6	2	8
Total	326	923	1026	244	2519	113	111	224

[*]Cell entries are weighted N's; see beginning of Appendix C for description of analysis groups.

TABLE C-7-1*

CROSS-TIME SELF-ESTEEM SCORES
FOR THREE LEVELS OF EDUCATION

		DATA LIMITED TO THOSE WHO CONTINUED PARTICIPATION THROUGHOUT THE STUDY				DATA INCLUDING ALL PARTICIPANTS AVAILABLE AT TIME OF MEASUREMENT			
		1 TIME 1	2 TIME 2	3 TIME 3	4 TIME 4	5 TIME 1	6 TIME 2	7 TIME 3	
GROUP 1	$\overline{X}$	3.60	3.71	3.81	3.82	3.59	3.75	3.83	
	SD	.51	.50	.51	.52	.55	.51	.51	
	N(Wt'd)	177	146	175	176	322	224	210	
GROUP 2	$\overline{X}$	3.65	3.77	3.82	3.87	3.67	3.77	3.81	TIME 4 SAME AS COLUMN 4
	SD	.50	.48	.50	.49	.51	.49	.50	
	N(Wt'd)	727	704	723	717	918	834	805	
GROUP 3	$\overline{X}$	3.86	3.90	3.96	3.94	3.86	3.90	3.95	
	SD	.50	.46	.48	.48	.50	.46	.48	
	N(Wt'd)	945	927	948	938	1021	996	1025	
TOTAL	$\overline{X}$	3.75	3.83	3.89	3.90	3.75	3.83	3.89	
	SD	.51	.48	.49	.49	.52	.48	.50	
	N(Wt'd)	1849	1777	1846	1831	2261	2054	2040	
Eta		.22	.16	.14	.09	.21	.15	.14	

TABLE C-7-2A*

CROSS-TIME NEGATIVE AFFECTIVE STATES
FOR THREE LEVELS OF EDUCATION

		1 TIME 1	2 TIME 2	3 TIME 3	4 TIME 4	5 TIME 1	6 TIME 2	7 TIME 3	
GROUP 1	$\overline{X}$	2.80	2.62	2.62	2.58	2.78	2.60	2.60	
	SD	.57	.61	.57	.55	.55	.60	.57	
	N(Wt'd)	177	144	174	175	321	218	208	
GROUP 2	$\overline{X}$	2.65	2.59	2.59	2.50	2.64	2.59	2.58	TIME 4 SAME AS COLUMN 4
	SD	.57	.55	.55	.55	.55	.55	.55	
	N(Wt'd)	721	703	712	715	909	830	792	
GROUP 3	$\overline{X}$	2.55	2.52	2.49	2.48	2.55	2.52	2.49	
	SD	.52	.52	.52	.51	.52	.52	.52	
	N(Wt'd)	940	923	941	933	1016	991	1017	
TOTAL	$\overline{X}$	2.61	2.55	2.54	2.50	2.62	2.56	2.54	
	SD	.55	.54	.54	.53	.54	.54	.54	
	N(Wt'd)	1838	1770	1827	1823	2246	2039	2017	
Eta		.14	.07	.10	.06	.15	.07	.09	

---

*See beginning of Appendix C for description of analysis groups.

TABLE C-7-2B[*]

CROSS-TIME HAPPINESS FOR
THREE LEVELS OF EDUCATION

		DATA LIMITED TO THOSE WHO CONTINUED PARTICIPATION THROUGHOUT THE STUDY				DATA INCLUDING ALL PARTICIPANTS AVAILABLE AT TIME OF MEASUREMENT			
		1 TIME 1	2 TIME 2	3 TIME 3	4 TIME 4	5 TIME 1	6 TIME 2	7 TIME 3	
GROUP 1	$\overline{X}$	3.67	3.75	3.69	3.72	3.65	3.76	3.72	
	SD	.64	.60	.65	.61	.63	.60	.64	
	N(Wt'd)	177	144	177	176	322	222	212	
GROUP 2	$\overline{X}$	3.74	3.78	3.77	3.79	3.74	3.78	3.77	
	SD	.61	.61	.60	.60	.62	.63	.61	TIME 4 SAME AS COLUMN 4
	N(Wt'd)	727	707	724	715	918	835	805	
GROUP 3	$\overline{X}$	3.84	3.85	3.81	3.78	3.85	3.86	3.82	
	SD	.60	.57	.57	.59	.60	.57	.57	
	N(Wt'd)	945	927	948	938	1022	996	1025	
TOTAL	$\overline{X}$	3.78	3.82	3.79	3.78	3.78	3.82	3.79	
	SD	.61	.59	.59	.59	.62	.60	.59	
	N(Wt'd)	1849	1778	1849	1829	2262	2053	2042	
Eta		.10	.07	.06	.03	.11	.08	.06	

TABLE C-7-2C[*]

CROSS-TIME SOMATIC SYMPTOMS FOR
THREE LEVELS OF EDUCATION

		1 TIME 1	2 TIME 2	3 TIME 3	4 TIME 4	5 TIME 1	6 TIME 2	7 TIME 3	
GROUP 1	$\overline{X}$	2.39	2.28	2.30	2.35	2.36	2.25	2.27	
	SD	.70	.72	.68	.70	.66	.68	.69	
	N(Wt'd)	171	149	174	177	315	222	209	
GROUP 2	$\overline{X}$	2.20	2.19	2.16	2.11	2.17	2.17	2.18	
	SD	.63	.60	.58	.56	.62	.59	.58	TIME 4 SAME AS COLUMN 4
	N(Wt'd)	709	708	722	719	895	839	805	
GROUP 3	$\overline{X}$	2.00	1.99	2.03	2.01	2.02	1.99	2.03	
	SD	.50	.49	.48	.50	.51	.49	.48	
	N(Wt'd)	945	923	945	940	1020	994	1022	
TOTAL	$\overline{X}$	2.12	2.10	2.10	2.08	2.13	2.09	2.11	
	SD	.59	.57	.55	.56	.59	.56	.55	
	N(Wt'd)	1825	1780	1841	1836	2230	2055	2036	
Eta		.22	.19	.16	.18	.20	.18	.16	

[*]See beginning of Appendix C for description of analysis groups.

TABLE C-7-2D[*]

CROSS-TIME IMPULSE TO AGGRESSION SCORES FOR
THREE LEVELS OF EDUCATION

		DATA LIMITED TO THOSE WHO CONTINUED PARTICIPATION THROUGHOUT THE STUDY				DATA INCLUDING ALL PARTICIPANTS AVAILABLE AT TIME OF MEASUREMENT			
		1 TIME 1	2 TIME 2	3 TIME 3	4 TIME 4	5 TIME 1	6 TIME 2	7 TIME 3	
GROUP 1	$\overline{X}$ SD N(Wt'd)	2.80 .84 175	2.57 .75 139	2.48 .73 169	2.44 .68 172	2.79 .84 309	2.52 .74 207	2.44 .70 203	TIME 4 SAME AS COLUMN 4
GROUP 2	$\overline{X}$ SD N(Wt'd)	2.55 .83 694	2.45 .69 701	2.45 .70 701	2.28 .64 706	2.54 .83 881	2.46 .70 830	2.45 .70 780	
GROUP 3	$\overline{X}$ SD N(Wt'd)	2.41 .75 936	2.40 .63 920	2.46 .62 929	2.41 .60 932	2.42 .75 1013	2.39 .63 988	2.45 .63 1005	
TOTAL	$\overline{X}$ SD N(Wt'd)	2.50 .80 1805	2.43 .67 1760	2.46 .66 1799	2.36 .63 1810	2.52 .81 2203	2.43 .67 2025	2.45 .67 1988	
Eta		.15	.07	.01	.11	.15	.06	.01	

TABLE C-7-3A[*]

CROSS-TIME NEED FOR SELF-DEVELOPMENT FOR
THREE LEVELS OF EDUCATION

		1 TIME 1	2 TIME 2	3 TIME 3	4 TIME 4	5 TIME 1	6 TIME 2	7 TIME 3	
GROUP 1	$\overline{X}$ SD N(Wt'd)	3.51 .58 179	3.47 .59 144	3.51 .55 176	3.53 .60 176	3.53 .55 323	3.53 .56 220	3.54 .54 210	TIME 4 SAME AS COLUMN 4
GROUP 2	$\overline{X}$ SD N(Wt'd)	3.53 .51 724	3.54 .49 703	3.56 .49 717	3.61 .51 714	3.53 .51 914	3.54 .50 833	3.56 .48 798	
GROUP 3	$\overline{X}$ SD N(Wt'd)	3.75 .50 945	3.72 .47 926	3.72 .46 941	3.66 .47 936	3.75 .50 1021	3.73 .47 995	3.71 .46 1017	
TOTAL	$\overline{X}$ SD N(Wt'd)	3.64 .52 1848	3.63 .50 1773	3.64 .48 1834	3.63 .50 1826	3.63 .53 2258	3.63 .50 2048	3.63 .48 2025	
Eta		.22	.20	.18	.08	.21	.19	.16	

---

[*]See beginning of Appendix C for description of analysis groups.

TABLE C-7-3B[*]

CROSS-TIME NEED FOR SELF-UTILIZATION FOR
THREE LEVELS OF EDUCATION

		DATA LIMITED TO THOSE WHO CONTINUED PARTICIPATION THROUGHOUT THE STUDY				DATA INCLUDING ALL PARTICIPANTS AVAILABLE AT TIME OF MEASUREMENT			
		1 TIME 1	2 TIME 2	3 TIME 3	4 TIME 4	5 TIME 1	6 TIME 2	7 TIME 3	
GROUP 1	$\overline{X}$ SD N(Wt'd)	3.78 .55 179	3.66 .62 145	3.72 .63 177	3.63 .59 176	3.78 .56 326	3.70 .59 223	3.75 .62 212	
GROUP 2	$\overline{X}$ SD N(Wt'd)	3.77 .54 725	3.73 .51 707	3.77 .49 724	3.72 .52 716	3.78 .54 916	3.73 .51 837	3.76 .50 806	TIME 4 SAME AS COLUMN 4
GROUP 3	$\overline{X}$ SD N(Wt'd)	3.94 .47 946	3.88 .46 927	3.91 .46 948	3.78 .48 938	3.94 .48 1023	3.88 .46 996	3.90 .46 1025	
TOTAL	$\overline{X}$ SD N(Wt'd)	3.86 .51 1850	3.81 .50 1779	3.84 .48 1849	3.74 .51 1830	3.85 .52 2265	3.80 .50 2056	3.83 .50 2043	
Eta		.16	.17	.15	.09	.15	.16	.14	

TABLE C-7-4A[*]

CROSS-TIME SOCIAL VALUES SCORES FOR
THREE LEVELS OF EDUCATION

		1 TIME 1	2 TIME 2	3 TIME 3	4 TIME 4	5 TIME 1	6 TIME 2	7 TIME 3	
GROUP 1	$\overline{X}$ SD N(Wt'd)	4.50 .60 172	4.57 .55 150	4.63 .54 172	4.58 .54 175	4.53 .61 317	4.63 .53 227	4.64 .55 207	
GROUP 2	$\overline{X}$ SD N(Wt'd)	4.64 .58 705	4.72 .52 693	4.73 .50 722	4.74 .52 716	4.66 .57 894	4.72 .52 820	4.72 .51 803	TIME 4 SAME AS COLUMN 4
GROUP 3	$\overline{X}$ SD N(Wt'd)	4.81 .50 937	4.82 .45 920	4.77 .42 938	4.69 .46 936	4.81 .51 1013	4.82 .46 991	4.77 .44 1015	
TOTAL	$\overline{X}$ SD N(Wt'd)	4.72 .55 1814	4.76 .49 1763	4.74 .47 1832	4.70 .50 1827	4.71 .56 2224	4.76 .49 2038	4.74 .48 2025	
Eta		.19	.15	.09	.09	.18	.13	.08	

---

[*]See beginning of Appendix C for description of analysis groups.

TABLE C-7-4B*

CROSS-TIME ACADEMIC ACHIEVEMENT VALUE SCORES FOR
THREE LEVELS OF EDUCATION

		DATA LIMITED TO THOSE WHO CONTINUED PARTICIPATION THROUGHOUT THE STUDY				DATA INCLUDING ALL PARTICIPANTS AVAILABLE AT TIME OF MEASUREMENT			
		1 TIME 1	2 TIME 2	3 TIME 3	4 TIME 4	5 TIME 1	6 TIME 2	7 TIME 3	
GROUP 1	X̄	4.90	4.85	4.99	4.76	4.88	4.89	4.97	
	SD	.82	.87	.82	.77	.87	.81	.85	
	N(Wt'd)	167	148	167	174	305	225	200	
GROUP 2	X̄	5.04	4.95	4.93	4.86	5.06	4.96	4.93	TIME 4 SAME AS COLUMN 4
	SD	.78	.75	.73	.74	.78	.74	.73	
	N(Wt'd)	692	675	716	709	877	800	796	
GROUP 3	X̄	5.29	5.11	4.95	4.75	5.29	5.12	4.96	
	SD	.62	.65	.67	.71	.62	.65	.67	
	N(Wt'd)	921	909	930	928	992	979	1005	
TOTAL	X̄	5.16	5.03	4.94	4.79	5.14	5.03	4.95	
	SD	.72	.72	.71	.73	.74	.71	.71	
	N(Wt'd)	1780	1732	1813	1811	2174	2004	2001	
Eta		.20	.13	.02	.07	.20	.13	.02	

TABLE C-7-5A*

CROSS-TIME RELATIVE JOB AMBITION FOR
THREE LEVELS OF EDUCATION

		1 TIME 1	2 TIME 2	3 TIME 3	4 TIME 4	5 TIME 1	6 TIME 2	7 TIME 3	
GROUP 1	X̄	4.84	5.09	5.13	5.10	4.87	5.11	5.15	
	SD	.77	.79	.77	.80	.76	.74	.78	
	N(Wt'd)	175	146	176	176	321	221	209	
GROUP 2	X̄	4.97	5.24	5.26	5.27	4.99	5.23	5.24	TIME 4 SAME AS COLUMN 4
	SD	.69	.70	.69	.68	.71	.70	.71	
	N(Wt'd)	719	702	706	717	906	832	786	
GROUP 3	X̄	5.25	5.34	5.33	5.25	5.24	5.34	5.32	
	SD	.62	.61	.59	.59	.62	.61	.59	
	N(Wt'd)	937	923	932	934	1014	994	1009	
TOTAL	X̄	5.10	5.28	5.28	5.24	5.08	5.27	5.27	
	SD	.68	.66	.65	.65	.69	.67	.67	
	N(Wt'd)	1831	1771	1814	1827	2241	2047	2004	
Eta		.22	.11	.09	.08	.21	.11	.09	

*See beginning of Appendix C for description of analysis groups.

TABLE C-7-5B[*]

CROSS-TIME INTERNAL CONTROL SCORES FOR
THREE LEVELS OF EDUCATION

		DATA LIMITED TO THOSE WHO CONTINUED PARTICIPATION THROUGHOUT THE STUDY				DATA INCLUDING ALL PARTICIPANTS AVAILABLE AT TIME OF MEASUREMENT			
		1 TIME 1	2 TIME 2	3 TIME 3	4 TIME 4	5 TIME 1	6 TIME 2	7 TIME 3	
GROUP 1	X̄	1.59	1.63	1.66	1.67	1.61	1.65	1.67	
	SD	.19	.22	.19	.21	.19	.21	.19	TIME 4 SAME AS COLUMN 4
	N(Wt'd)	170	147	175	178	314	221	209	
GROUP 2	X̄	1.64	1.68	1.68	1.70	1.65	1.68	1.68	
	SD	.18	.20	.21	.21	.18	.20	.21	
	N(Wt'd)	714	707	722	714	899	833	805	
GROUP 3	X̄	1.70	1.73	1.73	1.72	1.69	1.71	1.72	
	SD	.19	.20	.20	.23	.20	.20	.21	
	N(Wt'd)	937	923	945	940	1012	994	1022	
TOTAL	X̄	1.66	1.70	1.70	1.71	1.66	1.70	1.70	
	SD	.19	.20	.21	.22	.19	.20	.21	
	N(Wt'd)	1821	1777	1842	1832	2225	2048	2036	
Eta		.18	.16	.12	.07	.16	.15	.11	

TABLE C-7-5C[*]

CROSS-TIME TRUST IN PEOPLE SCORES FOR
THREE LEVELS OF EDUCATION

		1 TIME 1	2 TIME 2	3 TIME 3	4 TIME 4	5 TIME 1	6 TIME 2	7 TIME 3	
GROUP 1	X̄	1.50	1.47	1.11	1.32	1.50	1.47	1.17	
	SD	1.02	1.17	1.11	1.17	1.05	1.17	1.14	TIME 4 SAME AS COLUMN 4
	N(Wt'd)	167	146	174	175	310	220	209	
GROUP 2	X̄	1.47	1.50	1.38	1.53	1.47	1.50	1.41	
	SD	1.08	1.11	1.17	1.17	1.08	1.14	1.17	
	N(Wt'd)	701	701	719	710	884	826	802	
GROUP 3	X̄	1.56	1.68	1.68	1.74	1.56	1.68	1.68	
	SD	1.14	1.20	1.20	1.23	1.14	1.20	1.20	
	N(Wt'd)	933	923	940	935	1007	993	1017	
TOTAL	X̄	1.53	1.59	1.50	1.62	1.53	1.59	1.53	
	SD	1.11	1.17	1.20	1.20	1.11	1.17	1.20	
	N(Wt'd)	1801	1770	1833	1820	2201	2039	2028	
Eta		.04	.08	.17	.11	.04	.08	.15	

[*] See beginning of Appendix C for description of analysis groups.

TABLE C-7-5D[*]

CROSS-TIME TRUST IN GOVERNMENT SCORES FOR
THREE LEVELS OF EDUCATION

		DATA LIMITED TO THOSE WHO CONTINUED PARTICIPATION THROUGHOUT THE STUDY				DATA INCLUDING ALL PARTICIPANTS AVAILABLE AT TIME OF MEASUREMENT			
		1 TIME 1	2 TIME 2	3 TIME 3	4 TIME 4	5 TIME 1	6 TIME 2	7 TIME 3	
GROUP 1	X̄	3.53	3.36	3.27	3.23	3.54	3.43	3.31	
	SD	.68	.73	.65	.64	.69	.69	.68	
	N(Wt'd)	172	148	175	177	317	224	210	TIME 4 COLUMN 4
GROUP 2	X̄	3.62	3.52	3.48	3.29	3.63	3.52	3.47	
	SD	.68	.62	.62	.62	.66	.62	.62	
	N(Wt'd)	711	711	720	713	900	837	803	SAME AS
GROUP 3	X̄	3.76	3.55	3.51	3.23	3.75	3.55	3.51	
	SD	.62	.60	.57	.59	.63	.60	.56	
	N(Wt'd)	936	924	944	934	1010	994	1021	
TOTAL	X̄	3.68	3.52	3.48	3.26	3.67	3.53	3.47	
	SD	.65	.62	.60	.61	.66	.62	.60	
	N(Wt'd)	1819	1783	1839	1824	2227	2055	2034	
Eta		.12	.08	.11	.05	.12	.06	.10	

TABLE C-7-6A[*]

CROSS-TIME FREQUENCY OF DELINQUENT BEHAVIOR FOR
THREE LEVELS OF EDUCATION

		1 TIME 1	2 TIME 2	3 TIME 3	4 TIME 4	5 TIME 1	6 TIME 2	7 TIME 3	
GROUP 1	X̄	1.86	1.78	1.79	1.88	1.90	1.80	1.78	
	SD	.72	.71	.62	.71	.72	.68	.61	TIME 4 COLUMN 4
	N(Wt'd)	163	149	177	167	301	224	212	
GROUP 2	X̄	1.61	1.58	1.61	1.69	1.60	1.57	1.61	
	SD	.56	.55	.52	.56	.55	.55	.53	SAME AS
	N(Wt'd)	701	708	726	679	892	836	809	
GROUP 3	X̄	1.51	1.44	1.47	1.57	1.51	1.45	1.47	
	SD	.46	.48	.41	.44	.46	.49	.41	
	N(Wt'd)	930	924	943	940	1005	995	1020	
TOTAL	X̄	1.58	1.52	1.55	1.64	1.60	1.54	1.56	
	SD	.54	.54	.49	.53	.56	.55	.49	
	N(Wt'd)	1794	1781	1846	1786	2198	2055	2041	
Eta		.19	.19	.21	.18	.23	.20	.21	

[*]See beginning of Appendix C for description of analysis groups.

TABLE C-7-6B[*]

CROSS-TIME SERIOUSNESS OF DELINQUENCY FOR
THREE LEVELS OF EDUCATION

		DATA LIMITED TO THOSE WHO CONTINUED PARTICIPATION THROUGHOUT THE STUDY				DATA INCLUDING ALL PARTICIPANTS AVAILABLE AT TIME OF MEASUREMENT			
		1 TIME 1	2 TIME 2	3 TIME 3	4 TIME 4	5 TIME 1	6 TIME 2	7 TIME 3	
GROUP 1	X̄	1.58	1.55	1.50	1.58	1.60	1.51	1.46	TIME 4 SAME AS COLUMN 4
	SD	.69	.76	.66	.74	.72	.69	.64	
	N(Wt'd)	163	149	177	167	300	224	212	
GROUP 2	X̄	1.39	1.32	1.32	1.36	1.38	1.32	1.33	
	SD	.47	.51	.49	.52	.46	.50	.51	
	N(Wt'd)	701	708	726	679	891	836	809	
GROUP 3	X̄	1.30	1.22	1.21	1.27	1.30	1.22	1.21	
	SD	.38	.38	.35	.37	.38	.40	.35	
	N(Wt'd)	929	924	943	940	1004	995	1020	
TOTAL	X̄	1.36	1.28	1.28	1.33	1.37	1.29	1.29	
	SD	.46	.48	.45	.48	.48	.49	.46	
	N(Wt'd)	1793	1781	1846	1786	2195	2055	2041	
Eta		.18	.19	.19	.19	.21	.18	.18	

TABLE C-7-6C[*]

CROSS-TIME INTERPERSONAL AGGRESSION FOR
THREE LEVELS OF EDUCATION

		1 TIME 1	2 TIME 2	3 TIME 3	4 TIME 4	5 TIME 1	6 TIME 2	7 TIME 3	
GROUP 1	X̄	1.85	1.47	1.46	1.50	1.87	1.48	1.45	TIME 4 SAME AS COLUMN 4
	SD	.72	.64	.59	.70	.74	.63	.58	
	N(Wt'd)	162	149	176	167	299	224	211	
GROUP 2	X̄	1.55	1.29	1.27	1.31	1.54	1.28	1.28	
	SD	.58	.49	.46	.51	.57	.47	.48	
	N(Wt'd)	700	708	726	678	890	835	809	
GROUP 3	X̄	1.38	1.15	1.11	1.13	1.38	1.15	1.12	
	SD	.41	.33	.27	.27	.40	.35	.27	
	N(Wt'd)	929	924	943	940	1004	995	1020	
TOTAL	X̄	1.49	1.23	1.21	1.23	1.51	1.24	1.21	
	SD	.53	.44	.41	.45	.55	.46	.42	
	N(Wt'd)	1791	1781	1845	1785	2193	2054	2040	
Eta		.26	.22	.27	.27	.29	.23	.26	

---

[*]See beginning of Appendix C for description of analysis groups.

TABLE C-7-6D*

CROSS-TIME DELINQUENT BEHAVIOR IN SCHOOL FOR
THREE LEVELS OF EDUCATION

		DATA LIMITED TO THOSE WHO CONTINUED PARTICIPATION THROUGHOUT THE STUDY				DATA INCLUDING ALL PARTICIPANTS AVAILABLE AT TIME OF MEASUREMENT			
		1 TIME 1	2 TIME 2	3 TIME 3	4 TIME 4	5 TIME 1	6 TIME 2	7 TIME 3	
GROUP 1	X̄ SD N(Wt'd)	1.96 .84 162	2.05 .83 149	2.11 .73 177	2.29 .59 177	2.00 .85 300	2.09 .79 223	2.09 .74 212	
GROUP 2	X̄ SD N(Wt'd)	1.53 .59 701	1.64 .64 708	1.71 .62 726	2.09 .56 716	1.52 .58 892	1.63 .64 835	1.72 .64 809	TIME 4 SAME AS COLUMN 4
GROUP 3	X̄ SD N(Wt'd)	1.30 .40 928	1.30 .46 923	1.37 .46 943	1.91 .46 946	1.30 .41 1003	1.31 .48 994	1.38 .46 1020	
TOTAL	X̄ SD N(Wt'd)	1.45 .56 1791	1.50 .62 1780	1.57 .61 1846	2.02 .53 1839	1.49 .60 2195	1.53 .64 2052	1.59 .61 2041	
Eta		.35	.37	.39	.24	.38	.39	.38	

TABLE C-7-7A*

CROSS-TIME JOB INFORMATION TEST SCORES FOR
THREE LEVELS OF EDUCATION

		1 TIME 1	2 TIME 2	3 TIME 3	4 TIME 4	5 TIME 1	6 TIME 2	7 TIME 3	
GROUP 1	X̄ SD N(Wt'd)	15.28 3.65 178	15.70 4.64 152	16.70 3.74 177	16.64 4.28 179	15.48 3.65 325	15.94 4.62 230	16.81 3.73 212	
GROUP 2	X̄ SD N(Wt'd)	16.05 3.26 727	16.98 3.47 714	17.58 3.68 729	18.21 3.83 729	16.10 3.26 918	17.02 3.48 845	17.50 3.76 812	TIME 4 SAME AS COLUMN 4
GROUP 3	X̄ SD N(Wt'd)	17.87 3.00 943	18.92 3.08 930	19.82 2.79 948	20.42 3.13 949	17.82 2.99 1020	18.84 3.16 1001	19.74 2.86 1025	
TOTAL	X̄ SD N(Wt'd)	16.90 3.32 1848	17.88 3.57 1796	18.64 3.48 1854	19.19 3.78 1857	16.79 3.34 2263	17.78 3.64 2076	18.55 3.55 2049	
Eta		.30	.32	.35	.35	.29	.30	.34	

---

*See beginning of Appendix C for description of analysis groups.

TABLE C-7-7B[*]

CROSS-TIME POLITICAL KNOWLEDGE TEST SCORES FOR
THREE LEVELS OF EDUCATION

		DATA LIMITED TO THOSE WHO CONTINUED PARTICIPATION THROUGHOUT THE STUDY				DATA INCLUDING ALL PARTICIPANTS AVAILABLE AT TIME OF MEASUREMENT			
		1 TIME 1	2 TIME 2	3 TIME 3	4 TIME 4	5 TIME 1	6 TIME 2	7 TIME 3	
GROUP 1	X̄	1.79	1.54	1.17	1.30	1.86	1.58	1.18	
	SD	1.23	1.02	.82	.93	1.26	1.01	.81	
	N(Wt'd)	171	155	178	179	312	233	213	TIME 4 SAME AS COLUMN 4
GROUP 2	X̄	2.34	2.03	1.80	1.82	2.35	2.06	1.82	
	SD	1.36	1.08	1.07	1.12	1.36	1.10	1.08	
	N(Wt'd)	712	714	729	729	900	845	812	
GROUP 3	X̄	3.20	2.80	2.54	2.72	3.18	2.79	2.53	
	SD	1.42	1.23	1.36	1.38	1.41	1.22	1.36	
	N(Wt'd)	935	930	948	949	1010	1001	1025	
TOTAL	X̄	2.73	2.39	2.12	2.23	2.66	2.36	2.11	
	SD	1.47	1.24	1.29	1.35	1.46	1.23	1.29	
	N(Wt'd)	1818	1799	1855	1857	2222	2079	2050	
Eta		.35	.36	.36	.39	.34	.36	.36	

TABLE C-7-8A[*]

CROSS-TIME OCCUPATIONAL ASPIRATIONS FOR
THREE LEVELS OF EDUCATION

		1 TIME 1	2 TIME 2	3 TIME 3	4 TIME 4	5 TIME 1	6 TIME 2	7 TIME 3	
GROUP 1	X̄	48.41	42.81	40.03	38.50	47.89	42.52	40.29	
	SD	27.32	24.45	23.62	21.58	27.62	23.62	23.59	
	N(Wt'd)	133	128	129	161	252	189	151	TIME 4 SAME AS COLUMN 4
GROUP 2	X̄	53.19	48.53	45.85	44.95	54.13	48.62	45.68	
	SD	27.07	23.72	23.83	23.44	27.00	23.67	23.83	
	N(Wt'd)	534	556	596	637	669	653	660	
GROUP 3	X̄	71.31	70.01	69.91	69.32	70.93	69.58	69.43	
	SD	21.34	20.61	18.86	18.97	21.68	20.76	19.04	
	N(Wt'd)	745	780	832	872	803	835	899	
TOTAL	X̄	62.30	59.48	58.22	57.05	61.04	58.37	57.69	
	SD	26.06	24.91	24.74	24.69	26.49	24.96	24.76	
	N(Wt'd)	1412	1464	1557	1670	1724	1677	1710	
Eta		.37	.46	.51	.53	.36	.45	.50	

---

[*]See beginning of Appendix C for description of analysis groups.

TABLE C-7-8B[*]

CROSS-TIME COLLEGE PLANS[**] FOR
THREE LEVELS OF EDUCATION

		DATA LIMITED TO THOSE WHO CONTINUED PARTICIPATION THROUGHOUT THE STUDY				DATA INCLUDING ALL PARTICIPANTS AVAILABLE AT TIME OF MEASUREMENT			
		1 TIME 1	2 TIME 2	3 TIME 3	4 TIME 4	5 TIME 1	6 TIME 2	7 TIME 3	
GROUP 1	$\overline{X}$	.37	.36	.05		.39	.32	.04	
	SD	.49	.48	.22		.49	.47	.21	
	N(Wt'd)	179	155	172	NOT MEASURED AT TIME 4	326	233	205	TIME 4 SAME AS COLUMN 4
GROUP 2	$\overline{X}$	.44	.47	.23		.45	.45	.21	
	SD	.50	.50	.42		.50	.50	.41	
	N(Wt'd)	729	714	725		923	845	807	
GROUP 3	$\overline{X}$	.80	.84	.85		.79	.84	.86	
	SD	.40	.37	.36		.41	.36	.35	
	N(Wt'd)	949	930	948		1026	1001	1025	
TOTAL	$\overline{X}$	.62	.65	.53		.60	.63	.52	
	SD	.49	.48	.50		.49	.48	.50	
	N(Wt'd)	1857	1799	1845		2275	2079	2037	
Eta		.38	.41	.66		.37	.44	.69	

---

[*] See beginning of Appendix C for description of analysis groups.

[**] Coded so that 1=planning to go to college and 0=not planning to go to college

Appendix D
DROPOUTS WITH DIPLOMAS

This appendix presents a comparison between those dropouts who had obtained high school diplomas by mid-1970 and those who had not. Our primary reason for placing this information in an appendix rather than in the text is that the number of "dropouts with diplomas" is so small that we can view their data as only suggestive -- they represent, collectively, a sort of case study.

In Chapter 2 we defined several kinds of dropout categories. Some dropouts continued their participation in the study while others did not. Among those who did continue through the last data collection, a total of 32 respondents reported that they had returned to school or in some other manner had acquired a diploma after earlier dropping out. As we indicated in Chapter 2, any distinction between dropouts with and without diplomas is linked to a specific point in time. In the present instance, we are able to focus upon those dropouts who had acquired a diploma sometime within a year of the time they would have graduated if they had continued in school on a "non-stop" basis. Perhaps a later follow-up of the Youth in Transition panel will be able to examine those who attained a diploma within four or five years of the expected time of high school graduation.

The 32 respondents who dropped out but soon afterwards attained diplomas were, from the start of the study, somewhat different from the group of "dropouts without diplomas." Table D presents mean test scores and family background characteristics for the two dropout subgroups, and also for the three major analysis groups examined throughout this monograph. The dropouts who later obtained diplomas came from higher SEL families, on the average, than did other dropouts -- indeed their SEL averaged somewhat higher than those "regular" high school graduates who did not go on to college (Group 2).

The picture for test scores bears some resemblance to that for SEL, but it is more complicated. Quick Test scores for dropouts with diplomas averaged somewhat higher than those for Group 2. However, on the other tests the dropout with diploma group averaged the same as or slightly below those in Group 2. The pattern is one of scholastic underachievement; dropouts with diplomas were above the average for other non-college high school graduates when it came to intelligence, but they were only average when it came to vocabulary and reading skill.

If we were to limit our consideration to SEL and ability, we would conclude that the dropouts who later attained diplomas were not so different from those who went straight through high school

225

TABLE D

BACKGROUND AND ABILITY CHARACTERISTICS OF
DROPOUT GROUPS AND OTHERS

	Sub-group 1a	Sub-group 1b	Group 1	Group 2	Group 3
	Dropouts with diplomas (32)	Dropouts without diplomas (125)	All dropouts (286)	Graduates, no college (796)	College entrants (914)
FAMILY BACKGROUND					
Socio-economic level	4.93	4.56	4.60	4.76	5.34
Parental punitiveness	2.60	2.56	2.58	2.39	2.21
INTELLECTUAL SKILLS					
Quick test	110.15	100.40	103.55	105.93	113.00
GATB-J test of vocabulary	16.12	13.72	14.90	17.25	21.95
Gates reading test	34.47	31.73	32.89	34.99	38.44

NOTES: Table entries are mean scores. Subgroups 1a and 1b include only individuals who continued their participation through all four data collections. Groups 1, 2, and 3 include all participants who could be classified. See Chapter 2 for descriptions of analysis groups. See Table 6-1 for further data, including standard deviations and scores for the total sample.

but did not enter college (Group 2), except that dropouts with diplomas were actually a bit more advantaged in terms of intelligence
and family SEL. But when we turn to the set of dimensions which
most clearly differentiates dropouts in general from stayins, we
find dropouts with diplomas very similar to dropouts without diplomas. The delinquent behavior dimensions, presented in Tables
D-14 through D-17, show that the two dropout groups differed very
little from each other; and what differences there were showed
slightly higher delinquency for the dropouts who later attained
diplomas. Here as in our other analyses of delinquency, we find the
differences to be consistent over time. Getting a diploma did not
seem to lead to a sharp reduction in level of reported delinquency,
for dropouts with diplomas remained highly delinquent throughout the
study.

The two types of dropouts are similar also in terms of parental
punitiveness. This probably reflects the similarities in delinquent
behaviors -- parents of delinquent boys tend to be more punitive.

The above findings represent the clearest and most consistent
conclusions we have reached in this effort to contrast dropouts with
diplomas and those without diplomas. Additional data are presented
in the tables which follow. These tables parallel those in
Appendix C, specifically those corresponding to the figures in
Chapter 7. Thus by cross-matching the two sets of tables, it is
possible to contrast Subgroups 1a and 1b with Groups 1, 2, and 3
(as was done in Table D above).

We leave it to the interested reader to make detailed examina-
tions of the data, but a few general observations are in order.
The dropouts who later gained diplomas showed some signs of moderate
"improvement" along a number of dimensions: self-esteem, negative
affective states, happiness, physical symptoms, needs for self-
development and self-utilization, social values, and ambitious job
attitudes. Occupational aspirations and college plans, on the
other hand, showed a more marked drop than was the case for dropouts
in general or for graduates who did not go on to college (Group 2).
The drop in aspirations is not surprising. Given a group of fairly
bright young men from at least average SEL homes, we might expect
initially high aspirations; and given that they later dropped out
of high school and did not enter college, we could also expect a
lowering of aspiration levels. The "improvement" along attitude,
value, and affective states dimensions, on the other hand, represents a possible result of the sequence of experiences involving
dropping out and then later acquiring a diploma. This explanation
is plausible, and in some ways rather tempting. However, the
reader who examines the following tables in some detail will
recognize some of the reasons why we have been cautious about such
a conclusion. The changes are not especially large, and given the
small number of cases we cannot claim that the changes are statistically significant. Moreover, the pattern of change across time
is seldom steady and sometimes involves irregular up-and-down
movement; this adds to our suspicion that the picture is a rather

"noisy" one, due to the small number of cases in the dropouts with diplomas category.

Perhaps the most appropriate conclusion we can reach here is that dropouts who later acquire diplomas represent a very interesting subgroup for further study (with larger samples). We are very cautious about the apparent changes which have occurred in our small group of dropouts with diplomas, and thus have not laid much stress on these data. On the other hand, the pattern of background characteristics, test scores, and delinquency is stronger and more consistent. We find here, as we have throughout the monograph, that delinquent behavior and parental punitiveness are predictive of dropping out. But some dropouts are above average in intelligence (although somewhat underachieving when it comes to more specific academic skills), and these are the dropouts who are likely later to return to school or obtain a diploma in some other manner.

TABLE D-1

CROSS-TIME SELF-ESTEEM SCORES
FOR DROPOUTS WITH DIPLOMAS AND
DROPOUTS WITHOUT DIPLOMAS

		TIME 1	TIME 2	TIME 3	TIME 4
DROPOUTS WITH DIPLOMAS	$\overline{X}$	3.75	3.75	3.89	4.06
	SD	.55	.49	.54	.46
	N(Wt'd)	33	29	32	31
DROPOUTS WITHOUT DIPLOMAS	$\overline{X}$	3.56	3.69	3.79	3.77
	SD	.50	.51	.50	.52
	N(Wt'd)	144	117	143	145

TABLE D-2

CROSS-TIME NEGATIVE AFFECTIVE STATES
FOR DROPOUTS WITH DIPLOMAS AND
DROPOUTS WITHOUT DIPLOMAS

		TIME 1	TIME 2	TIME 3	TIME 4
DROPOUTS WITH DIPLOMAS	$\overline{X}$	2.70	2.61	2.55	2.43
	SD	.66	.67	.62	.49
	N(Wt'd)	33	29	32	31
DROPOUTS WITHOUT DIPLOMAS	$\overline{X}$	2.82	2.62	2.64	2.61
	SD	.55	.60	.56	.56
	N(Wt'd)	144	115	142	144

TABLE D-3

CROSS-TIME HAPPINESS
FOR DROPOUTS WITH DIPLOMAS AND
DROPOUTS WITHOUT DIPLOMAS

		TIME 1	TIME 2	TIME 3	TIME 4
DROPOUTS	X̄	3.62	3.56	3.59	3.86
WITH	SD	.72	.61	.63	.53
DIPLOMAS	N(Wt'd)	33	29	32	31
DROPOUTS	X̄	3.68	3.80	3.71	3.69
WITHOUT	SD	.62	.60	.66	.62
DIPLOMAS	N(Wt'd)	144	115	145	145

TABLE D-4

CROSS-TIME SOMATIC SYMPTOMS
FOR DROPOUTS WITH DIPLOMAS AND
DROPOUTS WITHOUT DIPLOMAS

		TIME 1	TIME 2	TIME 3	TIME 4
DROPOUTS	X̄	2.46	2.15	2.25	2.21
WITH	SD	.74	.61	.66	.64
DIPLOMAS	N(Wt'd)	32	29	31	33
DROPOUTS	X̄	2.38	2.32	2.31	2.38
WITHOUT	SD	.69	.74	.69	.71
DIPLOMAS	N(Wt'd)	139	120	143	144

TABLE D-5

CROSS-TIME IMPULSE TO AGGRESSION SCORES
FOR DROPOUTS WITH DIPLOMAS AND
DROPOUTS WITHOUT DIPLOMAS

		TIME 1	TIME 2	TIME 3	TIME 4
DROPOUTS WITH DIPLOMAS	$\overline{X}$	2.84	2.63	2.54	2.38
	SD	.92	.73	.65	.78
	N(Wt'd)	32	28	32	31
DROPOUTS WITHOUT DIPLOMAS	$\overline{X}$	2.79	2.55	2.46	2.46
	SD	.83	.75	.74	.66
	N(Wt'd)	143	111	137	141

TABLE D-6

CROSS-TIME NEED FOR SELF-DEVELOPMENT
FOR DROPOUTS WITH DIPLOMAS AND
DROPOUTS WITHOUT DIPLOMAS

		TIME 1	TIME 2	TIME 3	TIME 4
DROPOUTS WITH DIPLOMAS	$\overline{X}$	3.54	3.36	3.62	3.69
	SD	.64	.47	.53	.53
	N(Wt'd)	33	29	32	31
DROPOUTS WITHOUT DIPLOMAS	$\overline{X}$	3.50	3.50	3.48	3.49
	SD	.56	.61	.55	.61
	N(Wt'd)	146	115	144	145

YOUTH IN TRANSITION

TABLE D-7

CROSS-TIME NEED FOR SELF-UTILIZATION
FOR DROPOUTS WITH DIPLOMAS AND
DROPOUTS WITHOUT DIPLOMAS

		TIME 1	TIME 2	TIME 3	TIME 4
DROPOUTS	X̄	3.79	3.51	3.75	3.74
WITH	SD	.56	.54	.50	.57
DIPLOMAS	N(Wt'd)	33	29	32	31
DROPOUTS	X̄	3.77	3.70	3.72	3.61
WITHOUT	SD	.55	.63	.66	.60
DIPLOMAS	N(Wt'd)	146	116	145	145

TABLE D-8

CROSS-TIME SOCIAL VALUES SCORES
FOR DROPOUTS WITH DIPLOMAS AND
DROPOUTS WITHOUT DIPLOMAS

		TIME 1	TIME 2	TIME 3	TIME 4
DROPOUTS	X̄	4.40	4.39	4.69	4.66
WITH	SD	.55	.51	.55	.58
DIPLOMAS	N(Wt'd)	31	30	31	33
DROPOUTS	X̄	4.52	4.61	4.62	4.56
WITHOUT	SD	.61	.56	.54	.54
DIPLOMAS	N(Wt'd)	141	120	141	142

TABLE D-9

CROSS-TIME ACADEMIC ACHIEVEMENT VALUE
FOR DROPOUTS WITH DIPLOMAS AND
DROPOUTS WITHOUT DIPLOMAS

		TIME 1	TIME 2	TIME 3	TIME 4
DROPOUTS	$\overline{X}$	4.85	4.57	4.90	4.73
WITH	SD	.83	.92	.76	.72
DIPLOMAS	N(Wt'd)	30	29	31	32
DROPOUTS	$\overline{X}$	4.91	4.91	5.01	4.77
WITHOUT	SD	.82	.85	.84	.78
DIPLOMAS	N(Wt'd)	137	119	136	121

TABLE D-10

CROSS-TIME RELATIVE JOB AMBITION
FOR DROPOUTS WITH DIPLOMAS AND
DROPOUTS WITHOUT DIPLOMAS

		TIME 1	TIME 2	TIME 3	TIME 4
DROPOUTS	$\overline{X}$	4.94	5.03	5.12	5.28
WITH	SD	.71	.60	.66	.72
DIPLOMAS	N(Wt'd)	32	29	31	33
DROPOUTS	$\overline{X}$	4.82	5.11	5.14	5.05
WITHOUT	SD	.78	.83	.80	.82
DIPLOMAS	N(Wt'd)	143	117	145	143

TABLE D-11

CROSS-TIME INTERNAL CONTROL SCORES
FOR DROPOUTS WITH DIPLOMAS AND
DROPOUTS WITHOUT DIPLOMAS

		TIME 1	TIME 2	TIME 3	TIME 4
DROPOUTS	$\overline{X}$	1.61	1.60	1.68	1.67
WITH	SD	.20	.24	.20	.24
DIPLOMAS	N(Wt'd)	32	29	31	33
DROPOUTS	$\overline{X}$	1.59	1.64	1.66	1.67
WITHOUT	SD	.18	.21	.19	.20
DIPLOMAS	N(Wt'd)	138	118	144	145

TABLE D-12

CROSS-TIME TRUST IN PEOPLE SCORES
FOR DROPOUTS WITH DIPLOMAS AND
DROPOUTS WITHOUT DIPLOMAS

		TIME 1	TIME 2	TIME 3	TIME 4
DROPOUTS	$\overline{X}$	1.62	1.32	.99	1.41
WITH	SD	.99	1.20	1.08	1.32
DIPLOMAS	N(Wt'd)	32	28	31	33
DROPOUTS	$\overline{X}$	1.47	1.50	1.14	1.29
WITHOUT	SD	1.02	1.17	1.11	1.14
DIPLOMAS	N(Wt'd)	135	118	143	142

TABLE D-13

CROSS-TIME TRUST IN GOVERNMENT SCORES
FOR DROPOUTS WITH DIPLOMAS AND
DROPOUTS WITHOUT DIPLOMAS

		TIME 1	TIME 2	TIME 3	TIME 4
DROPOUTS WITH DIPLOMAS	$\overline{X}$	3.46	3.20	3.28	3.26
	SD	.74	.80	.57	.62
	N(Wt'd)	32	29	31	33
DROPOUTS WITHOUT DIPLOMAS	$\overline{X}$	3.55	3.41	3.27	3.23
	SD	.67	.71	.67	.65
	N(Wt'd)	140	119	144	144

TABLE D-14

CROSS-TIME FREQUENCY OF DELINQUENT BEHAVIOR
FOR DROPOUTS WITH DIPLOMAS AND
DROPOUTS WITHOUT DIPLOMAS

		TIME 1	TIME 2	TIME 3	TIME 4
DROPOUTS WITH DIPLOMAS	$\overline{X}$	2.02	1.95	1.82	1.94
	SD	.60	.68	.56	.54
	N(Wt'd)	32	29	32	29
DROPOUTS WITHOUT DIPLOMAS	$\overline{X}$	1.82	1.74	1.79	1.86
	SD	.75	.71	.63	.74
	N(Wt'd)	131	120	145	138

TABLE D-15

CROSS-TIME SERIOUSNESS OF DELINQUENCY
FOR DROPOUTS WITH DIPLOMAS AND
DROPOUTS WITHOUT DIPLOMAS

		TIME 1	TIME 2	TIME 3	TIME 4
DROPOUTS	X̄	1.64	1.63	1.54	1.67
WITH	SD	.58	.57	.52	.81
DIPLOMAS	N(Wt'd)	32	29	32	29
DROPOUTS	X̄	1.57	1.53	1.49	1.56
WITHOUT	SD	.72	.80	.69	.72
DIPLOMAS	N(Wt'd)	131	120	124	138

TABLE D-16

CROSS-TIME INTERPERSONAL AGGRESSION
FOR DROPOUTS WITH DIPLOMAS AND
DROPOUTS WITHOUT DIPLOMAS

		TIME 1	TIME 2	TIME 3	TIME 4
DROPOUTS	X̄	1.94	1.46	1.45	1.46
WITH	SD	.67	.48	.51	.67
DIPLOMAS	N(Wt'd)	32	29	32	29
DROPOUTS	X̄	1.82	1.47	1.47	1.51
WITHOUT	SD	.74	.67	.61	.71
DIPLOMAS	N(Wt'd)	130	120	144	138

TABLE D-17

CROSS-TIME DELINQUENT BEHAVIOR IN SCHOOL
FOR DROPOUTS WITH DIPLOMAS AND
DROPOUTS WITHOUT DIPLOMAS

		TIME 1	TIME 2	TIME 3	TIME 4
DROPOUTS WITH DIPLOMAS	X̄	2.12	2.25	2.10	
	SD	.83	.67	.71	
	N(Wt'd)	32	29	32	NOT MEASURED AT TIME 4
DROPOUTS WITHOUT DIPLOMAS	X̄	1.93	2.00	2.11	
	SD	.84	.86	.74	
	N(Wt'd)	130	120	145	

TABLE D-18

CROSS-TIME JOB INFORMATION TEST SCORES
FOR DROPOUTS WITH DIPLOMAS AND
DROPOUTS WITHOUT DIPLOMAS

		TIME 1	TIME 2	TIME 3	TIME 4
DROPOUTS WITH DIPLOMAS	X̄	16.24	16.47	17.88	18.00
	SD	3.79	5.55	3.91	3.98
	N(Wt'd)	33	30	32	33
DROPOUTS WITHOUT DIPLOMAS	X̄	15.06	15.52	16.43	16.33
	SD	3.60	4.40	3.66	4.29
	N(Wt'd)	145	122	145	146

TABLE D-19

CROSS-TIME POLITICAL KNOWLEDGE TEST SCORES
FOR DROPOUTS WITH DIPLOMAS AND
DROPOUTS WITHOUT DIPLOMAS

		TIME 1	TIME 2	TIME 3	TIME 4
DROPOUTS	$\overline{X}$	2.16	1.93	1.63	1.76
WITH	SD	1.32	1.11	1.04	1.06
DIPLOMAS	N(Wt'd)	31	30	32	33
DROPOUTS	$\overline{X}$	1.71	1.45	1.08	1.19
WITHOUT	SD	1.20	.97	.74	.87
DIPLOMAS	N(Wt'd)	140	125	146	146

TABLE D-20

CROSS-TIME OCCUPATIONAL ASPIRATIONS
FOR DROPOUTS WITH DIPLOMAS AND
DROPOUTS WITHOUT DIPLOMAS

		TIME 1	TIME 2	TIME 3	TIME 4
DROPOUTS	$\overline{X}$	66.09	50.08	45.11	47.90
WITH	SD	23.00	26.22	25.04	22.72
DIPLOMAS	N(Wt'd)	22	24	28	31
DROPOUTS	$\overline{X}$	44.91	41.14	38.62	36.26
WITHOUT	SD	26.84	23.85	23.15	20.77
DIPLOMAS	N(Wt'd)	111	104	101	112

TABLE D-21

CROSS-TIME COLLEGE PLANS[*]
FOR DROPOUTS WITH DIPLOMAS AND
DROPOUTS WITHOUT DIPLOMAS

		TIME 1	TIME 2	TIME 3	TIME 4
DROPOUTS WITH DIPLOMAS	$\overline{X}$	.52	.53	.13	NOT MEASURED AT TIME 4
	SD	.51	.51	.35	
	N(Wt'd)	33	30	30	
DROPOUTS WITHOUT DIPLOMAS	$\overline{X}$	.34	.32	.04	
	SD	.48	.47	.19	
	N(Wt'd)	146	125	142	

---

[*]Coded so that 1=planning to go to college and 0=not planning to go
to college

BIBLIOGRAPHY

Ammons, R. B. and Ammons, C. H. The Quick Test (QT): provisional manual. *Psychological Reports*, 1962, 11, (Monograph Supplement 7-VII).

Andrews, F. M., Morgan, J. N., and Sonquist, J. A. *Multiple classification analysis, a report on a computer program for multiple regression using categorical predictors.* Ann Arbor: Survey Research Center, Institute for Social Research, 1969.

Bachman, J. G., Kahn, R. L., Mednick, M. T., Davidson, T. N., and Johnston, L. D. *Youth in transition, volume I: blueprint for a longitudinal study of adolescent boys.* Ann Arbor: Survey Research Center, Institute for Social Research, 1967.

Bachman, J. G. *Youth in transition, volume II: the impact of family background and intelligence on tenth-grade boys.* Ann Arbor: Survey Research Center, Institute for Social Research, 1970.

Bachman, J. G. and vanDuinen, E. *Youth look at national problems: a special report.* Ann Arbor: Survey Research Center, Institute for Social Research, 1971.

Beinstock, H. Realities of the job market for the high school dropout. In Schreiber, D. (Ed.), *Profile of the school dropout.* New York: Vantage Books, 1967.

Bledsoe, L. C. An investigation of correlates of student withdrawal from high school. *Journal of Educational Research*, 1959, 53, 1-6.

Campbell, A. and Schuman, H. *Racial attitudes in fifteen American cities.* Ann Arbor: Survey Research Center, Institute for Social Research, 1968.

Cervantes, L. *The dropout: causes and cures.* Ann Arbor: The University of Michigan Press, 1965.

Cobb, S., Brooks, G. H., Kasl, S. U. and Connelly, W. E. The health of people changing jobs: a description of a longitudinal study. *American Journal of Public Health*, 1966, 56, 1476-1481.

Coleman, J. S., Campbell, E. Q., Hobson, C. J., McPartland, J., Mood, A. S., Weinfeld, F. D., and York, R. L. *Equality of educational opportunity.* Washington, D.C.: U. S. Government Printing Office, 1966.

241

Combs, J. and Cooley, W. W. Dropouts: in high school and after school. *American Educational Research Journal,* 1968, 5, 343-363.

Coopersmith, S. *The antecedents of self-esteem.* San Francisco: W. H. Freeman and Co., 1967.

Dentler, R. S. and Warshauer, M. E. *Big city dropouts and illiterates.* New York: Frederick A. Proeger, 1968.

Festinger, L. *Theory of cognitive dissonance.* Stanford: Stanford University Press, 1957.

Frankel, M. R. *Inference from survey samples: an empirical investigation.* Ann Arbor: Survey Research Center, Institute for Social Research, 1971.

Gates, A. I. *Gates Reading Survey—Form 1.* New York: Teachers College, Columbia University, 1958.

Gold, M. Undetected delinquent behavior. *Journal of Research in Crime and Delinquency,* 1966, 3, 27-46.

Goodman, P. The universal trap. In Schreiber, D. (Ed.), *Profile of the school dropout.* New York: Vantage Books, 1967.

Gurin, G., Veroff, J., and Feld, S. *How Americans view their mental health.* New York: Basic Books, 1960.

Hathaway, S., Reynolds, P., and Monachesi, E. Follow-up of the later careers and lives of 1,000 boys who dropped out of high school. *Journal of Consulting and Clinical Psychology,* 1969a, 33, (4), 370-380.

Hathaway, S., Reynolds, P., and Monachesi, E. Follow-up of 812 girls 10 years after high school dropout. *Journal of Consulting and Clinical Psychology,* 1969b, 33, (4), 383-390.

Hayghe, H. Employment of high school graduates and dropouts. *Monthly Labor Review,* 1970, 93, (8), 35-42.

Johnson, L. A message from the President for all who work with youth. *American Education,* 1965, 1, 27 (September).

Johnston, J. and Bachman, J. G. *Young men look at military service: a preliminary report.* Ann Arbor: Survey Research Center, Institute for Social Research, 1970.

Kelly, F. J., Veldman, D. J., and McGuire, C. Multiple discriminant prediction of delinquency and school dropouts. *Educational and Psychological Measurement,* Fall 1964, 24, 535-544.

Kennedy, J. The President's recommendations for education. *School Life,* 1962, 44, (4,5), 29-33.

Kennedy, J. The President's message on education to the congress of the United States, Jan. 29, 1963. *School Life,* 1963, 45, (4,5-7), 22-26.

Kish, L. Confidence intervals for clustered samples. *American Sociological Review,* 1957, 22, 154-165.

Kish, L. and Frankel, M. R. Balanced repeated replication for standard errors. *Journal of the American Statistical Association*, 1970, 65, 1071-1094.

Klinger, M. R. B. *A comparison between American and foreign student groups on certain moral values.* (Doctoral dissertation, The University of Michigan) Ann Arbor: University Microfilms, 1961, No. 2690.

Kohen, A. I. and Parnes, H. S. *Career thresholds: a longitudinal study of the educational and labor market experience of young male youth.* Columbus: Center for Human Resource Research, Ohio State University, 1971.

Lichter, S., Rapier, E., Siebert, F., and Sklansky, M. *The dropouts.* New York: Free Press of Glencoe, 1962.

Long, J. M. Self-actualization in a sample of high school boys: a test of some propositions regarding self-identity. (Unpublished doctoral dissertation, The University of Michigan) 1967.

Miller, S. M., Saleem, B. L., and Bryce, H. *School dropouts: a commentary and annotated bibliography.* New York: Syracuse University, Youth Development Center, 1964.

Namenwirth, J. Z. Failing in New Haven: an analysis of high school graduates and dropouts. *Social Forces*, 1969, 48, 1.

Orshansky, M. Children of the poor. In Schreiber, D. (Ed.), *Profile of the school dropout.* New York: Vantage Books, 1967.

Persella, V. C. Employment of high school graduates and dropouts. *Monthly Labor Review*, 1970, 93, 36-43.

Reiss, J. C. *Guide to using progressive matrices (1947) sets A, Ab, B.* London: Lewis, 1951.

Ribicoff, A. Plain words from Mr. Ribicoff on dropouts. *School Life*, 1961, 44, (3), 14-15.

Rosenberg, M. *Society and the adolescent self-image.* Princeton: Princeton University Press, 1965.

Rotter, J. B. Generalized expectancies for internal vs. external control of reinforcement. *Psychological Monographs*, 1966, 80.

Rotter, J. B., Liverant, S., and Seeman, M. Internal versus external control of reinforcements: a major variable in behavior theory. In Washburne (Ed.), *Decisions, values, and groups, volume II.* London: Pergamon Press, 1963.

Sampson, E. E. *An experiment on active and passive resistance to social power.* (Doctoral dissertation, The University of Michigan) Ann Arbor: University Microfilms, 1960, No. 3889.

Schreiber, D. *Profile of the school dropout.* New York: Vantage Books, 1967.

Scott, W. A. *Values and organizations.* Chicago: Rand McNally and Company, 1965.

Sellin, T. and Wolfgang, M. E. *The measurement of delinquency.* New York: Wiley, 1964.

Sherman, A. Dropouts' march. *Time,* 1964, 83, 76 (April 10).

Super, D. E. The multifactor tests: summing up. *Personnel and Guidance Journal,* 1957, 36, 17-20.

Swanstrom, T. E. Out of school youth, February 1963. In Schreiber, D. (Ed.), *Profile of the school dropout.* New York: Vantage Books, 1967.

Varner, S. E. *School dropouts.* National Education Association, Research Division, 1967.

Winch, R. F. and Campbell, D. T. Proof? No. Evidence? Yes. The significance of tests of significance. *American Sociologist,* 1969, 4, 140-143.

Young, A. Employment of high school graduates and dropouts. *Monthly Labor Review,* 1971, 94, (5), 33-38.

Zeller, R. H. *Lowering the odds on student dropouts.* New Jersey: Prentice-Hall Inc., 1966.

INDEX

The notation "t" indicates a table or figure in which the index entry appears.

245

linked to occupational aspira-
tions, 128, 129, 130t, 131
treated as a criterion, 127t, 128
College students, attitude change
among, 135
Combs, J., 6, 9, 53, 89, 101, 145,
150-152, 180-181, 242
Community size
as a predictor to dropping out
and college entrance, 40
Computer Services Facility of the
Institute for Social Research,
preface
Conclusions, 169-183 (*espec.* 169,
182-183)
Connelly, W., 78, 91, 241
Cooley, W., 6, 9, 53, 89, 101, 145,
150-152, 180-181, 242
Coopersmith, S., 78, 242
Cope, R., preface
Credential value of the high school
diploma, 3-4, 7, 137, 159-164,
174, 177-180, 182
Curriculum (*see* Program of study)

Data collection procedures, 15-16
Davidson, D., preface
Davidson, T., preface, 13, 14, 15, 75,
78, 108, 112, 115, 131, 241
Delinquency, frequency of (*see* Frequency of delinquency)
Delinquency, seriousness of (*see*
Seriousness of delinquency)
Delinquent behavior in school
as a predictor to dropping out
and college entrance, 93, 94t,
95t, 96-97, 99-104
in multivariate prediction, 97-98
treated as a criterion, 124t, 125
Delinquent behaviors, 91, 93-97, 123-
125
of employed versus unemployed
dropouts, 131-132
review of, 172, 173
Dentler, R., 53, 242
Depression, 80 (*see also* Negative
affective states)
Diploma
as a credential (*see* Credential
value of the high school
diploma)
dropouts' attitudes toward, 163-
164

Dropouts
at work or unemployed, 131-132,
175-176
definition of, 5
plans for getting diploma, 163-165
Dropouts' self-reported attitudes,
153-167
regarding earning a diploma,
163-164
regarding employment effects,
161-163
regarding leaving school, 159-161
regarding reasons for dropping
out, 154-159
regarding role-sending from
others, 164-165
Dropping out
as a national problem, 1-11
causes of, 25-110 (*espec.* 99-
105), 171-173 (*see also particular causal dimensions of
interest*)
dropouts' attitudes toward, 159-
161
dropouts' reasons for, 154-159
effects or results of, 111-152,
175-179 (*see also particular
outcome dimensions of
interest*)
estimated rate of, 21-23
issues in the study of, 4-7
Duncan socioeconomic status index
for aspired occupation, 87, 89
for occupations of dropouts and
graduates, 146

Educational attainment
a conceptual overview (as cause
and effect), 108, 109t, 110
as a continuum, 7-8, 105-108,
169, 173-174
categories of, 17-20
causes of, 25-110 (*espec.* 99-105),
171-173 (*see also particular
causal dimensions of interest*)
effects or results of, 111-152,
175-179 (*see also particular
outcome dimensions of interest*)
predicting occupational outcomes,
142-144
Employment
dropouts' attitudes toward, 161-
163

248

treated as a criterion, 120, 121t
Interpersonal aggression
 as a predictor to dropping out
   and college entrance, 93, 94t,
   96-97
 treated as a criterion, 124t, 125
Intervening variable, 48, 49t, 73t, 74
Irritability, 80 (*see also* Negative
   affective states)

Jacobs, M., preface
Job attitudes (*see* Ambitious job attitudes *and* Occupational aspirations)
Job characteristics (*see* Occupational
   outcomes)
Job information test
 treated as a criterion, 125, 126,
   127t
Johnson, L., 2, 242
Johnston, J., preface, 135, 242
Johnston, L., preface, 13, 14, 15, 75,
   78, 108, 112, 115, 131, 241

Kahn, R., preface, 13, 14, 15, 75, 78,
   108, 112, 115, 131, 241
Kasl, S., 78, 91, 241
Kelly, F., 89, 242
Kennedy, J., 2, 242
Kindness, 82 (*see* Social values)
Klinger, M., 82, 243
Kohen, A., 146, 243

Lamendella, R., preface
Lichter, S., 53, 89, 243
Long, J., preface, 75, 76, 243

McGuire, C., 89, 242
Mednick, M., preface, 13, 14, 15,
   75, 78, 108, 112, 115, 131, 241
Miller, S., 5, 20, 243
Monachesi, E., 4, 9, 78, 91, 242
Morgan, J., 47, 241
Multiple Classification Analysis, 46-
   48

Namenwirth, J., 91, 243
Navarro, H., preface
NEA Project on School Dropouts, 5
Need for self-development
 as a predictor to dropping out
   and college entrance, 75-76, 77t

treated as a criterion, 118, 119t
Need for self-utilization
 as a predictor to dropping out
   and college entrance, 76
 treated as a criterion, 118, 119t
Negative affective states
 as a predictor to dropping out
   and college entrance, 80, 82
 treated as a criterion, 116, 117t
Negative school attitudes
 as a predictor to dropping out
   and college entrance, 65, 67,
   68t, 99-104
 in multivariate prediction, 71-72
Niaki, R., preface
Norstebo, G., preface
Number of siblings (*see* Family size)

Occupational aspirations
 as a predictor to dropping out
   and college entrance, 87, 88t,
   89, 99-104
 in multivariate prediction, 97-98
 linked to college plans, 128, 129,
   130t, 131
 treated as a criterion, 126, 127t,
   128
 (*see also* Ambitious job attitudes)
Occupational outcomes, 137-152
 for dropouts and graduates,
   146-150, 177-179
 predicted from GATB-J vocabulary test, 141-144
 predicted from Gates reading
   test, 141-144
 predicted from educational attainment continuum, 142-144
 predicted from socioeconomic
   level, 141-144
O'Malley, P., preface
Orshansky, M., 25, 243

Paige, K., preface
Parental punitiveness
 as a predictor to dropping out
   and college entrance, 33, 34t,
   35t, 36, 99-104
 in multivariate prediction, 48,
   72
 review of, 171
Parents' attitudes toward dropping
   out, 164-165, 166t

and college entrance, 93
treated as a criterion, 123, 124t
Shapiro, S., preface
Sherman, A., 3, 244
Siebert, F., 89, 243
Sklansky, M., 89, 243
Social responsibility, 82 (*see* Social
  values)
Social skills, 82 (*see* Social values)
Social values
    as a predictor to dropping out
      and college entrance, 82, 84t,
      85
    treated as a criterion, 118, 119t,
      120
Socioeconomic level
    as a predictor to dropping out
      and college entrance, 26-27,
      28t, 99-104
    in multivariate prediction, 48,
      72
    of aspired occupation, 87, 89
    of occupations attained by drop-
      outs and graduates, 146
    predicting occupational out-
      comes, 141-144
    review of, 171
Somatic symptoms
    as a predictor to dropping out
      and college entrance, 80, 82,
      83t, 99-104
    in multivariate prediction, 97-98
    treated as a criterion, 116, 117t
Sonquist, J., 47, 241
Statistical procedures, overview,
  23-24
Statistical significance, 23
Status (*see* Socioeconomic level)
Super, D., 41, 244
Swanstrom, T., 4, 244
Symptoms (*see* Problems and
  symptoms)

TALENT (*see* Project TALENT)
Taylor, C., preface
Thomas, B., preface

Truax, D., preface
Trust in people
    treated as a criterion, 121t, 122
Trust in the government
    treated as a criterion, 121t, 122

U. S. Department of Defense, preface
U. S. Department of Labor, preface
U. S. Office of Education, preface, 5
Unemployed dropouts compared with
  employed dropouts, 131-132
Unemployment (*see* Employment,
  rates of)

Validity of measures, discussion of,
  176-177
Values (*see* Social values, Academic
  achievement values)
vanDuinen, E., preface, 122, 123,
  133, 135, 241
Varner, S., 4, 5, 25, 53, 244
Veerkamp, P., preface
Veldman, D., 89, 242
Verbal skills
    as background factors, 40-51
    relationship to intelligence,
      43, 46
    review of, 171-172
    (*see also* General Aptitude
      Test Battery)
Veroff, J., 80, 242
Vietnam dissent
    treated as a criterion, 134t, 135

Warshauer, M., 53, 242
Winch, R., 23, 244
Wirtanen, I., preface
Wolfgang, M., 93, 244

Young, A., 137, 141, 244
Youth in Transition project
    future research plans for, 183
    purposes of, preface

Zeller, R., 4, 78, 244